Read this for yo

"...Schirmer is a [illegible] storyteller, with an amazing account of how his family suffered through the WWII years in Singapore. The painful events are vivid and heartbreaking, and the celebration of courage, generosity and risk-taking is tremendously inspiring."

— Don Bosco;
Author of the *Time Talisman* series

A true "page turner" filled with romance, history and heroics!

"A must read for enthusiasts of WWII and Singapore history. Schirmer has painstakingly unearthed the real faces of heroes from the West who settle down in the East. Based on true life accounts, we are taken on a journey from one man named Edward Schirmer, and then through the personal life of his son Hans Schirmer—amidst the ravages of Japanese occupation in a small growing nation in Southeast Asia—and his dedication to the people around him."

— Shawn Peter;
Author of *Perseverance—The Power Is Within You*

I couldn't put this down!

"What a fantastic book! This had me up nights. A great combination of history and humanity, and splendidly written... It really got me thinking about the characters, and I learned a lot about Singapore during WWII. It sure had me feeling like I was witnessing events for myself, and I was in tears several times. A very worthwhile read. Can hardly wait for the next one!"

— Rachel Buck;
Language Teacher

EDMUND M. SCHIRMER

WHEN THERE WERE TIGERS IN SINGAPORE

A FAMILY SAGA OF THE JAPANESE OCCUPATION

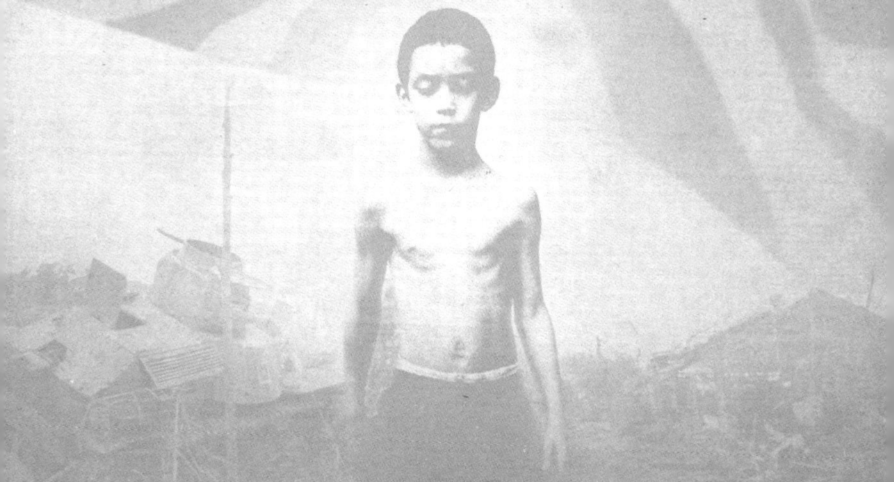

Marshall Cavendish Editions

This edition published in 2012 by Marshall Cavendish Editions
An imprint of Marshall Cavendish International
1 New Industrial Road, Singapore 536196

Cover design by Cover Kitchen
Designed by Benson Tan
Photographs of the Schirmer family are from a private collection. All other photographs are reproduced courtesy of Creative Commons Licenses and the Public Domain. Original sources include: Wikipedia Commons, U.S. Army, Imperial War Museum (U.K.), Australian War Memorial, German Federal Archive, the Japanese Government, the People's Republic of China, Yesterday.sg and Flickr.com. The reproduction of these photographs or images does not imply endorsement by any of these entities.

Other Marshall Cavendish Offices:
Marshall Cavendish Corporation. 99 White Plains Road, Tarrytown NY 10591-9001, USA • Marshall Cavendish International (Thailand) Co Ltd. 253 Asoke, 12th Flr, Sukhumvit 21 Road, Klongtoey Nua, Wattana, Bangkok 10110, Thailand • Marshall Cavendish (Malaysia) Sdn Bhd, Times Subang, Lot 46, Subang Hi-Tech Industrial Park, Batu Tiga, 40000 Shah Alam, Selangor Darul Ehsan, Malaysia.

National Library Board, Singapore Cataloguing-in-Publication Data
Schirmer, Edmund M.
When there were tigers in Singapore / Edmund M. Schirmer. – Singapore : Marshall Cavendish Editions, 2012.
p. cm.
ISBN : 978-981-4398-17-6

Singapore – History — Japanese occupation, 1942-1945 —Biography. I. Title.

DS610.55
957.5703092 — dc23 OCN794026178

Printed by KWF Printing Pte Ltd

Jan, 2017
Jan, 2019

DEDICATION

A heart-warming real life story of bravery, tragedy and family.

For my father, Hans Schirmer

This is a true story whose events begin in South East Asia, then Europe and finally back to S.E.A — Singapore.

Hans Schirmer's son, Edmund wished to record something of his family's history. Most of it revolves around Han's life in Singapore, the multicultural life, Japanese attack + occupation

Hans led quite a tragic life when young but thru perseverance, survived and was successful.

ACKNOWLEDGEMENTS

There is no way I could have written this book without the love, help and support of certain individuals. Simply saying the words "Thank You" seems to be such an insignificant gesture, in comparison to the gratitude I actually feel. Nevertheless, I would like to take this opportunity to express my appreciation.

To begin, Dad (without whom I would have nothing to write about!). For always being there for me...

Mom, for your love and patience, even when I drove you nuts all those years...

My sister Pat, for your critique and for being the Pooh to my Piglet...

My wife Corina, for too many reasons to list. Right there, reading and re-reading all the drafts, sharing Dad's history with me, pulling me back when I got lost. You could have run away screaming a long time ago. Glad that you didn't...

My sons Colton and Garret, for many reasons also, but most of all, for putting up with your old man. You are the future...

The Londons—Jim and Freda, Darrin and Tina. For all the encouragement over the years, for believing in me...

All my friends in Singapore, the Bedok Buddies (you know who you are!) but especially Choon, Colin and Chris Smith and your families. You guys have always been there when I really needed you...

The Sebana gang—Tim and Chris, Kevin and Winnie, and your wonderful families...

John and May Harding, for all the professional tips, support and encouragement throughout this process. Hans would have loved it...

Last but definitely not least, Chris Toh, Don Bosco, Mindy Pang, Lee Mei Lin and the good folks at Marshall Cavendish. For all your good ideas, your encouragement, your trust and your patience...

CONTENTS

Prologue 10
Author's Note 13

PART ONE: EDWARD
Chapter 1 — Singapore 22
Chapter 2 — The Mauritius Islands 26
Chapter 3 — Finding Home Again 35
Chapter 4 — When There Were Tigers In Singapore 45
Chapter 5 — Florence Chia 51
Chapter 6 — Courtship 60
Chapter 7 — Friends And Family 71
Chapter 8 — Florence Schirmer 79
Chapter 9 — Generations 87
Chapter 10 — Boys 93
Chapter 11 — Resentment 100
Chapter 12 — A Trip Downtown 108

PART TWO: LOSING PARADISE
Introduction 118
- *Winds Of War*
- *The Battle Of Malaya*
- *The Tiger Of Malaya*
- *The Battle For Singapore*

Chapter 1 — Calm Before The Storm 146
Chapter 2 — War In Paradise 151
Chapter 3 — Air Battles 159
Chapter 4 — Coming Under Fire 168
Chapter 5 — The Surrender 174
Chapter 6 — Meeting The Tiger 179
Chapter 7 — A Friend Of The Empire 185
Chapter 8 — Sook Ching 194
Chapter 9 — Farewell To The Tiger 198
Chapter 10 — Eng Guan 204
Chapter 11 — Betrayal 209
Chapter 12 — Everything Falls Apart 216
Chapter 13 — Where Do We Go From Here? 222
Chapter 14 — Where Is Everybody? 228
Chapter 15 — Carl And Eugene 235
Chapter 16 — The Journey Begins 239
Chapter 17 — Interrogation 245
Chapter 18 — The Outram Road Jail 254
Chapter 19 — Life On The Streets 261
Chapter 20 — I Will Always Be With You 268

PART THREE: HANS

Chapter 1 — Alone In The Crowd 276
Chapter 2 — The Cowboy And The Indian 282
Chapter 3 — Superfortress 289
Chapter 4 — The Americans 296
Chapter 5 — Back On The Streets 303
Chapter 6 — Operation Rimau 308
Chapter 7 — U-235 And Pu-239 314
Chapter 8 — Coming Down From Niitaka 320
Chapter 9 — The Relief 325
Chapter 10 — The Road To Recovery 332
Chapter 11 — Reunited 338
Chapter 12 — Aftermath 344

Epilogue 352
About The Author 364

PROLOGUE

December 8th 1941, approximately 0415 hour (local time)
Ubin Island—Located between Singapore and Malaya

"Wake up, Hansel ... it's begun. You'll want to see this."

The tiger is back!

Three year-old Hans Felix Schirmer sat up in his bed. He was still in that drowsy sort of state where he could never be sure what he was hearing was real or only a dream.

Papa will get him this time! But why is it so dark, though? And why are there bees buzzing?

Edward Henry Schirmer picked up his tired son. "We'll be safe enough here," he said in a reassuring voice. "The Japanese have nothing to gain by bombing this island. If it is indeed the Japanese flying over—I don't quite know yet. But we must not turn on any lights, alright? Come and see, though. This is unbelievable!"

Carrying the small boy, Edward walked through the dark house and out the front door. He put his son down. They stood together on the *attap* palm-frond covered porch and looked in the direction of southwest, toward the main island of Singapore.

"I couldn't sleep, so I got up to walk around. Then I heard these aeroplanes," Edward said, motioning upwards.

A flight of Mitsubishi twin engine bombers droned loudly overhead, invisible in the cover of the cloudy tropical sky.

So that's what that sound was. Funny! They do sound like bees...

A warm glow filled the southern sky. Edward turned toward it and watched incredulously. "The bloody fools! Why are all the street lights still on? Don't they know what they are doing?"

Within minutes, they could see fiery orange balls rising into the sky in the direction of the Sembawang Naval Base, which was to the west of them. These were immediately followed by the sound of explosions. The balls of flame seemed somewhat tiny because of the distance, and to little Hans, the explosions sounded more like the fireworks on Chinese New Year. Yet—even to the three year-old—it was obvious that these things were not happening for fun. Intermittent pops from the anti-aircraft guns rang between the explosions, while searchlights clawed the night sky.

By now, Hans was fully awake—there was no longer any doubt in his mind that this was not a dream. He clutched his father. Although there was no real need to, he kept his voice to a whisper, caution compelled by instinct.

"Papa, I'm scared!"

"Don't worry, Son. We're safe here. They know they would only be wasting their bombs on some silly coconut trees if they drop them here. I feel sorry for the poor buggers on the main island, though. I need to go and check on the others. Do you want to stay here and watch?"

Hans nodded, unable to take his eyes off the southern sky. Papa was always right, so he felt safe staying on the porch alone.

Edward went back in the house to find his young Chinese wife holding their two younger sons. Carl Johann was almost two and Franz Eugene had just turned one. Even though Edward could barely see her face, he sensed that Florence was glaring at him, as if everything was his fault entirely.

"*Aiyoh*, this is terrible! What is happening?" she asked.

"Well, war has finally happened, that's what. The British have said for months now that the Japanese would be fools to start a war with them. Well, I suppose we shall see whether that is true."

"The British, the British ... *we* are the British, you know! You act as if this is someone else's problem, but we are the ones here! You know what those bloody Japanese have already done in China. They hate us Chinese even more than they hate you Europeans! What if they come here?"

Edward rubbed his face in the dark and said nothing. He did not know what dawn would bring. Who did? But for now, they were alive, and he knew that in times of war, that was the best one could hope for.

Mitsubishi G3M bombers headed for Singapore—December 8th 1941.

AUTHOR'S NOTE

Just like what Bonasera the undertaker told Don Vito Corleone in the opening scene of *The Godfather*—life in America has been good to me.

Nevertheless, I did not grow up here in America. I was born and raised in Singapore, a tiny island country in Southeast Asia, a former British colony.

With the exception of the usual shenanigans that boys tend to concoct for themselves, my growing up there was fairly uneventful. It was certainly nothing like that of my father's. His was indeed a far more eventful childhood, for he had survived the Japanese Occupation of Singapore in World War II.

Listening to my father's life story and getting to know more about him in that way was a very important part of my childhood. That, in turn, has led to my life-long interest in the history of that particular place and time—of World War II and the colonial days.

Naturally, it also made me curious about our family history. When I asked him how and when the Schirmers had ended up in Singapore, he told me an interesting tale of their travel from Europe to South America, and then on to the British colonies in the East. He also showed me some old travel documents, as well as birth and death certificates belonging to his father and grandparents.

I still remember all those stories because Dad was the kind of guy who would repeat himself every now and then. Something would happen and he would say, "Boy that reminds me of the time... " He had always been that way, even when he was younger. It wasn't as if he grew old and began to repeat himself. Dad was just a natural storyteller and he enjoyed having a ready audience.

Each time, my mother would laugh and say, "*Aiyoh*, Dear! We've heard that one how-many-hundred times already. Someone should write a book about you and your life!" Nevertheless, I loved hearing his stories—even for the how-many-hundredth time—though I never really thought seriously about writing it all down. I guess I just got busy with my own life.

After I received my discharge from the Army (mandatory military service) at age twenty-one, I left Singapore for the United States to attend school. But that was where I met Corina, who became my lovely wife and companion for all these years. I decided to stay on in the country, raise a family and chase the dream. That sort of thing.

Since my move to the United States in 1992, I have been through different career paths over the years. For most of the time, I worked in the field of medical equipment supply, and that was when I came to meet some really interesting people.

Most of my clients were retirees, and many of them were in fact World War II veterans. Old soldiers who had fought across Europe under General Patton. Marines who served in the Pacific campaign. I once met a fighter pilot who used to fly P-38s—one of my favorite aircraft designs—over the Mediterranean.

Then I met a particular gentleman in a nursing home, a former tank commander in the Philippines who had survived the infamous

Bataan Death March and the horrors of a Japanese POW camp. As I gazed at the black-and-white photograph on his mantle—a picture of a young lieutenant posing beside an M3A Stuart light battle tank—it made me think of the American experience in the Philippines. The humiliating defeat, the torture and abuse at the hands of their Japanese captors. These things seemed to parallel what the British had gone through in Singapore and Malaya. I felt compelled to share some of Dad's stories with him. In turn, he shared his experiences with me. At the end of it, he said that I needed to put my father's accounts down on paper. "I don't think they tell the kids these days what really happened back then," he said. "There is too much revisionist history being taught in school. Write a book about it. Share it with people before they forget that whole era, especially this younger generation."

I had to agree with him.

Shortly after speaking with that gentleman, I came to know one of his neighbors as well, a gunner who had served aboard a medium cruiser during the closing days of the Pacific war. This man, a survivor of multiple *Kamikaze* attacks on his ship, had written a short memoir about his Navy days. After talking with him, he too felt that I should be writing down my Dad's story.

Then it got me thinking. How should I go about doing this? I had pieces of someone's life experiences rolling around in my head, events that I could certainly corroborate with hard historical data. But that, in and of itself, does not necessarily make a coherent tale, let alone one that anyone would want to read.

So in order to make this work, I had to invent some of the dialog, change some names and take a few liberties with certain details. But other than that, the story you are about to read is based on everything my father had told me.

This book started out being solely based on the experiences of my father, Hans Schirmer—a boy growing up in Singapore during the years of World War II. His life was a story of survival against great odds. However, there is more to the story than that alone. Before we can get into that, we have to go back to the years before the war—starting first with his parents and his grandparents, and how they came to be in British Singapore in the 1930s.

While this is certainly a personal story, as it involves my family, I believe it will be of interest to anyone. After all, it really is a tale of travel, romance, hopes, dreams, loss and recovery. And for all the history buffs, there is war, adventure, airplanes and guns.

This is also a tale of a different time and, for many Western readers, a very different place. Unless you grew up there, the history and geography of Singapore is about as familiar to most people as that of Turkmenistan. Because of this, it was necessary to inject some historical and geographical pointers along the way.

Singapore is located about eighty-five miles north of the equator, with the Malay Peninsula to the north and the islands of Indonesia, then known as the Dutch East Indies, to the south. The main island is diamond-shaped, about twenty-six miles from east to west and fourteen miles north to south.

The indigenous people were the Malays. Over the centuries, immigrants from India, China and the surrounding islands began taking up residence as well. Because of the blending of different cultures and languages, the local dialect, aside from their native tongues, became an evolving patois unique to the land. Today, that style of speech is called "Singlish" or Singapore English.

Singapore also had different names over the years. In ancient times, the Malays called the island Pulau Ujong, meaning "island at the end," while the Sumatrans called it Temasek, or "Sea Town" in old Javanese. One legend states that the modern name came from Sang Nila Utama, a thirteenth century Majapahit Indian prince of Palembang, who called the island Singapura, or "Lion City." At various times in history, Singapore came under the control of different Indian dynasties that were ruling in Sumatra and Java, and at one point the kingdom of Siam claimed it as a vassal state.

Singapore's modern history—as far the British were concerned —began in 1819. That was the year the entrepreneurial Sir Thomas Stamford Raffles of the English East India Company saw the potential of its location and founded an international trading port at the site of a small fishing village on the south end.

As time went on, the settlement at Singapore evolved into an actual city, with growth in commerce, population and international importance. By 1867, the island had become a port and Crown Colony ruled by a governor appointed by the British monarchy. It also formed part of the Straits Settlements, a group of British territories located in Southeast Asia, which included Penang Island and Malacca.

The success of the port was largely due to Singapore's strategic location along the old trade route linking the Indian Ocean to the Pacific. Even after ships had transitioned from wind to coal power, the location remained of prime importance, right to this day. Another important factor was the chain of islands that surround the deep natural harbor in the south. These islands formed a buffer that served to protect the ships from monsoon storms.

Over the years, the British built a world-class infrastructure, including a modern dock and shipyard, around these natural assets, making Singapore a very desirable possession from a maritime standpoint. The shipping facilities, along with tin and rubber resources in Malaya, became commodities that would eventually attract the eyes of the expansionist Japanese in 1941.

By the early twentieth century, the British knew that those assets could potentially be preyed upon by other powers. They then began to develop Singapore as a fortress.

The British called India the "Jewel in the Crown" for her contribution to the Empire's treasury. Singapore, on the other hand, gained the reputation as the Gibraltar of the East by the 1930s, with the Colonial Office promoting images of security, impregnability and formidability. The steady appearance of defense projects on the island compounded that image. An image which drew a ready influx of immigrants during the early twentieth century.

When the 1930s Great Depression came, it caused most of the world to be tied up in financial disarray. Singapore, on the other hand, remained relatively unhurt. Although international trade, the island's main source of revenue, had slowed down, it managed to pump Singapore's economic lifeblood sufficiently. That is not to say that the Depression had no effect at all on Singapore, but the country was just not as hard-hit as many other places. Compared to many in Europe who were suffering the high rates of inflation, unemployment and financial uncertainty, the colonials were living it up in Asia. The British colonial masters, as well as the other Europeans, were able to enjoy a relatively opulent life in Singapore during the Depression due to the lower cost of living. Even a government clerk could expect to have his own bungalow, with a full staff of servants employed at low wages. Not a bad way to live, from that standpoint.

Now, this book neither extols nor condemns European colonialism in the Orient. Enough authors have written volumes about the benefits of Western civilization in these places, while many others have written about the evil white man oppressing the natives. I don't get into that, or any such social commentary.

Today, political correctness dictates that it is acceptable to say certain things, and conversely, unacceptable to say other things. But this sometimes prevents us from telling the truth. Whether we like it or not, certain things happened just the way they did, whether right or wrong, and it is in this backdrop that history was written.

In this case, the history of a young Eurasian boy. The history of a family, their hopes and dreams. The history of a nation.

These days, I live somewhere in suburban America. Not very exciting, I must say, but this story isn't about me. It's about my father, and his father before him.

And a more interesting time.

1

EDWARD

1
SINGAPORE

March 12th 1932
Singapore Harbour

Johnston's Pier in Singapore Harbour was the disembarkation point for those entering the colony by sea. That morning, a liner of the British-India Steam Navigation Company was at berth, with passengers making their way down the gangplanks.

One of the passengers, thirty-seven year-old Edward Henry Schirmer, was a well-built European man, about six foot four tall (1.93 meters), with light gray eyes and short dark-blond hair. He stopped along the main deck and stood there for a moment, looking at the familiar sight before his eyes.

During the voyage, Edward had experienced many conflicting emotions about the prospect of returning to Singapore. He was sad about leaving his home and business behind, but happy to see his parents again. He was excited and optimistic about the possibilities that awaited him, yet apprehensive about whether it would all work out. But now that he was here, he was determined to make a success of things, no matter what.

Edward had been away for many years, but as he gazed about, the details of the senses, sights and sounds did not escape his attention. It certainly felt hotter and a little more humid than the place he had just come from, but Edward was no stranger to the warm tropics. He had, in fact, spent most of his growing up years in Singapore, with some of it on another small island on the Indian Ocean, not far from Madagascar.

This was now his home, again. Everything was coming back to him.

Each place has its own unique olfactory signature, which is one of the first things a traveler tends to take in. The moment he stepped off the gangplank, Edward closed his eyes and drew a deep breath. His sense of smell was hit by an amalgam of various local fruit, spices ... and something else. Some sort of fried food, perhaps?

It was all a welcome change from the subtle, yet constant odor of enamel paint, metal and fuel oil that he had smelled on board the ship.

Looking around the bustling center, Edward observed that there appeared to be a representation of just about every ethnic group. Sinewy *coolie* laborers from the south of China, dark skinned Tamil porters, fair skinned north Indian *chettiar* money changers, Malay taxi drivers, businessmen from the different parts of Europe—all were busying themselves in their tasks. For the first time since his return, Edward began paying attention to the fascinating sound of the different languages clashing in the constant din. Somehow, communication succeeded amid the commotion.

Edward straightened his straw hat and smoothed his linen suit. He then picked up a small travel bag and strode forward, determined to get the customs and immigration ordeal over with.

The immigration clerk was a slightly built Irishman, who appeared to be in his mid-thirties. Perhaps this one fancied himself rather as a ladies man—the Errol Flynn mustache and slick dark hair were indeed a nice touch—but the man's lack of a prominent chin did not bode too well for the intended image.

When it became Edward's turn, the clerk looked up from his desk without interest, and held out his hand for the proffered travel documents. Once the papers were in his possession, he looked down at them and reached for his pen and stamp as a matter of routine. However, upon reading Edward's full name, he paused for a moment and then looked up again.

"Schirmer ... You're a German. Why are you traveling under a British passport?" the clerk probed, raising one eyebrow.

Of course. Here we go.

"I was born in Plaines Wilhems, in the Mauritius Islands. Which—as I am sure you know—is a British protectorate," Edward replied.

Perhaps, if you'd read further, you might have noticed that little fact. He hoped his annoyance was not too apparent.

"Hmph ... yes, I suppose so. Which side...? I mean, where were you during the war, if I might inquire?" the clerk asked, still barely concealing his suspicion.

Every now and then, Edward ran into people like that—narrow-minded fools, bigots. He knew better than to have words with this petty bureaucrat, so he maintained a neutral expression while he spoke.

"I was in school. Engineering."

"Never been to the front, then?"

"No."

"Well, why ever not? You look healthy enough."

"As I've said, I was in school."

Edward struggled to maintain composure.

"So was I, but I heeded the King's call to arms, if you must know. Took a round in the shoulder from the Boche bastards, as a matter of fact!" the clerk declared, with the air of a man used to throwing about that claim in order to gain sympathy or respect.

Edward knew this was going nowhere. He was not an unreasonable man, and understood the need for proper security and documentation. However, this line of questioning had nothing to do with official procedure. It was also not the first time that he had to deal with this sort of thing.

In the meantime, the people standing in line behind him were growing impatient, and Edward could hear their grumbling. He glanced momentarily at the crowd, then he turned back slowly to rest his cold gray eyes on the clerk. After a second, he spoke. "My great-grandparents had no interest in continental politics, so they left Europe a long time ago. I myself have no interest either, having never lived there for any extended period of time. I do regret your injury, Sir, and applaud your patriotism. However, if you will observe, all my papers are in order."

He looked at the line behind him once more, then turned his eyes back to the clerk. Seeing all the impatient faces in the queue, the clerk quickly moved his focus back to the papers before him. A few quick stamps and a signature later, he handed them back to Edward. Nodding his chinless head at him, the clerk called out, "Next, please."

Edward picked up his bag and nodded back at the clerk. It was now time to take on the arduous task of retrieving his belongings, which were being unloaded from the ship.

Once we get these things settled, a cold beer is the next order of business.

2
THE MAURITIUS ISLANDS

In the early 1900s a German family, the Schirmers, owned of one of the largest sugarcane plantations on the Isle of Mauritius. This is the story of how that branch of the family came to be there. The Schirmers apparently were at one time landed aristocrats in the former Kingdom of Prussia, which is northeastern Germany today. Despite the family's privileged status, the constant wars in Europe had become a hardship with which many did not want to contend. So in the early 1800s, members of the Schirmer family, along with a large number of other Germans, headed for the Americas. While there are many Schirmers in the United States today, one branch of the family went south and settled in Argentina. It was to be a new land and a new life for them. A land with vast acreage and, unlike Europe, a land with many new opportunities. Just as it came to be in the United States to the north, many new immigrants became businessmen, tending to their own farms and ranches.

Carlos Juan Schirmer was born in Buenos Aires, on April 7th 1870. But he was the restless kind, always looking over the ocean to the far horizon. As soon as he came of age, he left Argentina to see what the rest of the world had to offer.

In the Isle of Mauritius, he met the beautiful daughter of a French merchant, who would become the future Mrs Schirmer. Marie Lucie Duclos was six years his senior, but Carlos Schirmer managed to capture her attention with his tales of travel on the high seas. Marie was in her late twenties—considered old in those days to have yet remained single. Her parents worried that if they did not do something about that, she would become an old spinster. They regularly dropped hints for her to not be so fussy.

The problem was that all the eligible bachelors who Marie knew were the foppish, spoiled sons of French aristocrats. Boy-men who had never been anywhere, who knew nothing about anything, and who expected their women to wait on them. Marie Lucie Duclos would rather die a shriveled old spinster than settle for any one of those fools.

Although Marie herself had not traveled—she was born in Port Louis, Isle of Mauritius on July 4th 1864—she inwardly yearned to see other places for herself.

When she first met him, Marie thought Carlos was a little odd. He had an intense stare that almost appeared disdainful. However, it was just the way he studied his environment, constantly analyzing it. A mutual friend introduced them during one of his lavish balls. They sat and talked for hours. She asked him about the places he had been, he asked her about her thoughts and dreams. Nobody had ever asked Marie what she thought about. She liked him immediately.

Although money was not on her list of priorities—she could have married one of her fellow Frenchmen if it was—Marie noticed that Carlos was financially comfortable. At least then her parents would not object to him, should a relationship continue.

Their courtship was quick. Carlos and Marie were married on September 8th 1893, in Plaines Wilhems, Isle of Mauritius. The following year, their son Edward Henry Schirmer was born to them, on August 12th 1894. Marie had named the boy after her father, Edouard. As expected, they were to raise their son in the manner of an aristocrat, educating him in the arts and languages.

Because of where they lived, Edward primarily learned to speak English and French. With his father, he conversed in German and was able to pick up some Spanish as well. For Edward, languages came fairly easily.

He also proved to be quite a marksman, even as a boy, during the times when he accompanied his father in game hunting on the African mainland and, later on, in the jungles of Malaya. Edward led a life of privilege, yet he was still able to enjoy the casual atmosphere of island living. It really was the best of both worlds.

By the turn of the century, Carlos had been in the Mauritius for a decade. He had become a successful sugar plantation owner and merchant, but his sea legs were beginning to get restless again. Since he had business dealings in the other British colonies, he would travel time and again to see how his other business holdings were doing. When Edward was little, Carlos traveled alone. Now that the boy was no longer a toddler, he felt it was a good time for the whole family to go places together.

While Marie enjoyed traveling to India and the Dutch East Indies, it was with Singapore that she fell in love. Compared to the Mauritius, Singapore was a bustling metropolis. There were concerts and cricket matches, fine dining and sartorial elegance. At the same time, there was also hunting in the Malayan jungles to the north and sailing in the islands to the south. Carlos was happy to be anywhere, as long as it was with his beloved Marie Lucie, so he moved his base of operations, and his family, to Singapore in 1901. Their only son, Edward, spent his early years there.

By the time Edward grew to be a young man, there was yet another war raging in Europe. The Great War, which would later be known as World War I, lasted from 1914 to the end of 1918. This time, the Germans were the enemy. Carlos and Marie Schirmer did their best to mind their own business and to avoid political discussions with their neighbors. Fortunately for them, this was a fairly easy thing to do in the cosmopolitan society of Singapore. It could potentially have been a difficult time, because of their German surname, however everyone knew that Carlos was from Argentina, and that Marie was French. For the most part, the English in Singapore treated them as friends. Once in a while, there were one or two snide remarks about their name, but these jibes were few and far in between.

Edward could pass off as an English gentleman and even considered himself an Anglophile at the time. However, that changed during his education in England after the war, when he received his first real taste of bigotry there. He learned, rather rudely, that he would never be considered "one of the lads."

Even though Edward was a British subject and had never even been to Germany, this did not seem to matter to some of his English hosts. A number of his fellow students still regarded his undeniably Teutonic surname with contempt. Many of the young men around him had been "battling the Huns" during the recent war, and had seen many friends fall to the devilish enemy. Even though this enemy had since been defeated, some were still feeling resentment toward them. Edward understood this, but nevertheless, their attitude toward him grew tiresome, especially when certain ones insisted on calling him "Herr Edvard," while goose-stepping around him. Even worse, some of his things began to mysteriously disappear or become broken, although there was nothing he could prove by that alone.

During his stay in England, Edward learned to keep to himself, focusing on his books and going on long walks. The narrow-mindedness of his adversaries had sowed the seeds of disillusionment within his heart. He learned that although he might have been British by way of birth, he was not English, and as such, would not be treated as an equal by many Englishmen.

While he would also learn that this behavior was certainly not representative of all English people, it remained enough to sour up his time there. It was a time that he had very much looked forward to, ever since he was a boy. Now, he simply wanted it to be over. But above all things, Edward hated the English weather, with all its rain and fog. He had grown up in a tropical paradise, where the Equatorial sun warmed the air every day. Here, he felt trapped and cold, his wings clipped. Needless to say, he longed for home.

In 1923, his studies were completed. Edward was very much ready to leave after having spent four long years in England. Although he missed Singapore and his parents, Edward still wanted to see the rest of Europe. It therefore made sense for him to do this before he went home, for he was certain that it would be a long time, if ever, before he returned to that part of the world.

Many parts of Germany both appalled and disappointed him. Unfortunately, what he was seeing at that time was a very defeated nation. Germany was going through its worst period under the Weimar Republic government.

After World War I, the victorious Allies had imposed punitive terms upon the German people by way of the Versailles Treaty. This created hyperinflation, which in turn was driving many people to acts of desperation. By late summer of that year—around the same time Edward was touring Germany—a fifty million Deutsche Mark note was only worth one US dollar.

Drunks, prostitutes and thugs roamed the streets of the major cities. In the meantime, Adolf Hitler and his fledgling National Socialist Party fed on the unrest, blaming Jews and other so-called degenerates in the government for their current situation. Yet another clever opportunist, vying for the attention and power that he would eventually gain.

It was nothing at all like what Edward had thought it would be. Nevertheless, he had finally been able to see where his family came from, and during his stay there, he met some very fine and hospitable individuals.

One of them was an old man he met in Berlin who had the same surname. The old gent did not know exactly in what way they might have been related, but he was sure there was some connection somewhere. As a parting gift, he presented Edward with a very ornate pewter beer stein. Edward had a hard time accepting such a gift, knowing the state of poverty that the German people were enduring. But the old man insisted, and Edward acquiesced. It would have been an insult to do otherwise.

After having spent some time in Germany, he wanted to go to Belgium next. This was for a very specific reason. During his stay in England, Edward had seen a certain three barreled combination shotgun-rifle made by Holland & Holland. Such guns were called Drillings—from the German word *drei*, meaning "three."

Edward was fascinated with the design, but what he wanted was a Belgian handcrafted model, one that he could present to his father. At the time, everyone knew that the finest personal firearms were of Belgian make. He knew that his father would appreciate it.

A gunsmith near Liège offered to make a custom Drilling, with any combination of barrels in any caliber desired. Edward selected an inverse triangle configuration with a pair of twelve bore shotgun tubes above one .303 British rifle barrel. He had chosen those particular calibers for versatility as well as the availability of ammunition in the places he knew they would be. The British army Lee-Enfield fired the same rifle cartridge, and twelve bore shotgun shells were also very common.

Edward stayed in Belgium long enough to personally observe the beautiful engraving workmanship being completed. It was certainly more a work of art than a mere firearm.

From there, he traveled through France and Spain. Portugal was his last stop. Although he had experienced many things—some good, some not so good—on the trip, he was now ready to return to Singapore. Edward boarded a ship in Lisbon that would take him on the long voyage home.

Carlos and Marie received him at Johnston's Pier as he came off the ship. After exchanging hugs and handshakes, Edward presented his parents with the gifts he had procured during his time abroad. Carlos could not believe his eyes, as he handled the Drilling for the first time. He turned it about and carefully studied the fine workmanship. "I dare not ask the price, my son," he commented dryly, but with a warm smile and moist eyes.

Not long after his return from Europe, Edward began to travel between Singapore and the Mauritius islands with Carlos, in order to learn how to take care of the family business and the plantation. Edward was about seven when they had left the islands for Singapore. Over the years, they made the occasional return to visit family, and for Carlos to check on things. Although Edward had always enjoyed those trips as a boy, at that time, he still preferred the more urban Singapore. Now that he was an adult, the serene atmosphere and the quietness of the Mauritius appealed to him in a way that it had not before.

On one of those business trips, Edward chose to stay behind. Carlos knew that he would miss his son, but he also knew that it was a good idea for him to learn to be a man on his own terms. Besides, it was relieving to know that the plantation would always have someone responsible to look after it.

There were to be a few more good years. Buoyed by the economy of the Roaring Twenties, Carlos had diversified his investments heavily. Then the stock market crashed on October 29th 1929, and his many investments became worthless in an instant. Following the crash, crop prices—including sugar—plummeted. Just like the thousands of businessmen who were millionaires the day before, Carlos lost most of his money overnight. After the crash, Edward turned away from his life of relative ease. He quickly had to learn to handle a multitude of menial roles on the plantation, as he reluctantly cut back on workers in order to minimize operating costs.

Although the change was not easy, it taught him many skills. More importantly though, he learned a valuable lesson—respect for those who work with their hands. It also served to reshape his attitude toward those whom he once haughtily looked upon as lesser men than he was, simply by virtue of their race. When he was younger, he associated only with other Europeans, as was the custom. But working side-by-side with the Indians and the few Chinese on the island slowly made him realize how insipid the racial barriers were.

Their financial situation, however, continued to decline. They had to make some tough choices. By the end of 1931, it was obvious that things were not going to improve any time soon. In the end, with costs outweighing profits, the family made the sad decision to totally close operations on the island. Instead, they would consolidate their assets in Singapore. It was the end of an era, and the start of a new one.

Carlos Juan Schirmer—early 1900s

3
FINDING HOME AGAIN

Edward Henry Schirmer, trained as he was in design and engineering, had an affinity for anything mechanical. In fact, tinkering with engines of any sort gave him more joy than the dry calculations and projections involved in engineering.

Shortly after returning to Singapore, he witnessed a demonstration of the new Marston Seagull marine outboard motor. It was the first of its kind, designed from the ground up with an actual marine engine. Edward immediately saw the potential in the simple, rugged design, with its reliability and fuel efficiency. For sure, it would not win any prizes in speed or aesthetics, but it certainly was a workhorse.

What he now had in mind was a gamble. He had come back to Singapore without much in his pocket, and his parents had limited savings themselves. Nonetheless, what little he had, he invested in a sales and service center for Sunbeam Marston, manufacturer of Seagull Marine Engines. Edward Schirmer thus became a regional sales distributor, earning the official title of "Commissioned Agent."

Business was slow at first, and that scared him. As a boy, even as a young man, he had always had access to money without having to think about it. Now, he became worried—was he doing the right thing? Was he throwing away what little they had left?

Fortunately, the word did get around about the new outboard motors. Even the most die-hard sailing purists were coming around to the practical application of the Seagull as an auxiliary power source when maneuvering around moorings, or simply when there was no wind.

Interestingly enough, Edward noted, it was the Europeans who were somewhat slower coming around to the little motors. The locals seemed fascinated by anything new, and every fisherman wanted one. Unfortunately, many of the locals were underpaid and consequently, not able to afford such an investment. Edward felt bad, and tried to help where he could. However, a business cannot afford to be a charity, if it was to succeed at all. Nonetheless, the humble Seagulls continued to sell. For £26 at the time, a fisherman could power his fifteen-foot *sampan* with the 1.5 horsepower standard model. Larger motors with longer shafts were also available for other applications.

While this may not seem like much money today, it was a lot for the local fishermen then, who barely made enough to feed their families. Because of it, those who could afford the investment took meticulous care of their Seagulls, and this gave them years of dependable use. Only when they had a major problem did they call on Edward.

There was this one time when an old Malay fisherman dropped his Seagull engine while unfastening it from the boat transom, whereupon it sank to the bottom of the muddy bay. He was practically in tears when he brought it in, imploring *Tuan* to do something about it. The first thing Edward did was to flush out the salt water and silt that had deposited inside the drive, from sitting at the bottom of the bay. Next, he drained all the fluids and disassembled the motor—not a very difficult process because of the simple design. He finished up with drying and lubricating the parts before reassembly. Once he was satisfied that it was safe to do so, Edward fired it up in a barrel of water. It started up without hesitation. Such was the ruggedness of the Seagull.

Edward's small shop with the thriving business was located in the Loyang area, up in the northeast corner of Singapore, near Changi. There was sufficient dwelling room for a bachelor in the small upstairs apartment, but not much more. It was definitely not going to be enough room for his parents.

At one time, his parents used to own a large mansion on the lower east coast beach, but they had since sold it and moved inland to a smaller place. The new place was fairly comfortable, very modest, but he could tell that they still missed the beach house with the sprawling garden. Above all things, Edward wanted to remedy that situation someday soon.

Not long after he had started his business, Edward met a young Chinese man who would become his close friend, playing a part in certain factors that were to change Edward's life.

It was an afternoon in mid-1933. Edward stopped to have lunch at a small coffee shop, known by the locals as a *kopitiam* (despite the name, these places do serve much more than just coffee and are still popular in Singapore today).

Unlike his parents, Edward was not one to waste money on the snobbish "Whites Only" restaurants. He had changed over the years, especially during his time alone in Mauritius. For one thing, he had become more frugal, but more than that, he honestly felt more comfortable among the local people.

From his experience, Edward knew that the simpler local establishments actually served much better, much more interesting cuisine at very reasonable prices. As such, he usually chose to eat at these places when he was by himself, without his clients.

As usual, there was much to choose from, with the vendors of different ethnicity offering a variety of cuisine. It was not his first time at a *kopitiam*, of course, but it was his first time at that particular one. He ignored the curious glances thrown his way. Having seen a familiar sight, he attracted the attention of a food vendor and pointed at a pot consisting of different cuts of meat stewed in a dark soy sauce broth, served with flat rice noodles on the side. The food vendors, or hawkers, smiled at each other beatifically while ladling out the hot soup and meat into a bowl.

They were probably thinking something on the lines of, "The stupid *angmoh* doesn't know what he is about to eat!" *Angmoh*, literally meaning "red hair," is the Hokkien Chinese collective term for Caucasians.

During this transaction, a young Chinese man stood nearby, watching. He appeared to be in his twenties, small framed with short, tufty black hair, wearing a well-worn pair of khaki trousers and a singlet undershirt only—a typical working man on his lunch break. The young man looked on and shook his head. "*Wah*, I didn't know *angmoh* people know how to eat this kind of meat," he said, stepping up to Edward and pointing at the bowl. The Chinese, especially the Hokkien or Teochew, can come across as extremely blunt, but the heart of their crudeness is usually well-intentioned.

"I beg your pardon," Edward replied amicably. "Is there something wrong with 'this kind of meat' as you called it?"

"No, no ... nothing wrong with it. But usually *angmoh* throw away this part," the Chinese man replied. He seemed genuinely concerned for Edward.

"This part?" Edward asked, feigning confusion. He was amused—he knew what he had ordered, but somehow he still felt like playing a game with the earnest young man.

"Ah ... not sure how you say this one in English..."

The young Chinese man looked around, trying to remember what it was called. "*Eh, chi eh angmoh kio simi*?" he asked the hawker. Translated, what is this called in English?

The hawker shrugged, of no help at all. Suddenly the young man remembered the word he was searching for. "I think you call it intestines—pig intestines," he said, very proud of himself.

"Ah! Well, then I shall like it very much," Edward replied.

"Really?" The young man was incredulous.

"Yes. I'm German. We eat every part of the pig."

The young man laughed. "Just like Chinese people!" he said. A moment later, he added, "My name is Lee Eng Guan. You don't mind, I want to see."

"See?"

"Yes, see if you really can eat this or not."

"You want to watch me eat?"

"Uh, if you don't mind," Eng Guan said. Suddenly his demeanor changed, as he realized that he was being far too forward with this strange European. He looked down uneasily.

Edward took a liking to the outgoing young Chinese man. "Well, why not? But only if you eat as well. Don't want to be the only one with my mouth full, you know!" he said.

Eng Guan looked nonplused. "No *lah*, *Towkay*. I cannot..."

"I insist! Then you shall see me eat this stuff," Edward said as he reached out his hand to shake. "My name is Edward, by the way."

Eng Guan looked at the big hand tentatively, and then he shook it with a big grin. "You don't mind ... I call you *Towkay*. It means 'boss'."

"Well, I'm not your boss, or anyone's boss for that matter, but suit yourself. Come, I'm hungry after all this talk. Let's eat!"

Turning to the hawkers, who had been observing the exchange with interest, Edward ordered another bowl for Eng Guan. They sat and shared the meal. Eng Guan could not disguise his amazement at watching the unusual European man eating the very food at which other Europeans would normally have scorned.

After they had dined for a while, Edward turned to the young Chinese man. "I have a confession to make, Eng Guan. This is not the first time I have had *kway chap*," he said.

"*Aiyah, Towkay*! You pull my leg, ah?" Eng Guan exclaimed, his eyes widening.

Edward shrugged and smiled. "I'm sorry—I just could not help myself," he said.

Eng Guan burst out laughing and shook his finger at Edward, as if chiding an errant child. A friendship was born.

Late 1933
Changi Point, Singapore

"*Wah, Towkay*, this one very nice! I never before see gun like this one," Lee Eng Guan commented as he marveled at the handmade Belgian firearm hanging from Edward's shoulder.

Edward smiled. "Yes, I am quite fond of it. Actually it belongs to my father, but since he doesn't hunt much these days, he lets me have it from time to time. Would you like to take a look at it, then?" he asked, unshouldering the weapon.

"*Wah*, thank you!" Eng Guan said with his eyes widening. He carefully took the weapon from Edward, handling it with respect. When he first glanced at it, Eng Guan had assumed it was a normal double barrel shotgun of a side-by-side configuration. However, there appeared to be another barrel between and below the two twelve bore shotgun tubes—a rifle barrel forming an inverse triangle configuration with the breech opened.

"The rifle barrel here is chambered for the .303 cartridge, which is fairly easy to obtain around here. Enough power for the famous tigers, what say you?" Edward said.

In recent days, the Ubin villagers had reported seeing a tiger on the island. Whether these sightings could be substantiated or not, Edward thought it was still better to be safe than sorry. Eng Guan agreed with the precaution.

"Yes, the tigers better watch out for *Towkay*!" he said with a smile.

He carefully handed back the gun, as if it was made of glass. He then picked up the pack beside him and placed it on his shoulder as he slowly made his way down to the *sampan* moored to the slimy jetty. Edward carefully climbed into the boat next and sat at the stern, while Eng Guan sat at the bow facing him.

The young Chinese man smiled again, his gold teeth glinting in the morning sun. He was eagerly awaiting the start of the mechanical device behind Edward.

The device of interest was the Marston Seagull outboard motor. Edward turned toward it, grasped the starter cord coiled around the magneto, and pulled it quickly. The little motor sputtered to life without hesitation. "Most reliable thing in the world. You really should think about getting one, you know!"

Eng Guan grinned. "Maybe if *Towkay* buy one for me! Otherwise wait long, long time!"

Edward laughed. "I like you, Eng Guan, but not that much!"

They both laughed. Eng Guan cast off the moorings, and the boat got underway. The small Seagull motor propelled the *sampan* towards Ubin Island. It was by no means a quick ride, but certainly less effort than rowing or even rigging a sail.

For some time, Edward had been making inquiries about houses that were for sale with a sizeable property attached. Unfortunately, most of the places that he had looked at cost more money than he cared to spend. Through a relative, Eng Guan heard about a place for sale on Ubin Island. It seemed to fit the criteria and came with a very reasonable price tag. As soon as he heard about it, he told Edward the good news and offered to show him the place.

The tide was low that morning, which actually made the approach to Ubin easier, with the rocks around the island becoming more visible. Edward retarded the throttle and then killed the motor as the little boat glided alongside a crude wooden jetty. Eng Guan leapt out with a rope in hand. With the boat secure, Edward handed him the packs and the gun, then climbed out himself. Shouldering the gun and one of the packs, Edward followed him up the narrow steps from the jetty.

"So *Towkay* ... this place that I show you, ah ... my wife's uncle, he say very nice one!" Eng Guan said, leading the way with enthusiasm. They walked along a beaten red earth footpath lined with trees. "I never see the place before, but he tell me where to find. Yes, he say very nice!" he repeated. Edward smiled in reply, as they walked along the path.

Actually, it turned out to be a rather forlorn and dilapidated place that may have, at one time or another, been "very nice." But the passage of time, a lack of use and maintenance, coupled with the oppressive tropical heat and moisture, had all taken their toll on the property. The *attap*-covered porch sagged sadly. All exterior walls were covered in the ubiquitous tropical mildew and paint that was peeling. True to its nature, the indomitable jungle was steadily reclaiming the ground that had once been cleared for an English-style garden.

Eng Guan had a horrified expression on his face as he carefully turned his head toward Edward. His embarrassment was quite apparent and Edward felt bad for the eager young Chinese man.

He could not help bursting out in laughter at the situation. "Well, it looks like the place could use a little work here and there. But I tell you, I could not find so much land to go with a house on the main island at such a good price. And it is so close to the beach. Let's take a closer look inside and see what needs to be done, alright?" he suggested.

"You sure or not?" Eng Guan said, a mixture of both relief and concern evident on his tan face.

"Yes, I'm quite sure." Edward smiled to reassure him. *Poor fellow, he looks so embarrassed! It really isn't his fault, and I don't think the place is as bad as it looks at first glance, I'm sure. I'll need to invest in some supplies for certain, but I don't believe it would take too long to repair.*

A careful look around on the inside confirmed Edward's thoughts. While there was some wood-rot in places, the extent of it was fairly minimal. Most importantly, the structure was sound. Remembering that Eng Guan was a carpenter by trade, Edward voiced his thoughts to him, asking his opinion as well. Lee looked around thoughtfully and nodded.

"Eh *Towkay*, don't worry. You want help, I help. Cut wood, climb roof, anything! This kind of work is no problem!" Eng Guan said, sincerity showing on his face.

"*Ach*, Eng Guan! That is most kind of you, but I couldn't take you away from your family or your work. And I most certainly wouldn't expect you to help for free, alright?"

Eng Guan furrowed his brow and waved his hand. "Ahh! Don't worry *lah*. If I can help, I help. If I am busy, I will tell you. And no need to pay money! Buy me some *makan* to eat … enough already. Alright?"

Edward was touched by his sincere kindness. Many of the locals preferred to keep their distance from the Europeans, and no doubt the opposite was also true. Yet, here was Lee Eng Guan, a Chinese man, extending such selflessness that one could only have expected from a close friend. Throughout the years, Edward had made many acquaintances, yet very few friends. He appreciated Eng Guan's frank honesty and uncomplicated manners, and knew that he was someone with whom he could become close as brothers.

Edward smiled and placed a hand on the young man's shoulder. "Alright then. Thank you, my friend."

Eng Guan flashed his gold-toothed grin. "So I tell my wife's uncle you like this place?"

"Yes, please. Tell him I like it."

4
WHEN THERE WERE TIGERS IN SINGAPORE

1934

By then, the outboard motor business had been steadily growing, and Edward began adding other marine equipment to the inventory. Between his work and rebuilding his newly purchased home, Edward had little time for other distractions, which was fine by him.

The social scene in Singapore was very established, but unlike his parents, Edward had found it to be most unappealing. He felt that his reception from some of the English had been cool, to say the least, and he found that he really had nothing in common with the tiny German community, or any of the other Europeans on the island, for that matter.

His parents, on the other hand, enjoyed balls at the Raffles Hotel and concerts at the Victoria Memorial Hall. If there was any coolness toward them because of their German name, they ignored it entirely. They had been in Singapore for far too long to care.

They did not press Edward to join them, but hinted now and then that he needed to do something other than work. Marie was hoping to introduce her son to a certain young English lady, whose family she knew quite well.

However, Edward found himself to be more comfortable with the local people—the Chinese, Malays and Indians. This obviously did nothing but alienate himself further from many of the Europeans, but there was nothing he could do about that. He regarded such ones as stuffy and snobbish, anyway, and he had no desire to befriend them.

Although most of the local people were wary about him initially—they were that way with all Europeans—he quickly proved to them that he was no regular *orang puteh*, or "white man." One thing that Edward had found to be an effective icebreaker was to address people in their own language. He then resolved to learn some phrases in the more common dialects.

East Asian languages have certain tones and consonants that do not exist in Western tongues, and pronunciation can be tricky. As a young man growing up in Singapore, Edward had not learned any of the local languages. Now that he was older, it became more of a challenge. While the locals could more or less understand what he was saying, his accent usually brought on laughter. To them, Edward was a paradox. He appeared to be a giant of a white man, yet he ate like a local, thought and spoke—albeit with his funny accent—like a local. He even remembered their names and inquired with sincerity about their families.

Edward shortly came to be a fond figure in their community. And with the passage of time, he continued to improve on his vocabulary of local dialects, as well as the proper pronunciation of words. But he never quite lost the accent.

With his good friend Eng Guan's help, Edward completed the work on the Ubin house in late 1934. It had taken a year. Both men were often busy with their regular jobs and could only schedule what spare time they could afford to the endeavor.

As soon as the house was ready, Edward moved his belongings, including some furniture he had purchased on the main island, to Ubin. Eng Guan, who had also helped him move, smiled as he watched the house slowly becoming a home for his friend. But for Edward, it was much more than that. It was the beginning of a dream's realization.

His parents had lost so much to the world of finances, but they had stayed close as a family. Carlos once told him, "If you lose your money, you can always make it back as long as you are healthy. But if you lose your family, there is no amount of money in the world that can buy it back for you."

Now that he had made back some of their former wealth—at least enough to provide his parents with a better home—he knew that they could start dreaming again. At that point, he felt comfortable inviting Carlos and Marie to stay with him. Initially, they had said no—a man should have his own place. He replied that it was not just his place, but it was theirs as well. It was what he had in mind when he started the project.

After some persuasion, his parents finally agreed to move in, but they still kept their house on the main island. Carlos had reasoned that Marie still enjoyed the concerts from time to time, and they needed a place to go back to on those nights. However, she was starting to show her years and the idyllic life on Ubin turned out to be better suited for her.

Edward kept the staff in the house to the necessary minimum. He hired a young Tamil man in his twenties to cut back the ensuing jungle vegetation and maintain the property. An elderly Chinese housekeeper, or *amah*, would also come by twice a week from the village, or *kampong*, on the island to clean, launder and cook some meals. Whenever he was hungry, he would also head to the *kampong*. There was an old Malay couple in the village who owned a simple hawker stall that served very good food. *Satay*, seasoned skewers of barbequed meats; *nasi lemak*, which was rice cooked in coconut milk, served with fish, peanuts and a spicy chili paste; mee *rebus*, boiled noodles served in spicy gravy—these dishes were usually on the menu, as well as other quintessential Malay fare.

Evenings and nights were indescribably peaceful on Ubin. After a long day at work, Edward enjoyed coming home to spend his evenings sitting on a comfortable chair on the porch, while sharing a beer or glass of Johnnie Walker's Black Label Scotch with his father.

The one thing that remained extremely annoying, and even potentially dangerous at the same time, was the ubiquitous swarm of mosquitoes that seemed to become only worse at dusk. The local remedy for that was to burn coconut fronds, which produced a sweet, smoky odor that was somewhat effective in deterring the pests.

Night time could also bring another danger. In those days, tigers from the jungles of Malaya to the north would swim across the narrow channel from time to time. Sometimes, they would even go beyond Ubin, on to the main island of Singapore.

There were nights when Edward would wake up to the eerie moan of a tiger. Unlike the famous roar of lions, tigers tend to make low, quiet moans that are most unnerving. They also preferred to roam alone, seeking unattended chickens or even goats. Typically, they stayed away from humans, but there were some stories of attacks on children.

One night, Edward heard the familiar moan sounding closer than he had ever heard before, just as he was going to bed. He was by himself that night, with his parents spending the night on the main island. In the dark, he slowly moved to the Drilling mounted onto the wall. Breaking open the action, he slid two "00" buckshot shells into their respective chambers, followed by the .303 rifle cartridge. With the safety off, he silently moved toward the back door, which was facing the jungle. There, he stopped and listened. Another grumbling moan emanated from beyond the door.

My God, it sounds as if it is just outside this door!

Edward carefully reached for the door with his right hand, left hand firmly gripping the narrow forestock of the gun held across his chest. As he opened the door, he could see a movement in the clearing behind the house. A large male stood barely twenty feet away, the moonlight clearly defining its silhouette. It stopped in its tracks at seeing the movement of the door.

For an indeterminable moment, Edward and the tiger both stood and stared into each other's eyes, neither of them moving a muscle. Then, the tiger turned its whole body toward Edward and snarled. Immediately, Edward snapped the Drilling to his shoulder and drew a bead on the magnificent beast before him. In that instant, the tiger leapt to the left and disappeared into the jungle just as Edward squeezed off the rifle round. There was no evidence of a hit, and by the time Edward had recovered his aim, the tiger was long gone into the darkness.

That was the one and only time Edward had ever seen the famous tiger up that close. He became a legend on Ubin after the incident. However, it seemed to him that somehow the stories coming from the encounter were becoming bigger and bigger, the more times people told it.

From time to time, Edward would still hear the moans, and villagers would complain of missing livestock, but the elusive old king of the jungle did not show his magnificent head in the open. At least not that anyone saw.

The Malayan Tiger was not formally recognized as its own subspecies until 2004. Prior to that, zoologists regarded it to be the same as the Indochinese Tiger. Today, the *Panthera Tigris Malayensis* is an endangered species, numbering only a few hundred in the wild. As their natural habitat—the Malaysian rainforest—makes way for further urbanization, that small number will only continue to decline.

In Singapore, that age-old clash between man and beast resulted in the complete eradication of tigers before the start of World War II, with the last official recorded killing sometime in the 1930s. Since then, there have been only a few sightings over the years, most of which are unsubstantiated. With the only jungle left in Singapore being the urban kind, it is no wonder.

The Victoria Theatre and Memorial Hall in downtown Singapore—one of Marie Schirmer's favorite places.

5
FLORENCE CHIA

March 1937

Over the course of the past four years, Edward maintained few dealings with Winston Chia, the man who had sold him the Ubin house. Everyone called him Old Mr Chia, and the story was that he used to be a wealthy businessman in the old days. However the market crash, as well as an addiction to gambling, had wiped him out. Now, any money that he could scrape up from old debts was promptly squandered on cognac and the horses.

Edward did not particularly care for Chia. He found the man to be a crude and obnoxious drunkard, the kind of person who would verbally abuse anyone whom he perceived to be subordinate, while shamelessly groveling before anyone he felt might be of use to him. Nonetheless, Edward dealt with him cordially when he had to, as there were these necessary transactions from time to time. But other than that, he tried to keep his distance.

By then, Edward had been close friends for years with Lee Eng Guan, whose wife was related to Chia. One evening, Eng Guan dropped by to convey Chia's compliments, as well as an invitation for Edward to his house, to talk about a certain business proposal over dinner.

Knowing that he could be frank about it, Eng Guan added, "The bloody Old Bugger probably wants to *ketuk* you." Meaning that the old man was going to try and hit him up for some money.

Somehow, Edward still felt obliged to be nice to the old man. Reluctantly, he accepted the invitation. Eng Guan had that "better you than me" look as he left to convey the reply.

Winston Chia lived on the main island of Singapore in Katong, a well-to-do suburban district on the lower east side. His was a grand old mansion that appeared somewhat ostentatious on the outside. However, once inside, it proved to be rather threadbare and lacking in fixtures, missing items that had obviously been sold to accommodate the old man's habits.

Dinner was delicious, albeit somewhat rich in coconut milk and oil—typical of Peranakan cuisine. The Peranakans, also known as Nyonyas, are Straits-born Chinese whose forefathers had blended in with the indigenous Malays for generations. A typically jovial and excitable lot, they reveled in food that reflected a unique mix of the two cultures.

Mrs Chia was a plump, smiling matron who kept urging Edward to eat, also very typical of her culture. She grinned sheepishly when her husband scolded her like a child to leave his guest alone. It was all a little uncomfortable for Edward. But what caught his attention was the sight of their daughter, a beautiful yet somewhat sullen looking young woman wearing her wavy hair in a neck length bob, and dressed in a traditional *cheongsam* dress. She approached the table carrying plates of food.

"Florence, you bloody idiot! Put the food down and get Mr Schirmer here something to drink!" Chia barked at his daughter, who in turn glared at Edward.

Embarrassed, Edward opened his eyes wide and barely shook his head, as if to tell her she did not have to wait on him. For a brief moment, Florence seemed intrigued by his clear gray eyes. She turned away when her father barked, "Go, go, go!"

"These bloody women—I tell you, Mr Schirmer—will be the death of me. You're a bachelor, so you don't know, but mark my words, you have to know how to *tekan* them, or nothing gets done," Chia said. *Tekan* literally means to push or press in Malay, but used in this context, it denotes force.

What a pontificating bastard! I should hope his daughter dumps something on his fat head! How does she put up with such nonsense?

Edward said nothing in reply, choosing instead to fill his mouth with food rather than dignify the boorish old man. He could not wait for the night to end, but he knew it had really only just begun. To his surprise, he found his mind drifting back to the image of Chia's daughter.

Florence returned with a glass of Hennessey in one hand and the bottle in another. Edward thanked her and smiled his warmest smile. Her cold edge seemed to come off momentarily. Then, with her father barking at her to leave the bloody bottle and go, she stormed off and did not return for the rest of the evening.

For the remainder of that uncomfortable evening, Chia kept on pouring for himself more Hennessey, all the while going on about some hare-brained business proposal. The details of said proposal were lost to Edward after the first few minutes. Finally, the flush-faced old man—barely able to speak coherently—began nodding off. Edward heaved a sigh of relief.

Before leaving, he looked around for Mrs Chia so he could thank her for dinner. He found her in the kitchen, listening to the radio. She grinned widely and begged him to please come back again.

How does such a sweet soul end up with a monster like him? he wondered to himself, shaking his head as he walked from the mansion.

The next day, Eng Guan came over to visit Edward. He found him in his office, finishing up with some paperwork.

"So, how did it go?" he asked, although his expression was clear that he already knew how it had gone.

"Eng Guan, I should strangle you, my old friend. Good God, what a night!" Edward said as he shook his head, smiling.

"Eh, how you think I feel? I'm related to The Old Bugger!"

Edward contemplated his words. Slowly he said, "Perhaps you can still make up for things somehow."

"Huh?"

"Tell me about Florence..."

Eng Guan's usually small eyes went big. "You're joking! Eh, she's a bit young, you know!"

"How young?"

"Just turned sixteen!"

"What? You're pulling my leg! I thought she was in her twenties, at least."

Eng Guan shook his head and laughed. "Yes, yes, she look all grown up, but I'm not bluffing—she just only turn sixteen!"

Edward felt even more awkward. Sixteen! That made him, what, twenty-six years her elder? He was old enough to be her father!

Now he felt foolish. He did not want to come across as a dirty old man, but the truth was, he did find Florence very attractive. That being said, he also knew he was probably feeling a great sense of sympathy toward her because of her situation, having to live with such a tyrant. Yet sympathy, he realized, was probably not the best basis for any real relationship.

This was a new experience for Edward. In his younger years in Mauritius and Europe, there were the occasional dalliances with Flapper girls he had encountered during those daring days of the Roaring Twenties. Since arriving in Singapore, however, he had kept himself busy, and really had no interest in pursuing romance of any sort.

Up to now. But on the other hand, this was different. Or at least, he felt it was different. Perhaps it was because he was past forty and not getting any younger. Perhaps it was out of pity for Florence, and a need to rescue her. For whatever reason, he kept thinking of the beautiful, sullen young woman he met the night before. For right or for wrong, he decided to proceed anyway.

"Eng Guan ... this is most awkward for me. We've known each other for some time now, and you know that I don't take relationships with women very lightly..." Edward said.

"Yes, yes! Su Ling and I were wondering when you were going to join the monastery!" Eng Guan laughed.

Edward smiled warmly. "Not every man has the good fortune to marry someone like your wife! You know I have no time for these stuck up English ladies, yet it is expected that I marry someone of my ... well ... you know, color."

Eng Guan smiled back and put his hand on Edward's shoulder. "Edward, you know you can tell me anything. You are like a brother to me, or maybe more like an old-old uncle..." His smile turned impish.

"Yes! Thank you for reminding me of my age, you *kurang ajar!*" Edward retorted with a laugh. The Malay term which meant "lacking education" was often used to scold a disrespectful youth.

They both laughed. Then Eng Guan spoke. "But seriously *lah*, Edward, you don't have to explain yourself. I know you are a good man, never give people any trouble, not stuck up like most *angmoh*. But Edward ... this kind of thing ... people will talk. Especially those other *angmoh*. Maybe not so good for business, you know. Don't get angry. I say this as one friend to another."

"Thank you, Eng Guan. You are a true friend, and I know you speak the truth. Don't worry, I'm not angry at what you say. You are right, after all. But as far as I am concerned, all these bloody *angmohs* and their stiff upper lip can go to the Devil!"

"I also know that you can be very stubborn. Maybe that's good, maybe that's bad. But what about your parents?"

"Don't worry, my friend—I'm a big boy now!" Edward laughed. Then he added seriously, "Such things are not altogether uncommon. They knew a few people in the Mauritius who married local women."

"True, true. But how will they feel about their own son marrying one? That is different!"

Edward nodded—his friend had a point. He would have to cross that bridge when he reached it.

"I'm sure it will be fine with them," he said, simply.

Eng Guan looked doubtful. "If you say so. I still think you should not hurry into these things," he said.

"You are right. That's why I'm asking you to tell me more about her. Don't worry, Eng Guan. I know what I am doing."

Eng Guan sighed. He could not believe he was going along with this. "Okay, *lah*. I must warn you, though—that one is also very stubborn. She don't like people to tell her what to do."

"Perhaps it is because her father only knows how to scold her, and shows no kindness."

"You think so!" Eng Guan replied, although he did not look convinced. In fact, he was looking at Edward as if he thought Edward was only fooling himself. He continued, "But one thing

I know, if she like you, she is very kind. She don't like you, you better watch out!"

"How is she with you, then?"

"Don't know. Usually she ignore me. Got no money, what!"

That does not sound too promising. Is her kindness only based on one's wallet size? I must find out more…

"Other than that, you know her family story. You sure you know what you're doing?"

Edward was not sure, really. But he did know that if he did not pursue this, he would always wonder about her.

"How do I go about meeting her, without involving her father at first? At least until I can make a decision."

"Like that ... you cannot do. You have to talk to him first. And don't forget, he will be expecting something from you in the end."

Eng Guan made a sign—rubbing his thumb against the index and middle fingers—for money.

A dowry! Well, that seems absolutely archaic. But, I suppose, if it is the custom, although it rather seems like buying a human being...

Then the idea angered him. He knew that none of the money would make it to the family, but instead be squandered on the old man's selfish habits. But there really was nothing to be done about such things.

I must see her again.

Despite his reticence, Eng Guan arranged for Edward to visit the Chias on a social basis, whereupon Edward would be able to make his intentions known to Florence's father.

"I knew you would be back! It's a good idea, is it not? Plenty of money to be made by all!" Winston Chia greeted Edward, pumping his hand with great enthusiasm.

Good God! I can't even remember what rubbish you were going on about the other night, you old goat!

Edward wished he could say his thoughts out loud, but instead politely said, "Good to see you again, Mr Chia! Don't worry, I'm still thinking about things, you know. But I am here about a different matter altogether."

"Oh?" The old man looked at Edward warily.

Edward chose his words carefully. He disliked the awkwardness of it all. "Yes, Mr Chia ... this is a rather delicate matter, so I had better come right to the point. The other night when I was here, I could not help but notice your daughter. She is ... a very attractive young lady, and I ... well, I would like to become better acquainted with her. With your permission, of course," he said.

Although Edward had meant nothing lascivious by his words, Chia immediately took them in the worst possible manner. His eyes went big. Then they grew small again, as he laughed in delight. "Oh, ho! Young Florence has captured your attention, I see! Yes, she is quite beautiful. But rather young for you, what?"

A wicked gleam seemed to flash in his eyes.

"Yes, Eng Guan did tell me her age. I found it ... hard to believe. Really, she does seem much older."

"Mmm ... yes. They do grow up very quickly, it would appear. Why, it seems like only yesterday that she was a little girl!"

Chia seemed to take pleasure in Edward's discomfiture. Not quite sure how to respond, Edward smiled awkwardly and took a sip of the Oolong tea that Mrs Chia had set in front of him on the sitting room table.

"So, what exactly are your intentions, Edward? I should call you Edward, shouldn't I, under these circumstances? Just don't call me your Papa quite yet!" Chia laughed, full of glee.

You wouldn't want to know what I would like to call you, you filthy old devil!

Edward laughed politely and replied, "Of course! Please call me Edward. Well, as far as my intentions are, I would like to begin by getting to know Florence better. As a friend, of course. Certainly, marriage is something serious to consider, and two strangers are hardly suited for matrimony."

The old man nodded solemnly. Then he turned and bellowed up the stairs, "Florence! Come here now!"

Florence dreaded the sound of her father's grating voice. Sighing, she put down the clothes that she was mending and obediently headed for the stairs.

What now?

6 COURTSHIP

Edward was flustered. The truth of it was that it had been a long time since he went out with a young lady, and he was not quite sure what to do, or what she might be expecting of him. *I suppose dinner followed by a motion picture at the cinema or dancing is the typical thing to do. But what if that is much too typical? She will think I am a boring old man! You know, I probably am making too much out of this whole thing. How do I know her father will even let her out? For all I know he will insist on having us sit across each other in the sitting room, while he and his wife stare at us all evening!*

But that did not happen. Winston Chia had come straight out and told his daughter that Edward wanted to take her out, surprising everyone. Really, this was not because he was such a modern Dad, but in fact, it was because he had seen a golden opportunity in the making. For one thing, he would be rid of his daughter, whom he saw as nothing more than a financial liability. For another, he would possibly have some leverage against this European.

"But you are so much older!" Florence remarked. She immediately put her hand to her mouth, as she realized how impulsive her words had been.

"Florence!" her father barked, and moved toward her with his hand raised above his head. She cringed. Realizing the scene he was about to make, Chia lowered his hand.

"How rude!" he said after a moment.

Edward's heart sank. For a brief moment, he wanted to quickly turn around and run, to escape the humiliating situation. What was he even thinking? *But I have to remember that she is only sixteen. Apart from the candor of youth, what she said is quite correct.*

Because of the absurdity of the situation, he laughed. Slowly, everyone began laughing as well. "Well my dear, where can this old man take you, then? I promise not to trip you up with my walking cane!" Edward said, smiling.

She laughed. Her eyes softened and she smiled back at him. When she spoke, her voice had a slight giggle about it. "Not tonight. How about Friday night? And I want to go to the pictures after dinner! Maybe some dancing, even."

Winston Chia was one of many Chinese in those pre-war days who were English-educated, and essentially indoctrinated in the superiority of the white man, especially the British white man. This belief had its evidence in the apparently indomitable British Empire and the strong, efficient way it was run. In other words, as far as Chia and his fellow believers were concerned, power, money and influence equaled superiority.

Somehow, this notion of superiority came to include other aspects such as language, culture, dress and manners. Even one's beauty or handsomeness was based on the occidental perspective.

Hence, any alliance with a European, be it commercial or social, raised one's standing. This was a double-edged sword, however. Many people, of either race, considered a young Asian girl who was going out with a European man to be quite simply a harlot. Nonetheless, Chia viewed the prospects before him as more beneficial than not, and sought to exploit the situation.

Before the date, Chia spoke with his daughter about this great opportunity. Initially, she had found the idea of one of her father's business associates showing interest in her to be an appalling one. After all, Edward was old enough to be her father! Yet at the same time, she found it all somewhat intriguing. She also had to admit that the attention that he was giving her was somewhat flattering.

But more importantly, Edward, as her father had pointed out, had money, was tall, handsome and a European. Chia highlighted these attributes and downplayed the age difference. Any reservation Florence might have had left in her slowly dissipated as her father cunningly pointed out that she would also be the envy of friends and neighbors, every time Edward took her to places.

This was not quite true. Because of the social taboos, it was more than likely that she would encounter quite the opposite. However, he deftly steered her away from that as well, appealing to her young naïveté. He never once alluded to marriage or responsibility. Quite the opposite, he assured her that she would have a good time away from the usual chores. That closed the deal, as far as she was concerned. Anything to break free from the bonds of her tyrannical father, even for one evening!

Somehow, it never occurred to her young mind that her father was being disingenuous, or that he might be having ulterior motives for this sudden bout of friendliness and reasonableness.

At five o'clock Friday evening, Edward came to pick her up, arriving in a taxi. He had on a quality gray double-breasted wool suit, which he seldom wore, but felt it was necessary this time to make a good impression.

Florence appeared at the door, looking elegant in a jade silk *cheongsam* dress, which was well juxtaposed by a Western hairdo—the finger wave style of the day. She smiled at Edward and walked toward him, as he held open the door of the taxi for her.

Chia stood at the entrance of his big house, waving amiably at them with a big smile on his face. "Stupid *angmoh*! That girl will be wrapping him round her little finger in no time at all. Must see what can be gained from that!" he muttered to nobody in particular.

"So, what did you have in mind, Florence?" Edward asked, as the taxi started to move. Although he was familiar with places to go in Singapore, he wanted to make sure Florence was happy with the choice of destination. He was also being a little cautious about suggesting anything that might come off as old and boring.

"I want to go to the Raffles Hotel! However, while *you* can go in, they would throw *me* out for being a Chink, did you know that?" she replied, raising her eyebrows peevishly.

"I never go there. Waste of my time. Come, let's not talk about such things. Where is a good place that you like to eat?"

Florence gave directions to the taxi driver. He drove them through the suburbs down to the coastal Beach Road. They went past shophouses and droves of people walking about. In that part of town, one could truly experience the cosmopolitan nature of Singapore—English, Europeans, Arabs, Farsi, Chinese, Indians, and Malays, all mingled in commerce.

The driver turned this way and that, until finally pulling over in front of a row of two-story buildings on Victoria Street. After paying the driver, Edward got out and opened the door for Florence.

She put her arm in his and led him to a door on the side of one of the buildings that bore a large signboard with Chinese characters on it. The moment Edward opened the door, a pungent yet delicious aroma came wafting out, stirring his appetite. He particularly enjoyed the unique blend of the different regional Chinese cooking styles, which was quintessentially Singaporean.

The dimly lit stairway led them to a rooftop restaurant. A cool evening breeze blew gently, and it felt refreshing. It was a little unnerving though, as the other diners, all Chinese, turned to look at them. Edward smiled slightly and nodded at some, as Florence led him to a table.

"Europeans never come here, you see. Would you like me to order the food?" she asked.

"Yes please. Whatever you like. I'll eat anything."

Florence called a young woman over. Edward had no idea what was transpiring in the animated conversation between her and the waitress, but every now and then, they would turn to look at him. The waitress came back with a pot of tea and two small cups, and then she left.

"She is worried you may not be able to eat the food. It's quite spicy, you know," Florence said as she poured the tea.

"Oh! Is this a sort of test, then?" Edward smiled.

"Perhaps!" Florence returned the smile with a small amount of mischief.

When the food arrived, Edward took in the sights and smells. Then he ate. This was certainly some of the best Chinese cuisine he had experienced! However, some of it surprised him, especially a fried chicken dish served in a Szechuan style hot-sweet sauce with dried chilies. Upon ingesting a dried chili quite by accident, his eyes went round as saucers. Immediately, he shoveled some plain rice into his mouth, and then slowly sipped the hot tea.

Florence laughed at how flushed his face had become. "Well, I am most impressed, Edward! I thought for a moment there that I would have to call out the fire brigade," she said.

"You still might have to!"

After dinner, they walked to the Capitol Theatre, where a romantic drama entitled *Camille*—starring Greta Garbo—was playing. At that time air-conditioning was still a new concept in Singapore, and the old Capitol had not been upgraded yet. Even with the fans blowing, Edward regretted wearing his woolen suit. *The price we pay for trying to be fashionable!* He took the jacket off and draped it over the arm of the chair between them. Florence smiled at him, and became absorbed by the flickering lights on the screen.

The movie ended after nine. Edward was not sure if he should suggest that they end the night then, out of propriety, and risk appearing to be boring and old, so he said nothing. Florence spoke first.

"Edward, I still want to go dancing!"

"Well, I believe there is still enough time for that. Where do you suggest we go?"

Florence gave a thought about it. "There is that dance place at the New World Park. It's in the same direction as my house."

Edward knew exactly right where it was. "Sounds ideal. Let's hail a taxi."

The New World Amusement Park, just off Jalan Besar, was an enormous location featuring everything from a classy dance hall to seedy striptease cabarets, boxing and wrestling rings, an opera house and movie theaters. It was a very popular venue in Singapore, attracting both young and old, servicemen and civilians, locals and Europeans. As it was a Friday night, the boardwalks were overflowing with people.

Edward offered his arm to Florence. They stepped through the park's main entrance and gazed up at the bright neon lights to find directions to the main dance hall.

As they walked down the central boulevard, a small group of Australian infantrymen stumbled by, obviously having had too much to drink.

"Oi, fellas! Take a look at the Sheila with the big bloke over there," one of them said. His friends turned to look at Florence.

"What are you doing with the fella in the stuffy suit? You want a real good time, you come with us. I'm sure we've still got a few shillings left between all of us," he said, to the hooting laughter of his mates.

Edward pushed Florence behind him. He had not had to fight since his school days, and now he was facing four well-built soldiers who were half his age. On the upside, they were clearly inebriated and did not seem able to stand up very well.

Before things could get out of hand, their young lieutenant came rushing up to straighten things out, apologizing to Edward as he shuffled his men away. All the while, Florence was looking down, fidgeting with her purse.

"Are you alright, Florence?" Edward asked, concerned.

Florence looked up, nodded her head and gave a wry smile. "I'm fine. Come, we're here to dance. Let's go."

It had been a long time since Edward had stepped out on a dance floor. Fortunately for him, when they arrived, the orchestra had started the set with a rendition of the Ray Noble Orchestra's *Midnight, the Stars and You*—an easy fox-trot number. The American swing craze and audacious Lindy Hop dancing had, by then made its way around the world, but it was still viewed at the time with some disapproval among the more conservative British in Singapore. As far as Edward was concerned, that was quite all right. He personally thought that anyone performing such audacious dance moves looked as if they were crazy.

Florence danced with elegance and, by outward appearances, seemed to have forgotten the unpleasant encounter earlier and was enjoying herself. But when they sat down between dances, she grew sullen again. Hoping to keep things going, Edward began asking questions to find out more about her. Florence replied to these cursorily, but was not very chatty, otherwise. She seemed to be preoccupied with something else.

"I know they were drunk, but what do you think about what they said?" she remarked after a moment, obviously referring to their encounter with the Australian soldiers.

Edward felt embarrassed. He hated talking about such social topics, as he believed they were ridiculous in the first place. If everyone could behave themselves and mind their own business, then there would be no foolish social rules that really did nothing but create walls and dissension. But he knew that his Utopian ideals were only that—nothing more than ideals.

Furthermore, he knew deep down that, once upon a time, he was just another bigoted European, with their same disdain for people of a different color. It still embarrassed him somewhat.

"Well, that's just it. They were drunk, and drunkards talk rubbish," he replied after a while.

Florence rolled her eyes. "I'm not a little girl. I know they were drunk, but I also know, had they been sober, they still would have seen me as nothing more than a Chink and a harlot!"

Edward was feeling even more embarrassed. He had chosen not to give much thought to the social ramifications of interracial dating, but as his friend Eng Guan had reminded him earlier, it was not something that he could simply ignore just because he chose to.

"Come on now, that's not true. I'm sure they wouldn't be thinking of such things!" he mumbled.

"You really think so, Edward?"

Florence looked Edward in the eye, a piercing glare. She could see that he thought otherwise.

"Alright, then. So there are all sorts of stupid people out there, who go out of their way to make others miserable. Why bother about them and what they have to say?" Edward said after a moment.

"Because their talk affects me! I can't pretend that they don't exist when they are right there, in front of me. Maybe you can choose to ignore them, but my kind cannot!"

Edward had nothing to say about that. She was right. As a man—and to be precise, a white man especially—he had the ability to make his own decisions, and to make them stick. He knew that the same privilege did not necessarily extend to women and Asians.

Even much less then, to an Asian woman.

"Florence, you are right. You are not a little girl, and you do know how the world around you works. I'm just sorry things are not right with this foolish world we live in."

On an impulse, he leaned over and kissed her on the cheek. She smelt like a sweet mix of powder and jasmine flowers. Sitting upright, he looked away, blushing.

Florence was surprised by his gesture. She felt a warm, tingling feeling on her face and was not sure how to react. Having received little warmth from her own father, this sort of attention was a new thing for her altogether.

It was exciting.

She reached out and took his hand in hers. Edward turned to look at her. She laughed. "Oh my, Edward! Are you blushing?"

That made him blush even more. Looking down at his feet, he smiled. Then once again he looked up at her and squeezed her hand gently.

"Florence, I cannot lie to you. The first time I saw you, I was drawn to your beauty. But more than that, I really wanted to talk to you, to get to know you."

It was now her turn to blush. Unaccustomed to praise and kindness as she was, but still yearning desperately for it as any young lady would, Florence swelled up inside.

"*Aiyah,* Edward! You're so silly!"

"I do mean it, Florence. I'm sorry to be so single-minded, but these are the things I think of. Who are you? What kind of thoughts are going on in that pretty head of yours? What makes you happy? I want to know about these things! Not about what some stupid people have to say. Do you understand what I'm saying?"

Florence nodded. Never had anyone paid so much attention to her, other than her mother. *But she's my Mummy. She's supposed to say nice things about me!* she rationalized in her head. Florence felt that she could spend the entire night just listening to Edward say nice things about her.

The Capitol Theatre at the corner of Stamford Road and North Bridge Road.

The main entrance to The New World Park, as one would have seen in the 1930s.

7
FRIENDS AND FAMILY

After that successful first date, Edward began calling on the Chia household regularly to see Florence. Sometimes, it was for a meal with the whole family. Other times, they strolled around the neighborhood, talking and occasionally popping in to the small shops that lined Katong Road.

She really wanted to know about Europe and other lands that he had seen. In turn, Edward was curious about her family, which—as he had discovered after the first few conversations—seemed to be quite extensive.

"Appears to me you're related to half the island, dear!" Edward remarked during one of their walks, with a teasing smile on his face.

"Don't be silly. It's not that bad!"

"Well, at least I know a couple of your relatives. You know my friend Eng Guan and his wife Su Ling?"

"Yes, of course. Well, actually, I don't really know him all that well. I'm related to his wife, you see. She is a second cousin or something like that."

"Well, I think we should all have dinner together sometime."

"If you say so."

"You don't really like the idea, Florence?"

"No, it's not that. It's just that I am, well, not very close to that side of the family."

Edward was concerned.

"Anything bad that I should know about, perhaps?"

"No, no. We just grew up very differently. Never really spent much time together."

"Well, if you have nothing against it, I think we should all have dinner together then. Get to know each other. I think you would like them. They really are most kind, you know."

Florence smiled apprehensively.

"If it will make you happy, then yes."

Edward arranged for dinner at a restaurant famous for its fresh seafood. People in Singapore, both then and now, love to eat, and social events always take place around a meal of some sort. The restaurant was located somewhere east of Katong, toward the Bedok area. It was actually somebody's house with a large courtyard in front, where the proprietor had set tables up in the open for the customers. In those days, there were very few actual restaurants and for the most part, people went out to eat at informal set-ups such as these.

Edward insisted that Eng Guan should order the meal, saying that he had best defer to someone who knew what they were doing. They sat in the open courtyard, a dim light from kerosene lanterns flickering upon them. The cool, ocean-scented evening breeze gently blew by every now and then, while a delicious aroma from the cooking of fresh seafood, meats and vegetables swirled around them. When the food arrived, it was served on big platters, family style. Everyone took portions, placing the food on small plates or in bowls set before them.

"This is quite amazing, Eng Guan! Thank you for suggesting this place. I had no idea it even existed," Edward said, in between mouthfuls.

Eng Guan smiled, bowed his head and replied, "Yes, not many *angmoh* know this place. Eh, by the way, Edward, thank you for inviting us. Very kind of you!"

Su Ling gave a shy smile and nodded in agreement. Even though her husband and Edward were close friends, it was not customary for traditional Chinese women then to hold conversations with men other than their spouses, especially those outside of their race.

Edward understood this, and reciprocated by simply smiling back at her and nodding his head once as if to say, "It's nothing."

Florence remained somewhat aloof. It did appear that she was attempting to be friendly toward Eng Guan and his wife, but just not sure how to go about it. Edward was uncertain if he should be trying to break the ice, or just letting things take its course. He decided on the latter, chatting with Eng Guan mainly, but now and then asking Florence how she was doing. Slowly, Florence and Su Ling began their own conversation, mostly asking about this relative or that.

As young girls, they had very different upbringings. Florence had a life of privilege—at least for the first nine or ten years—while Su Ling came from a working family. Su Ling was also quite a few years older and, because Chinese girls then did not typically have much schooling, she was already working while Florence went to an all-girls school with other children of similar background. While Florence was educated in English, Su Ling spoke mostly Hokkien, the somewhat coarse southern Chinese dialect prevalent in Malaya and Singapore. Since Florence's servants spoke that same dialect—her parents did as well on occasion—she was fairly fluent in it, and thus able to communicate with Su Ling that evening.

Still, it was uncomfortable for Florence initially, as her father had raised her to look down on the less affluent Chinese-educated ones. As much as she recognized Su Ling's and Eng Guan's sincerity, they were just "not her type." She also found it somewhat astounding that Edward, a European, could be so comfortable with those whom she ashamedly thought of as peasants.

But the most unbearable part for her was realizing that the appearance of class or status was just a façade. Financially, her family was now actually worse off than Su Ling's hardworking family who made *beehoon,* rice vermicelli noodles, for a living.

However, the night moved along pleasantly. The men, aided by a few beers, were laughing about the antics of a mutual friend, while the women slowly warmed up to each other, catching up on the years. Finally, it became the time to say goodnight.

"Hey, Eng Guan, I don't believe your wife has seen the Ubin house since we repaired it, has she? I cannot believe how the time has flown by!" Edward remarked. "I think we should all go there sometime. Florence hasn't seen it, either."

"Sure, sure. Maybe on Sunday?" Eng Guan replied.

"Florence, would you like to go then?" Edward asked.

She thought about it and replied, "Yes, I'm sure Daddy will not mind. But only after I go to Church in the morning."

The boat crossing from Changi Point to Ubin was a rather precarious affair in the narrow wooden *sampan* powered with the Seagull engine. The four of them, plus supplies, were more than the boat was built for, and the water seemed alarmingly closer to the gunwale than usual. Edward knew it was time for a bigger boat.

Once on the island, they made their way to the house, following the primitive footpath. Florence looked around as they walked, and recognition slowly came to her.

"Oh my, I remember this place! We used to come here when I was little. Daddy had a house around here somewhere..." She stopped as the house came into view. "So it was you who bought it! Daddy said he sold it some time ago, but I didn't know all the details."

She quickly walked up to the house. Florence had not seen the place since she was seven years old. She had no idea of the state the house had fallen into, or that Edward and Eng Guan had taken great pains to restore it only a few years before.

"It looks just as I remember it ten years ago. Even better! This is quite amazing!" she said. Edward and Eng Guan looked at each other and smiled.

"Come inside, come inside," Edward invited. "The *amah* has been here since morning and she has cooked us a splendid meal."

They left their shoes out on the porch and went inside. The smell of cooking beckoned them, and they made their way to the dining table, which had already been set.

Roast pork with a salty and crispy skin sat on one plate in the middle. Next to it was another plate with a whole roast duck, its skin shiny with a seasoned red glaze. Two large bowls, one filled with a clear fish soup and the other with steamed rice, were alongside the main serving platters.

To complement the meal, the *amah* had also set a pot of Kuan Yin tea and small bowls of various sauces, neatly arranged around the main dishes.

Just as they were about to sit at the table, the *amah* came out of the kitchen with a platter of sautéed vegetables in her hands, thus completing the culinary picture.

"We'll eat very well today, no doubt," Edward said with enthusiasm. "This looks delicious, Aunty!" In Singapore, it is still customary today to address one's elder as Uncle or Aunty.

The old Chinese housekeeper smiled, dipped her head and gestured for them to sit down. "*Towkay* ... Uncle, Aunty already *makan.* They go for walk," she said to Edward, referring to his parents, Carlos and Marie, who had left earlier.

"Oh, good! I trust they enjoyed the food as well," Edward replied. To his friends, he said, "Come, let's eat."

A few bites confirmed his prior visual assessment of the food. It was indeed delicious. His friends settled in to the meal before them, commenting in between bites about the idyllic setting of the house on the island, and how nicely it had all turned out.

Indeed it was a very beautiful place, inside and out. The young Tamil gardener had a gift for transforming the overgrown jungle backdrop into a paradisiacal blend of natural tropical beauty and a manicured English garden. This had taken a few years of patience and consistency on his part, but at this point it was almost self-maintaining.

After lunch, they brought their drinks out on the porch to enjoy the breeze while staying out of the scorching sun.

Over generations of Colonial rule, the English had established two of the most refreshing daytime drinks for the tropics—sweet iced lemon tea and freshly squeezed lime juice. The iced tea was made by mashing thin slices of lemon in sugar syrup, then pouring crushed ice and English black tea over. The lime juice came from the kaffir lime, a small thin-skinned tropical variety, sweetened with sugar.

Initially, Su Ling was feeling a little uncomfortable being waited on, so she made an attempt to help with the dishes. However, the *amah* gently waved her away, telling her to go join the others. The older woman was quite adamant too, so Su Ling reluctantly went out on the porch and sat behind her husband, who was talking in his usual animated way with Edward.

Florence remained oblivious to this exchange. She put on a pair of sunglasses and sat next to a small table. As she sipped on her lime juice, her mind started wandering to a bygone time, back to when her family would stay at this very house, while servants waited on them.

She remembered playing in the sand on the beach, and wading out until the water reached her neck to cool off every now and again. Her mother would then call out in concern for her to be careful, every time she went in the water—just like clockwork. Her father would either be sitting with his nose in the papers, or passed out from too much beer.

Simpler times. Could she go back to them?

Edward observed the small smile that appeared on Florence's face and felt happy. He could easily imagine a future with her in this very house, with his friends coming to share good times. It was very satisfying to reflect on the day, and how it could always be this way.

From a distance, Carlos Juan Schirmer watched the group of people sitting on the porch and smiled to himself. His son appeared to be having a good time with his friends.

He was happy for Edward, that he was finally finding a life outside of work and his aging parents. Because of that, earlier on Carlos had said that he would be taking Marie for a walk after an early lunch. He gently added too that they would only be getting in the way if they stayed around. Of course, Edward had objected to that—his parents were always welcome to join in with his friends, he told his father. Carlos smiled, patted his son's hand and wished him a good time.

But there really was more to what Carlos had said. He actually was trying to spare his son any embarrassment. Marie was beginning to display signs of senile dementia, and sometimes she said the most inappropriate things, or would forget that she had already asked a question and begin to repeat herself.

Carlos was happy watching his son find happiness, but he did not altogether approve of Florence, from what he could see. Admittedly, the race issue was part of it—one should marry their own kind, he believed—but there remained something else about her that he did not quite like. A certain coldness perhaps, he thought. There were just some things a parent can see—the things that their children cannot, or will not. Carlos did not want to hurt Edward's feelings, so he kept his thoughts to himself.

He knew it was time to go back to the old house on Lim Ah Woo Road. With Marie's health declining, he could honestly say that they needed to be closer to the doctor.

8
FLORENCE SCHIRMER

May 1937
Katong District, Singapore

When Edward proposed to Florence, she did not hesitate. While it did seem terribly romantic in her young mind, above all, it was a ticket out of her present situation. Although she was still unsure about her feelings toward Edward, she reasoned that she could grow to love him. After all, it was how things had been done for generations: marriage before love.

Her father, having anticipated the proposal, immediately counter-proposed with a certain dowry sum. Edward, having anticipated this arrangement, accepted the terms and forked out the money. The date was set.

The couple's first argument was about the wedding itself. Edward had been raised only in name as a Catholic. He did not believe the teachings of the Catechism, and in fact had been disdainful of the Church's involvement in the Great War. Catholics killing Catholics, both invoking God's name on their side. He did not want a big church wedding, but Florence, an ardent churchgoer, insisted on having one.

The debate went on, and Edward was getting frustrated. Finally he asked, "What does your father think about it? What would he want?"

Florence rolled her eyes. "He has not stepped in a church for as long as I can remember. He will not care about what I want!"

True enough, when asked for his opinion, her father replied, "*Aiyah!* What nonsense! Who cares where you get married? Keep it simple! No need for all this Church rubbish. You take him, he takes you ... done already!"

In other words, since it had not been openly decided who was financially responsible for the wedding, he did not want to be the one to have to spend any money on the deal.

Florence kept her disappointment to herself. It was no use arguing with her father. His word was always final. She expressed her unhappiness by pouting. Edward found himself in a quandary. He did not want to start out their marriage on this note. However, he really did not want a big church wedding. Finally, he offered a compromise. "Florence, I don't want you to think of me as cruel or selfish, but I just don't want a big church wedding with all the hullabaloo. What if we had it at the church, but kept it a simple ceremony?"

Still pouting, she replied, "Well, I suppose that's better than nothing."

Her father threw his two bits in again. "*Aiyah!* Edward, I don't know why you give in to her like that. See if that doesn't become trouble for you down the road! Well, it's your wish. Sure, have it at the church, but just keep it simple, if I were you."

It was a simple ceremony at the Holy Family Catholic church in Katong. The Chias invited a small group of friends and family to the wedding. After that, they proceeded to a formal dinner, hosted by Edward. His new father-in-law had indicated that it was customary among the Chinese for the groom's family to pay for the wedding, so Edward acquiesced. It was something that he had expected anyway.

Edward and Florence enjoyed a brief honeymoon at Cameron Highlands, in the north of the Malay Peninsula. The highlands is a range of mountains with peaks that experience temperate climates year round, an unusual yet pleasant change from the tropical jungles that lie at their base. Europeans—the ones who could afford it—built their holiday mansions in these highlands. Edward could not yet afford to take Florence to Europe right then—a trip which would have been her dream—but promised her instead that they would go one day, soon. For now, they would enjoy a stay at the charming Tudor cottage, with its manicured English garden, with sunny yet cool days and dark chilly nights by the fireplace. It was an almost-European holiday, thousands of feet above the equatorial balminess of the Malayan jungle.

Barely a week after their return, Florence began to experience light-headedness. Was it perhaps the climate change, or the altitude? Then, the nausea kicked in.

Mrs Chia knew right away what it was. In her jolly manner of speech that interpolated English, Malay and Hokkien words, she gleefully pronounced the diagnosis, "*Alamak, darling! Lu ada anak, lah!*" You are with child!

Florence was aghast. A baby! She was certainly not ready to be a mother, of all things. "This is hardly fair! I just got out from Daddy's clutches. We just got our life started. How are we going to be able to go to dances and have fun? How am I going to have my holidays?" she muttered. Thoughts raced through her mind. She felt—understandably so because of her age—that her life was imploding. This was not what she had expected. But then, what had she really expected?

When Edward came home from work that night, he stopped a distance from the house to survey the scene before him. He felt a warm satisfaction inside. Things were starting to shape up nicely. What more could a man ask for in life? He was certainly not expecting the surprise that greeted him—Florence had obviously been crying.

"My dear! What is the matter?"

Florence glared at him. "I think I'm pregnant," she said.

Edward's warm, satisfied feeling doubled at this announcement. "Why, that's wonderful, Florence!"

"For you, maybe! I'm not ready! You had all your life to do all sorts of things. I'm just now starting to live, and this happens."

"Well, what did you think would happen?" Edward said, but immediately he regretted his words. "I mean, I thought it was something you would want as well. I forget sometimes, well ... you just seem so much older."

"Well, I'm not! All these years the only thing I ever did was go to school and then come home to be my father's slave. I suppose I'm your bloody slave now!"

"Florence, please don't say such things. I will never treat you the way he did. I love you, you know."

Do I really? I still don't know!

"So you say. I guess it doesn't really matter. We will find out if I have a baby in a short time. But I'm quite certain. The symptoms are all there."

Edward was hurt by her callous words. On one hand, he understood the apprehension that arose from her youth. However, for him, becoming a parent finally was a joyous feeling. Was he being selfish? But what did she really think would happen when people were married?

Now he wondered if his feelings toward her were driven only by selfish desires on his part to settle down—damn the consequences and never mind if it wasn't the right thing for her. Was she better off staying in that abusive relationship with her father? How could that even be so? Yet, here she was, unhappy with the way her life was headed. Edward thought about these things and made up his mind to do his best to make her happy.

Making Florence happy was not going to prove to be all that easy. As Eng Guan had mentioned at the start, she was indeed strong-headed. Now that she was also pregnant—as the family doctor had confirmed—her emotions ran high and low. Florence had a need to test the waters. She was not used to having her way at home with her father, but Edward really did seem to go out of his way to mollify her when she made demands. She became used to this idea, and as time went on, she would make even more demands, expecting them to be met. This did not always work out the way she expected.

One thing her father had made clear in the Chia household was that servants held their place at the bottom. There was a trickledown effect in abusive speech—her father yelled at her, she yelled at the servants. In her father's house, she expected the help to *kowtow* to her. Now that she was the mistress of this abode, she expected the same here.

It was no problem getting Arul the gardener to treat her the way she wanted. He came from a long line of servitude—his forefathers were originally convicts brought over by the British from India to perform manual labor. Although Edward had never treated him poorly, Arul was used to hearing his previous employers speak at him harshly. In return, he would bow profusely to them while promising to fulfill his tasks.

At the time, this was not considered ritual humiliation. It was just how things were done.

The *amah*, Ang Poh Yin, was a different case. In her younger years, her employers treated her harshly as well, and she accepted it then. However, she had reached an age when one has quite had enough of that sort of nonsense. Poh Yin had been initially hesitant to work for Edward, or anyone else for that matter, because she was getting ready to retire. She had some money saved up, not much but enough to live out her years if she was frugal, along with some help from her grown-up children. However, Edward had proven to be an easy master—he was seldom home anyway—so she stayed on. Even after his parents had moved in, they were kind to her and made her work pleasant. Now though, the *towkay's* young wife—who was only as old as her own granddaughter—was bossing her around with no respect. On top of that, there had also been some history between them, although Florence was unaware of it at that point.

The Chia family, in the good old days, would come to stay at that very house. Poh Yin remembered them well. How could she forget the uncouth abusive father and the bratty girl? The mother was nice, but a little insipid. Poh Yin remembered that there had also been another daughter, who seemed quite nice, but she was a bit older than Florence and mostly off on her own.

But here again was Florence, ten years or so older, but still bossy as ever. Poh Yin did her job, but she was not going to *kowtow* to her. It was one thing if an *angmoh* bossed her around, but quite another when it was some other *tng lang*, or Chinese person. Especially, one who was so young.

Florence felt that the *amah* was not giving her face, and decided that her husband should have to do something about that.

"Edward, I don't like that *amah*. You need to let her go," she said one day.

Edward was rather taken aback. "Poh Yin? Are you serious? What has she done wrong?"

"She's rude to me."

"What? I've never noticed her being rude to you."

"Well, she is. I tell her to do something, she doesn't even acknowledge me. That bloody woman!"

"I can't believe that! She always gets things done, it seems."

"That's not the point! Yes, she does what I tell her, but she doesn't say 'Yes Ma'am' to me or bother being polite at all."

"You think she should bow to you as well?"

"Don't make fun of me, Edward! She's a servant and she knows what is expected of her."

"Look, I'll be honest with you. I've observed you ordering her about, and you are very rude to her. You didn't seem to like how your father treated you, so why do you think it's fine to treat others in such a manner? Besides, she's much older than you. It doesn't matter that she works for us. She still deserves our respect."

Florence glared at him. "Well, are you or are you not going to take care of things? I'm your wife now. Are you saying that the servant is more important than me?"

This was beginning to get on Edward's nerves. He remained silent, but Florence went on grumbling about Poh Yin. Finally, he had had all that he could handle.

"ENOUGH!"

Florence stopped, her mouth agape.

Edward spoke again, but in a much gentler tone. "Florence, that's enough. I am not letting Poh Yin go. She does a fine job and I trust her. Frankly, I think you need to learn to treat the help with more respect. You will then find that they treat you back with respect. I'm sorry, but my decision is quite final."

Florence stormed away to sulk, and Edward let her go. Things settled down gradually in the Schirmer household, after some of these initial hiccups. Such moments are typically inevitable for any newly establishing family. However, the age and cultural differences between them did nothing but compound the issues further.

Edward still tried his best to give Florence what she wanted, but within reason. She would, on occasion, push a little too far or too much, and he would have to put her in her place.

Sometimes, he felt as if he was dealing with a petulant child, and then he would have to stop and think. *What do you expect, old man? She really is not that much older than a child.*

One had to deal with the choices made in life.

9
GENERATIONS

February 10th 1938
Ubin Island, Singapore

Within days of turning seventeen, Florence gave birth to a boy. It was not an easy delivery. After eight hours of labor, with the aid of a midwife from the village, the seven and a half pound bundle took in his first breaths of air.

For as much as Edward had been in anticipation of the moment, there was no preparing him for the overwhelming sense of joy that now enveloped him, the moment he held his son for the first time. His parents were also there to share the celebration, and for a moment, Marie almost seemed to be her old self as she cradled the infant. Becoming a grandparent had taken a while, but it had finally happened.

Naming the child then became a topic of debate. For some time, Edward had felt a need to be true to his German heritage. Although he had no desire to return to Germany, he felt pride in his ancestry. *Not that I agree with everything that fellow over there, that Hitler chap, is saying, mind you, but there's nothing wrong with simple pride in one's roots. The English are proud of their history, so are the Chinese, the Japanese and so on. My son should have some awareness of his heritage.*

Edward wanted his son to have a German first name, for a change. His father had a Spanish first name, and he himself had an English one. After some deliberation, he chose to name the boy Hans Felix Schirmer.

Florence wasn't so sure at first. She felt that an English name would be better suited, considering that they were living in a British colony. There were some who did not want to forget the last war, and many could see that Germany was again becoming belligerent.

Edward considered her opinion, but in the end remained adamant. He reasoned that their children should stand out from the crowd, that common English names were, well, just common. Florence finally agreed, and the more she thought about it, she found that she did rather like the exoticness, the foreignness of the name Hans.

And so, Hans Felix Schirmer came to be. His father affectionately called him Hansel—"Little Hans." He was a healthy boy, growing stronger every day. He suffered no major illnesses apart from the usual child-related ones.

It was the beginning of a new generation. Unfortunately, it also became the time for the old one to move on.

January 30th 1939
Singapore

Carlos Juan Schirmer did not stop to wipe his eyes, as he signed the paper certifying the death of Marie Lucie Schirmer, née Duclos.

A tear rolled down his nose and landed on the paper, smudging the ink. He did not care.

A few months before, they had celebrated their forty-fifth anniversary. When he had first met Marie, he was barely twenty-three. They had been through the proverbial thick and thin; they had grown old together. The last year or so he found himself pushing her about in a wheelchair, and cleaning her up when she soiled herself, but he would not have traded that for anything.

Now, she was gone.

For the most part, Carlos had hung up his sailor's hat when he married Marie—it was what he wanted to do, never had she forced him. Now he felt it was time to dust it off, and go with the tide. What else was there for him to do?

October 9th 1939

As Carlos left the Argentinean embassy, he looked over his reissued passport once more to make sure everything was in its place. The face in the photograph staring back still did not look familiar to him. No matter how old one gets, one always thinks of themselves as being much younger.

It had taken time to get things in order. Since the day his wife died earlier that year, he had been busy arranging her affairs and getting the house sold. He was now all packed up, and had made arrangements to vacate the house by the end of the week. The replacement passport was the final detail.

With all the moving over the years, he had lost his passport some time ago—he had no idea when exactly that had happened. The original had been issued in 1926, and the last time he traveled was in 1929. He could not believe it had been ten years already.

When he arrived at Edward's shop, he found his son on the telephone with a supplier. Edward held up one finger—the "I will be right with you in a moment" sign. Carlos nodded and sat down.

"So, Papa. How did things go?" Edward said, replacing the telephone handset onto the cradle.

Carlos shrugged. "I have my passport," he said.

"One last attempt to get you to stay..."

"We've been through all this before, son. I don't want to die on dry land. God knows how much time I have left anyway. Maybe get to see Buenos Aires one more time, I don't know."

"Just like the elephants, Papa? Going away to die?" Edward said with a sad smile.

Carlos laughed. "Yes! Just like that. That's an idea—I should see the Congo once more as well."

A moment of silence.

After swallowing the lump in his throat, Edward spoke first. "Well Papa, you know you can't go back to Africa without the Drilling. Let me go back to Ubin and get it for you," he said.

Carlos held out his hand. "You keep it, Edward. Over the years, it has given me great pleasure, but my hunting days are over. I will just go and say goodbye to the animals."

Tears rolled down Edward's cheeks. He nodded quietly. As soon as he could speak without his voice breaking, he said, "Make sure you write, Papa. I want to know all about your adventures."

Carlos snorted. "Ha! If you can read my handwriting, it will be a miracle!" he said.

Edward came around the counter and stood in front of his father. Papa was old-fashioned. Real men did not hug, they shook hands. But now was not the time for mere handshakes.

Carlos wrapped his arms around his son.

Edward received few letters over the months, but each time he did, he would smile as he read them. His father was finding peace with the world, even though it was a world that was by then seeing war in more and more places. Carlos did live to see the Congo and Buenos Aires again, just as he said he would.

The last letter Edward received came from Peru, of all places. Then, almost two years after his beloved wife's death, Carlos Juan Schirmer went to sleep aboard an ocean liner somewhere in the Pacific and never woke up again. The ship company forwarded his passport and other personal effects to Edward with profound regrets.

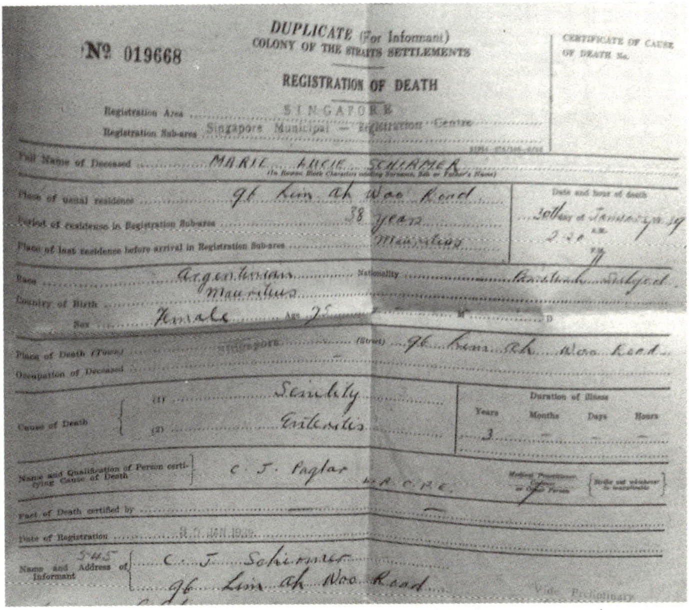
No. 019668

DUPLICATE (For Informant)
COLONY OF THE STRAITS SETTLEMENTS

REGISTRATION OF DEATH

CERTIFICATE OF CAUSE OF DEATH No.

Registration Area: SINGAPORE
Registration Sub-area: Singapore Municipal — Registration Centre

Full Name of Deceased: MARIE LUCIE SCHIRMER

Place of usual residence: 96 Lim Ah Woo Road
Period of residence in Registration Sub-area: 38 years
Place of last residence before arrival in Registration Sub-area: Mauritius
Date and hour of death: 30th day of January 1939, 2.20 P.M.

Race: Argentinian
Nationality: British Subject
Country of Birth: Mauritius
Sex: Female
Age: 75

Place of Death (Town): Singapore (Street): 96 Lim Ah Woo Road
Occupation of Deceased: —

Cause of Death: (1) Senility (2) Enteritis
Duration of Illness: Years 3, Months —, Days —, Hours —

Name and Qualification of Person certifying Cause of Death: C. J. Paglar L.M.C.P.E.

Fact of Death certified by: —

Date of Registration: 30 JAN 1939

Name and Address of Informant: C. J. Schirmer, 96 Lim Ah Woo Road

Death certificate of Marie Lucie Schirmer, dated January 30th 1939.

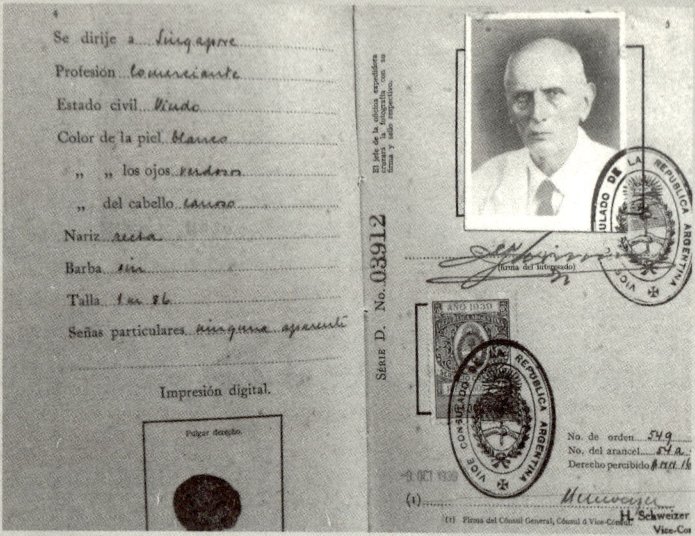

4

Se dirije a Singapore

Profesión Comerciante

Estado civil Viudo

Color de la piel blanco

„ „ los ojos pardos

„ del cabello canoso

Nariz recta

Barba sin

Talla 1 m 86

Señas particulares ninguna aparente

Impresión digital.

Pulgar derecho.

El jefe de la oficina expedidora cruzará la fotografía con su firma y sello respectivo.

Série D. No. 03912

5

(firma del interesado)

VICE CONSULADO DE LA REPUBLICA ARGENTINA

AÑO 1939

No. de orden 549

No. del arancel 54 a

Derecho percibido

-9 OCT 1939

(1)

(1) Firma del Cónsul General, Cónsul ó Vice-Cónsul.

H. Schweizer

Vice-Co

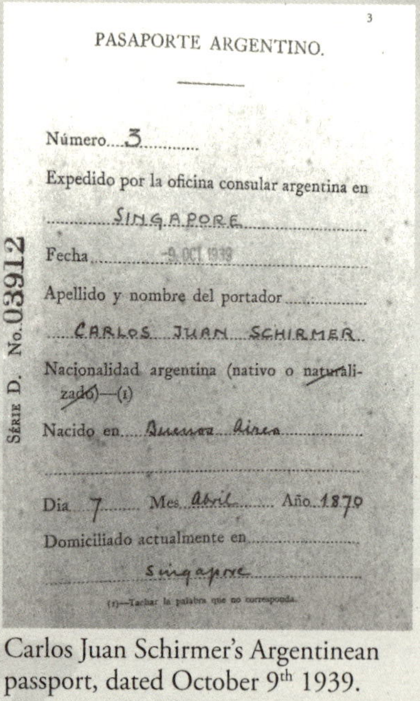

3

PASAPORTE ARGENTINO.

Número 3

Expedido por la oficina consular argentina en

SINGAPORE

Fecha -9 OCT 1939

Apellido y nombre del portador

CARLOS JUAN SCHIRMER

Nacionalidad argentina (nativo o naturalizado)—(1)

Nacido en Buenos Aires

Dia 7 Mes Abril Año 1870

Domiciliado actualmente en

Singapore

(1)—Tachar la palabra que no corresponda.

Série D. No. 03912

Carlos Juan Schirmer's Argentinean passport, dated October 9th 1939.

10
BOYS

Florence had little more than a year to recover from the first birth before she found herself pregnant again. In January of 1940, she gave birth to another boy. Edward named him Carl Johann, after his father.

When Carl was only ten months old, and Hans was two, Florence gave birth to yet another boy, Franz Eugene. He became known as Eugene, or Genie. Edward was as happy as he had ever been, a proud father to his three boys. He wished his parents were around to see them born.

As Hans grew into that chubby toddler stage, he became a little powerhouse, running everywhere. His parents observed that he was either asleep or at full steam. As soon as he was able to go outdoors himself, he liked to run around the property, terrorizing the chickens and laughing when he got them to run in fright, clucking loudly. For some reason, that sound amused him greatly. Whenever he heard them giving out the alarmed burst of clucking that can only be brought on by fright, he laughed even harder.

Typical of most boys, little Hans was never satisfied with the status quo. While chasing chickens could be amusing, he realized that it was even funnier to sneak up on them and throw a well-aimed stone at one. The thud of a stone hitting a chicken's feathery side, immediately followed by the surprised, indignant volley of clucks was downright hilarious to him.

Edward was silently observing this cruel stalking game one day while standing on the porch. Instead of shouting at Hans to stop, which had been his initial thought, Edward went back through the house and out the back door. He stealthily approached the giggling little boy from behind, who by then had armed himself with another stone and was waiting for an opportunity to strike again. Once Edward was close enough, he rushed in with a roar, picked up the unaware child and swatted his behind. Hans let out a shriek of terror, and Edward put him down.

When he saw who it was, Hans started sobbing. Then he furrowed his brow and folded his arms. Edward tried his hardest not to laugh.

"You sc ... you sc ... you scared me, Papa!" Hans grumbled between sobs.

"Well, how do you think the chickens feel?"

Hans thought about that, but did not want to answer.

"You know how they feel when you hurt them, or scare them. What if somebody was to throw stones at you? How would you like that, then?"

Still pouting, the little boy shook his head slightly.

"Well then, are you going to do this again?"

Another small shake of the head.

"See that you don't. Besides, if you hit them like that, they can only lay scrambled eggs. Did you know that?"

Hans furrowed his brow even more. Full of doubt, he asked, "Papa, is that really true?"

Edward laughed. "No, I'm just joking. But seriously, I don't ever want to see you hurting the animals like that again. It is cruel to them. Do you understand, Hansel?"

Hans nodded slowly. Edward picked him up and placed him on his broad shoulders.

"Let's go find something else to do, alright?"

Hans quietly rode on his father's shoulders. His quick little mind thought about Papa's words. He reasoned that if Papa didn't want to *see* that again, then he would just have to be careful to scare chickens only when Papa was not around to *see* it.

Edward could not have been prouder of his three sons, but since Hans was the oldest, he experienced the most time with his Papa. Hans would follow him everywhere, running with his short little legs to keep up with Edward's ranging stride. Whenever he tired, Edward simply picked up the boy with a smile and placed him on his shoulders.

Hans was at a good age to be taken places and taught about life. Edward began taking him to the shop sometime after the boy turned two, with some basic rules: ask before touching anything, be quiet when customers come in, and no interrupting adults. Hans complied easily, as it was his nature to observe quietly before doing anything. He was also eager to please his Papa, and dreaded the forbidding glare he would receive when doing something wrong. From following his father around, Hans learned many life skills, as well as his ethics, through observation. What Hans really looked forward to was when Papa would take his special gun off the wall and show it to him. As he became older, he was even allowed to handle it. Papa would then tell him about the hunts he had been on as a boy in far off Africa, which sounded so mysterious and exciting. But most of all, the story of the tiger thrilled him.

"When can you take me to go hunt the tiger, Papa?"

Edward smiled. "Oh, I don't want to go hunt the tiger, Hansel. We have a secret agreement, you know. He leaves me alone and I leave him alone. Besides, I haven't seen him in years. I do hear him once in a while, but I never see him anymore."

Hans was disappointed, Edward could see. He had an idea.

"But you know what we can do, though? Maybe we can go on a wild boar hunt!" he said with enthusiasm. "We can take a drive up to Johor and do that. You're certainly old enough for that."

"Really, Papa?"

"Yes. I will need to make some arrangements with someone over there, but I believe we might be able to go very soon."

October 1940
Johor, Malaya

As Edward did not own a car, he had made arrangements to borrow one from a good customer of his. Edward seldom drove, so he took his time to familiarize himself with the vehicle—a ten year-old Ford open tourer—before heading out.

It was the perfect day for a hunt, a clear Sunday morning. They drove across the Causeway that bridged Singapore to the Malayan mainland. Hans was excited, as he seldom had the opportunity to ride in a car. He sat in the back seat and waved at people on the street. Sometimes they waved back, sometimes they did not. Eng Guan sat in the front passenger seat and talked with Edward.

They stopped for breakfast at a coffee shop in Johor Bahru, the main city in the state of Johor. After that, they drove northeast for some time. The narrow road that they drove on was lined by jungle mostly, with rubber tree plantations in some parts.

In a little over a year from that day, an aggressive, determined Japanese army would fight a tired and confused force of British, Indian and Australian defenders down those very roads, all the way to Singapore.

After driving northeast for almost an hour, Edward slowed down the car and came to a stop at the edge of the rubber plantation where they were to meet a man named Malcolm Atkinson. He was the owner of the estate, and also a customer of Edward's. Atkinson would show them where they could hunt. When they arrived, they saw that he was already there, waiting in a car parked in the shade.

As they were pulling up in their car, they also noticed a small group of Tamil men waiting nearby. These men were rubber-tappers by trade, laborers who worked for the plantation owner. They were there that day to act as guides on the hunt.

Atkinson opened his door and walked up to Edward, waving. "Good to see you, old boy," he said, extending his hand to Edward and, somewhat hesitantly, to Eng Guan. Then he looked down at Hans. "This must be your son. Handsome lad!"

Hans smiled at him.

"Thank you for all this, Mr Atkinson. Good show! Your men all look quite ready," Edward replied, in his best English Gentleman manner.

"Quite, quite! Now, I'm sure you know how this all works, but just in case you don't, do allow me to explain," Atkinson said. "These fellows will take you into the plantation, and after a while, you will see them split up. They will be clapping their hands and making a row, but this is all quite normal. Their job is to flush out the pigs with their hullabaloo, yours is to shoot them. The pigs, that is, of course! Do try *not* to hit the Darkies, please. Rather difficult to replace, you know!" He laughed at his own joke.

"Yes, yes, I would imagine so," Edward said, with a polite but awkward laugh. He had known Atkinson for some time, and was familiar with his rather dry sense of humor. Despite the jibe, Atkinson was a fair employer, and treated his men well.

"Well, Schirmer, it looks as if you are all ready to have a splendid time. I must be getting back to the missus—she has plans for the afternoon, you see—or I'd think of joining you myself. Fine day for a hunt, eh?" he said.

With that, the two men shook hands once more. Edward thanked the older man profusely. Atkinson smiled and bid them a good hunt before driving away, tooting the horn and waving as he went off.

Edward went back to their car to retrieve his Drilling and a custom hand-tooled ammunition bandolier, which was made to hold a combination of .303 rifle cartridges and twelve bore shotgun shells. He then gave strict instructions for Hans to follow closely behind, and to never get ahead of him. Eng Guan just wanted to follow along and see the show, so he said that he would keep an eye on the boy.

As soon as they had collected all the things they needed, Edward waved at the Tamil men with a smile. They smiled, waved back and walked into the plantation. Edward's small party followed them.

Some distance in, the workers performed as Atkinson said they would. Edward slowed down on the edge of a clearing and listened. The clapping and shouting grew faint, then louder again as the men walked around to flush the wild boar toward Edward. Their job was a dangerous one. Wild boars, when startled, oftentimes charge blindly toward the source of their alarm. Armed with dangerous tusks, they can gore a man to death or at the very least, cause some serious damage.

When such an attack occurred, the agile young Tamil men would quickly jump on the trunk of the nearest tree and propel themselves upwards with their bare feet. Their solidly calloused feet rendered footwear unnecessary. Many of these men actually spent their entire lives without ever wearing shoes.

Just as Edward was about to move again, he heard a loud rustling from the undergrowth toward his right. Turning toward the sound, he snapped the Drilling to his shoulder and kept his eyes fixed on the brush ahead.

Suddenly, a large grayish male burst out from the brush. Edward squeezed the rifle trigger and the gun barked sharply. Both Eng Guan and Hans plugged their ears. The bullet hit the boar directly on the face, but the large animal kept on coming, its heavy body propelled by momentum. Edward moved his finger to the separate shotgun trigger and squeezed once. Again the gun barked, but with a different note—deeper and more percussive. This time, the boar crashed to the ground, its legs twitching spasmodically.

"*Wah*, good shot! Good shot!" Eng Guan exclaimed. Hans stood in stunned silence, his ears ringing.

The men came running out from all directions, calling excitedly to each other in Tamil.

Edward spoke. "Well, men! Think we can get another?"

The workers gave the thumbs up. They knew that the more meat he bagged, the more they would get to take home as well. Edward smiled and the men went back to their role in the hunt. He ejected the spent casings and inserted fresh rounds into the gun.

All in all, it was a most successful morning. Edward managed to shoot another two large pigs, a male and a female. The workers busied themselves with the slaughter of the animals, and everyone went home with plenty of meat that day.

Hans went to bed that night remembering in vivid detail everything he saw. He would never forget that day. "When I grow up, I want to be just like Papa," he said, as he drifted off to sleep.

11
RESENTMENT

For all her dreams—the glamorous grown-up life that Florence had pictured in her mind when she married—none came to fruition. Instead, all that she could see before her was yet another life of servitude.

Certainly, Edward was not abusive toward her. Quite the contrary, he was actually rather kind. Nonetheless she was still, in her mind, subject to him and his desires. He had simply replaced another authoritative figure.

But what had ultimately darkened her spirit was having three sons in three years—before she had even turned twenty. That was something she had never planned for.

It was also very obvious, more so than ever, that the European holiday Edward once promised would never take place, as far as she could tell. They could finally afford it now—money was no longer the issue—but instead, a new obstacle thwarted her dreams.

Europe had been in a state of war since September 1939, and travel was becoming more restricted. The other issue was the family situation, again. Even if the war ended tomorrow and they could begin the trip, she would rather die than go with three screaming brats in tow.

"As for leaving them behind, Edward would never stand for that—he is so ridiculously fond of his bloody spawn. Again, life sees fit to slap me in the face!" she raged to herself.

In all fairness to her, the situation that Florence had found herself in was indeed very overwhelming—more so than most young ladies her age would have wanted for themselves. However, what she had concocted for herself was a fairytale rescue from her wicked father's clutches—an imagined life that had excluded the very real possibility of becoming a mother before she was quite ready for it. Now, after reality had set in, she began to view her life as only just a little different from the one she had just escaped.

There was a small part of her that knew she was not entirely being fair to Edward. He was nothing at all like her father, and he actually did try his best to keep her happy. Still, she remained inconsolable.

On Edward's part, it had been unrealistic as well for him to assume that it would all turn out fine. Florence was young, immature, as well as mentally scarred from abuse and disappointment. Furthermore, as Eng Guan had pointed out to him, she was used to having her way with everyone (other than her father, of course) and that she was a strong-headed individual.

The feelings of resentment slowly grew deeper for both parties. Florence resented her life, and she channeled that resentment down to her husband and children. Edward grew tired of trying so hard to please her, only to be received with implacable coldness. Gradually, they grew apart, with Edward seeking solace and companionship in his children and his closest friend, Eng Guan.

Florence performed her obligatory maternal duties, but she resented the children nonetheless. She felt as if she was constantly tending to the two younger ones. Fortunately, Hans was old enough by then to follow his father everywhere, and so he did.

The tension was obvious in their household. Edward spent less time at home as he was more comfortable meeting Eng Guan in town or down at the shop. This unfortunately only served to compound the idea in Florence's head that she was indeed a prisoner on that island.

She knew though that the man of the house was king of his castle. A product of the times she lived in, she knew that ultimately, women had their place, so she did not fight it altogether. However, she was not happy, and when she was not happy, she made sure everyone knew it as well.

December 1940

For some time, Winston Chia had not been feeling well. The first time he passed blood in his urine, he nearly fainted from the shock. Then the sharp aches and pains from within his body began to hit him more and more frequently. Still, he refused to mention it to anyone. He knew what the doctors would say, and did not want to hear it.

"I don't want to live anyway if I can't have a smoke or a drink, and have to start eating like an old woman!" he grumbled to himself.

Even when he lost consciousness one day, he still refused to see a doctor. His wife was worried, but she knew the futility in pressing her husband to do anything that he was dead set against. He explained it away as nothing more than exhaustion.

"But exhaustion from doing what?" she wondered. "He sits around all day, doing nothing."

As the pains and fainting spells grew more frequent, malaise and fatigue also began to consume him. It was not long before he became completely bedbound with a fever. By this point, he was falling in and out of consciousness. His wife then called in a doctor, who took one look and insisted the patient be hospitalized right away. But it was already too late; Winston Chia never regained consciousness and his irregular breathing ceased altogether.

The traditional Chinese funeral in Singapore is typically a loud and somewhat elaborate ceremony—wailing mourners follow the cortege procession to the final resting place, with priests and other religious members chanting prayers along the way.

As strange to the Western mind as this may be, the family will sometimes hire professional mourners to bolster the procession numbers. The belief is that the gods will see how loved the deceased one was, and kindly admit that one to heaven. Loud funeral orchestras with clashing cymbals and blaring trumpets follow the procession, driving away wicked spirits as well.

In order not to offend or turn away newly converted parishioners, some churches chose to turn a blind eye to these customs, reasoning that if these ones were turned away completely, how then were they to gain salvation?

Winston Chia received none of the elaborate rites. His squandering of the family's fortune ensured that his own funeral remained a simple one. To Florence, this was possibly the only good thing that came from his selfishness. She was a devout Catholic, and did not approve of the mixing of pagan customs with what she believed to be proper Christian practice.

After a simple mass, Florence's father was laid to rest at the Bidadari Cemetery off Bartley Road, located in the central part of Singapore. The turnout for the funeral was indeed modest. As it was, the old man really did not have any friends, and most of his relatives did not want to waste their time honoring a man who had treated them with no respect. For them, a poor turnout would be their final payback to the old man.

Eng Guan and Su Ling had attended the funeral mainly out of respect to Edward, but also for the affable Mrs Chia, who stood by the open grave sobbing. They came wearing the traditional Chinese mourner's garb, consisting of baggy black trousers and tunic. Despite carrying their umbrellas, everyone was dripping wet with the rain blowing sideways from the wind, typical weather for that time of year.

Florence stood stone-faced at the graveside with a sleeping infant in her arms, while Edward struggled momentarily with a restless toddler who wanted to get down. Carl had just begun to walk and wanted to exercise his newfound ability. When Edward whispered something in his ear, the boy relaxed a little and then put his head down in resignation.

Hans stood quietly by himself, looking at the coffin in the ground. He was also observing the actions of the mourners. This was the first funeral that he could recall; he had been too little to remember the time when Marie died or when Carlos had left.

Although he did not really know the old man, and could not yet fully grasp the concept of death, Hans knew well enough that it was a somber occasion.

"Ma, what are you going to do now?" Florence asked her mother, later that evening.

"*Tak tahu, lah, Sayang,*" Mrs Chia replied, a blank look on her face. I don't know, my Love.

She started sobbing again. Florence silently put her hand on her mother's arm, waiting for her to speak.

Having caught her breath, Mrs Chia continued, "You know, Uncle Ah Neo told me that the bank will now come and take back the house! When he said that, I really *terperanjat*! I almost fainted! Here I was, thinking that your Daddy paid up for the house long time ago, but now I find out that he borrowed money again. What to do!"

Florence clenched her jaw in anger. "Even when he dies he has to make things difficult for people, that swine!"

"*Cheh!* Cannot say such things, *lah*!" her mother wailed. "Your Daddy loved you! How can you say such things, now that he's dead?"

"Ahh! I cannot believe this rubbish! He only loved himself, and you know that. You can lie to yourself about how wonderful he was—maybe you need to, or you'll go mad. But don't tell me he loved me. That's a lie!"

Feeling her world crumbling around her, Mrs Chia burst into tears. Reaching behind, she lowered her rotund frame on to an old rattan chair, sobbing helplessly. It was truly a most pitiful sight. Florence closed her eyes and pictured her father's face.

You filthy old bastard! All she's ever done was to serve you and now you leave her like this. I hope you rot in Hell! she mentally cursed, but having decided to further spare her mother's feelings, said nothing aloud. After a moment, Florence spoke, "You come stay with us on Ubin. Take all your things that you want and Edward will have someone move them for you. No choice *lah*. The bank will come and take the house anyway."

She did not mean to be brusque with her mother—her anger lay solely with her father—but she knew that she had to be the one to make the decisions now.

Her mother looked up at her and burst into tears again. "So many years here! You and your *chie chie* were both born here. How many *makan* times, birthday parties, wedding anniversaries... All nothing but memories now!"

Florence felt sorry for her mother. Her simple expectations and blind optimism, all dashed by the selfishness of one man. Softening her voice, she spoke again to her mother. "Mummy, there's really nothing we can do about that. We have to face the facts."

Mrs Chia tried to smile. "You are a good daughter, you know that?"

Florence put on her warmest smile and held her mother's hands gently in hers.

"We can make this work out. We'll take care of you, Ma."

January 1941
Ubin Island, Singapore

Florence did actually look forward to her mother moving in with them. On one hand, by taking care of her aging parent, she was fulfilling the obligations of filial piety indoctrinated in Chinese culture. On the other hand, she would also have someone to take care of the children when she needed it.

Edward was by nature a person who preferred his privacy, but he had no issue with his mother-in-law moving in. Taking her in had been the only kind thing to do. Although she could be somewhat annoying and constantly indulging in empty chit-chat, he chose to ignore such things, focusing instead on the fact that she was really a kind soul. One who had been dealt a very poor hand in life.

Just as Florence had been, Mrs Chia was delighted when she first saw the house on Ubin. For the first time in days, she moved with purpose, and it appeared that hope was returning to her.

"*Ala, Sayang!* You have done a wonderful job on the place! It has been such a long time since I've been here ... such wonderful memories we had here..."

She stopped when she noticed the *amah* standing by the kitchen, smiling. "*Alamak,* Ah Yin! Is that really you? *Aiyah, mai kek kee*! Come over here, *lah*!" she exclaimed in delight. Don't be so formal, in other words.

Poh Yin came over and grasped her hands. "Good to see you, Aunty!" she said. "Sorry to hear about Uncle. May the gods watch over him."

Old Mrs Chia became teary eyed again, but she smiled at Poh Yin. "What to do, what to do? Life's like that. But never mind, how are you? All the children grown up, ya?"

The two older women spoke excitedly in Hokkien, exchanging information about family and people they knew from the old days. Edward watched them for a moment and, knowing that he was out of his element, smiled and busied himself with carrying the bags and other belongings.

Florence also stood by, observing her mother.

"I can't believe she's carrying on with the help as if she was one of them. How embarrassing! Well, at least she can deal with that Ah Yin, so maybe I don't have to. Hopefully this all works out for the best..." she muttered to herself.

Mrs Chia's moving in proved to be beneficial to all. Always optimistic, always wanting everyone to get along, she continued her old role as the perpetual buffer. Even Florence began to warm up a little. Perhaps it was the reminders of being a little girl again.

After a few days, Mrs Chia began to cook again, which was her passion. Whenever she did, she insisted that Florence should watch and learn from her, just as if she was still a little girl. Each time that happened, Florence smiled, rolled her eyes and complied, even though she had heard it all before. Secretly, she enjoyed it. Besides, she knew it was giving her mother such joy to feel useful again.

The quiet island, unlike the busy Katong roads, was very therapeutic for Mrs Chia. Watching the children play and the chickens pecking, listening to the breeze through the coconut trees, it was not a bad way to spend the later years of her life.

12
A TRIP DOWNTOWN

February 10th 1941

Hans Schirmer's third birthday fell on a Monday. Edward had kept the shop closed that day and promised his son a special time downtown on the main island, just the two of them. The boy was bouncing off the walls with excitement. It was not his first time downtown, but the previous times had been to accompany his father on business and, truth be told, they were rather boring. This time, he knew it was going to be a special trip.

Several times, Edward had to remind him that the trip would be cancelled if he did not behave himself. Although bursting with excitement, he quieted down. His mind, however, continued racing.

Their day began with a simple but filling breakfast of *nasi lemak* at the village. After breakfast, they pushed off in the powered *sampan*, arriving at Changi Point on the main island. Both were dressed in their downtown attire. Edward wore a lightweight linen suit while Hans had on a collared shirt, wool dress shorts and socks with his new buckled sandals. Because of what they were wearing, they took extra care when walking up the slippery jetty.

From the jetty, they walked to the bus stop at Changi Village. Before long, Hans heard the *put-put* combustion sound of a small four-cylinder engine, and a funny looking vehicle came into view. Known as Mosquito Buses, these vehicles were small and underpowered motorized carriages with the entrance in the rear. Locals—even with their smaller size—always felt squeezed when they sat on the two narrow benches that ran the length of the vehicle, facing toward each other.

For Edward, it might have been an uncomfortable ordeal, but it was also the only means of transportation downtown. The stiff suspension riding on narrow wheels ensured a rough ride as the bus driver took nerve-wracking turns through the winding Changi roads. But for Hans, the ride was an adventure itself, almost on par with the hunting trip up to Johor.

It was a long journey to Singapore's downtown district, lasting a little over an hour through the various winding roads. The excited three year-old was ready to bolt as soon as the tiny bus came to a stop at Raffles Place, but his father had already warned him beforehand that he must not run off while they were downtown. So he patiently waited while his father, hunched over, made his way out the rear of the bus.

"Don't tell your mother I said so, but today you can have anything you want to eat! Ice-cream, cake, fruit, whatever. Just make sure you go slowly. I don't want you to make yourself sick," Edward said, smiling.

If there was one thing Hans loved, it was food! He hugged his Papa and held his big hand. This was going to be the best day ever! Hans was excited to see so many busy people walking about; certainly it was quite different from the sleepy pace on Ubin. Street vendors with their push carts sold different snacks and beverages.

Edward, knowing how much his son loved fruit, bought some fresh cut pineapple. The sweet juice invigorated them after the long, hot bus ride.

"This afternoon, we can go to the cinema. But first, let's walk around and look at some shops. After that we should have lunch. Don't eat too much, because I know of a good place around here where we can get some cake and ice-cream," Edward recommended.

They walked through busy Raffles Place to the popular Robinsons department store. Edward had also promised Florence that he would buy some clothes for the boys when they were downtown. He knew that they would find everything they needed, right there in one place.

As Hans tried on clothes, the look on his face said it all—this doesn't seem like much fun. But his expression changed to excitement when Edward took him to the toy department.

"Papa, can I have a gun like yours?" he asked.

"I don't know if they have anything quite like that, but let's see what they have."

The toy gun aisle presented a fairly large variety. There was nothing like the Drilling, as Edward had guessed, but his eyes fell on a Daisy non-firing model. It was a scaled down replica of Winchester's Model 94 lever-action carbine.

"Oh look, Hans. Just like what the cowboys carry in their saddle!" he said, holding the toy out for Hans to see.

Hans's eyes opened wide. He reached out for the carbine.

"Here, hold it like this. And let's pretend it is a real gun. That means you cannot point it at people. You don't want to be shooting them accidentally, right?" Edward said. He presented the carbine to his son in a port arms position, with the weapon held across his chest diagonally, the barrel pointed upwards.

Hans nodded as he accepted the toy, a serious look on his face. Keeping his finger off the trigger just as he had seen Papa doing,

Hans slowly worked the lever action. Just like the real thing, that action cocked the hammer backwards.

"Aim it toward that open wall over there. Let's see what it does," Edward said.

Hans shouldered and aimed the gun, just as he had seen Papa do many times before. Closing one eye, he squeezed the trigger. The hammer fell with a click.

"Not bad at all, Hansel! You just have to pretend it fires a real bullet, and BOOM!"

"Can I have it, Papa?"

"Yes, of course!"

Hans hugged his father with one hand, the other still holding the forestock of the toy gun. As they walked down some other aisles toward the register, they passed by a box of slingshots. Hans stopped to look at them, but he remembered the toy gun in his hands, and glanced down at it.

Edward stopped and turned to see what had caught his son's attention. He looked at the boy's face and saw the longing on it.

"Would you like a catapult as well?"

"Papa, I can have two presents?"

"Why not? But you must promise me something. No shooting at chickens or people, alright? And make sure you don't break any windows, either."

"I promise, Papa."

After shopping, it was time to eat. The dessert shop that Edward had in mind turned out to be a small café that also served light lunches, so he recommended that they have their afternoon meal there as well. Edward opted for a cream style soup and a chicken sandwich, while Hans went for the fish and chips, which came served in the authentic English style, in newspaper. It was blazing hot from the fryer. After nearly burning his mouth and fingers, Hans blew cautiously at each bite.

"For dessert, what if I ordered a cake and you ordered ice-cream? That way we could try both," Edward suggested.

Hans nodded; his mouth was full. Edward called the waitress.

"Miss, I noticed a very nice looking chocolate torte in the showcase. I would like a big slice of that, please. My son would like a banana split sundae, but without strawberry ice-cream, please. He doesn't like that flavor," he said.

The desserts came just as Hans ate the last of his lunch.

"Perhaps I should have waited a little before ordering dessert. Do you need to wait a few minutes, son?"

Hans shook his head and reached for the spoon. Edward laughed, reaching for his dessert fork. Between the two of them, both desserts disappeared completely.

That afternoon, Walt Disney's feature film *Fantasia* was playing at the new air-conditioned cinema in the Cathay building. The show was brand new to the screen, with animation that was the most vivid and detailed at the time. Everyone had been talking about it, and Hans was very excited.

They took a bus there, as it was some distance from Raffles Place. Edward, paying for the tickets, said that he did not think they needed snacks for the show. Hans nodded in agreement.

As they stepped into the dark air-conditioned auditorium, an usher with a flashlight took their tickets and pointed out their seats. For Hans, it was his first time in an air-conditioned place.

Just as Edward had anticipated, Hans became enthralled with the color, music and animation of *Fantasia*, right from the beginning. There were even some moments when he had to grip his father's hand. Edward laughed and held his son tight in those moments to reassure him.

As they left the cinema, the little boy still had lights and stars flashing in his eyes, while music swirled in his head. He could imagine himself as the sorcerer's apprentice, in place of Mickey

Mouse, whenever he closed his eyes.

While the show was perhaps not quite what he would have picked for himself, Edward enjoyed watching his son have a good time. He felt a warm glow inside as he observed the boy smile, close his eyes and hum the tunes he had just heard. There was nothing in the world better than seeing his son happy.

After the show, they walked around for a while, but it was becoming late in the day. Edward said they needed to catch the bus back to Changi before it got too dark. By then, Hans was tired from all the excitement and needed to be carried on his Papa's broad shoulders every now and again.

The Mosquito Bus to Changi Point arrived just before six. They boarded it along with the other passengers and settled down on the narrow benches once again. It was another crowded, uncomfortable affair. Edward took off his jacket and loosened his tie, heaving a sigh of relief. The journey proved uneventful most of the way. However, once the bus came to the winding, hilly road just around the notorious Changi prison, it started having problems. The already underpowered engine could not propel the overloaded bus up a certain stretch, so the bus driver pulled over and turned off the engine to let it cool. The disgruntled passengers sighed and grumbled about the delay.

Edward stepped outside to stretch his legs and cool off, having been squashed next to a large, older Malay lady. As he slowly walked around in the dusk, he heard an old familiar sound that raised the hairs on his arms—a low, grumbling moan emanating from beyond the tall *lalang* grass that grew alongside the road.

Oh, shit!

"TIGER!" he shouted. "Driver, start the engine! There's a tiger nearby and we have to get the bus moving!"

Immediately, everyone sprang to life with shouts of alarm. The driver hopped back in his seat and turned on the ignition. The hot engine coughed and spluttered, but refused to start. After a few more attempts, it reluctantly turned over and rumbled to life.

"Rev the engine! Make noise, everyone!" Edward ordered.

All the passengers began shouting, in the hope of scaring the unseen tiger away. In reality though, everyone was shouting more out of terror than anything else.

Edward threw his jacket at Hans. "Stay inside, boy!" he ordered. To the bus driver he shouted, "Start driving! I'll push from behind."

As Edward braced himself to push the bus, two Chinese men hopped out and lined themselves up beside him to help push as well.

The bus slowly and painfully climbed the hill. Just before reaching the crest, Edward felt it start to slip backwards. With a shout, he leaned in and pushed with all his strength. The bus inched forward. At the crest, it suddenly lurched forward and Edward stumbled, almost falling to his face. The two Chinese men jumped in just as the bus cleared the crest and began its descent.

"Hey, hey, wait for me!" Edward called. He jumped to his feet and ran after the bus, which was rapidly gaining speed downhill. The bus driver looked in the mirror and saw the large European man running behind and waving. He stepped on the brakes immediately. Edward hopped into the bus and shouted, "Go! Go! Go!"

The bus quickly descended the hill, and before reaching the next hill, the driver floored the accelerator in order to gain momentum. Edward flopped in his seat, breathing hard. Slowly, he looked around at the faces staring at him. One by one, they burst out laughing, with Edward laughing the loudest.

For Hans, that was one of his happiest, most exciting days. One that he would remember for the rest of his life. Many years later—as an adult—he would recount the tale of that day to his family, many times over. It was for him the height of his childhood innocence and bliss. Unfortunately, those moments are so very fleeting.

Raffles Place in the 1930s.

The Cathay Cinema

2

LOSING PARADISE

INTRODUCTION

The disaster that was the British defense of Singapore and Malaya has been covered in many forms, among them the fine book *Singapore Burning* by Colin Smith. I do not present my book as a treatise on the subject, but I feel it is necessary to briefly cover the events that led to the British capitulation, and subsequent Japanese Occupation of Singapore, in order to tell my family's story.

Like many Singaporeans, I grew up believing a mixture of fact and myth about our history. This section is for the purpose of separating the two, as well as providing a background for the Schirmer family's story, for anyone unfamiliar with that part of history.

WINDS OF WAR

On the first day of September 1939, Germany invaded Poland, marking the beginning of World War II. Two years later, in the summer of 1941, there was still no sign of the war ending any time soon.

Although Hitler's previously unstoppable military forces were not successful in invading England, after having taken France with relative ease, it was definitely not the end. On the North African front, which had opened in 1940, joint Axis forces of Germans and Italians were still enjoying success.

Then, on June 22nd 1941, the Nazis opened another front with the launch of Operation Barbarossa—the invasion of the Soviet Union—in violation of the non-aggression treaty that they had signed with Stalin earlier. German forces stormed east of occupied Poland with frightening blitzkrieg speed. The successes of the earlier "lightning war" campaigns repeated themselves, and by the late summer of 1941, German victory in the Western hemisphere once again seemed imminent.

At the same time, on the other side of the world, the overseas British were still enjoying a peaceful existence on sunny Singapore. The closest conflict was in China, but for many Europeans, it really had nothing to do with them, or so they believed. In their opinion, the Sino-Japanese War consisted of Asiatics fighting among themselves. Better to let them settle things on their own.

Nonetheless, there were a few in the military who saw things differently. These few were absolutely convinced that the Japanese were trying to expand their borders, and would very soon be taking on the West and their colonies in Asia. They were certain that it was not a matter of if, but when.

It was no secret that both American and British resources were already spread much too thin. Britain was tied up in the war in Europe, the Middle East and the Mediterranean. Many Americans favored the isolationist policy, so military spending was not the top priority. Common sense dictated that the Japanese would sooner or later be taking advantage of the situation.

Unfortunately, the warnings of the few remained ignored by the many. For the majority of civilians—including a good many in the government—it was unimaginable that an Asian power would even attempt such an ambitious enterprise. Many people in the West were still ignorant of the degree to which the Japanese had been building up their military since the 1920s. To them, Japan still seemed backward and almost comical—hardly a real threat.

During the 1930s, the outside world still knew very little about Japan's military, apart from news reports of the hostilities in China. At that time, newspapers were still portraying the Japanese army more as an invading barbaric horde, capable only of committing atrocities upon unarmed women and children, not as a modern fighting force on par with any Western nation. So when the military experts in America and Britain evaluated the Japanese expansion and decided that it was of no serious threat, unfortunately much of it had been based on misconceptions that went back many years.

By European standards, Japan was still a relative newcomer among modern nations. After all, the modernization of Japan really only began in the 1860s, after Commodore Perry of the US Navy showed up in feudal Japan with a steam-powered frigate, forcing them to open up trading. But inadvertently, that action had shown Japan the desirable power of modern fighting equipment. In doing so, the West had stoked an inextinguishable fire. What they also did not realize was how quickly this industrious and disciplined race could rise to the challenge of modernization.

By 1905, the Japanese possessed a navy that was capable of defeating a Western power, namely, Czarist Russia. Japan took on a giant, and came out victorious. In 1914, the Japanese were ready to fight again. Their role as Britain's friends in World War I mainly involved naval actions and patrols in the Indian and Pacific Oceans against the German *Kriegsmarine*.

But despite these success stories of the Japanese military, many Westerners continued to ignore their capabilities. Yet again, more misconceptions—no doubt partially fueled by racism—seemed to be at play. For instance, because Japan's military hardware during the early twentieth century comprised of equipment either purchased from Western nations, or manufactured copies thereof, this gave the very false impression that the Japanese were unable to innovate for themselves. Also, the Japanese contribution to the Allied victory in World War I was looked upon as merely riding on the coat-tails of their much admired British. What the world overlooked was that Britain had actually requested Japan's assistance in naval support.

Furthermore, Imperial Japanese Navy uniforms of the day appeared to be more from the 1800s, giving a somewhat comic or operatic image—very Gilbert and Sullivan. Many Westerners just could not take the quaint Japanese seriously, with their smaller stature and stiff martial moves.

Because of these factors and others, too many key members of the Allied military and government came to the unfortunate conclusion that—despite obvious signs of a growing modern military—Japan was still merely a second-rate copycat of the West and therefore, of no real danger.

After 1918, the victorious French, British and Americans were in a post-war euphoria, and thus paid little attention to the ambitions of their wartime ally, Japan. During the course of the war, the Japanese had seized German holdings in the Asia-Pacific region, such as Shandong Province in China and the Mariana Islands in the Pacific. As one of the co-victors, the Japanese were given these territories to keep, after the end of the war. They began the building of military installations at these locations.

However, when the leading Allied nations began drawing up arms treaties in the post war years, ostensibly in the interests of preventing another world war, Japan was the one to receive the raw end of the process. While these treaties remained more generous to Britain and the United States, they severely limited warship size and quantity afforded to Japan.

For the Japanese, after supporting the Allies in their time of need, this came to be a slap in their face. They understood the message to say that while Japan had been useful to the West from time to time, they were not welcome to share world power.

Ignoring the stipulations of said arms treaties, Japan went on to build larger and more powerful warships than her former allies, in preparation for the inevitable. By early 1941, Japan's Imperial Navy outclassed the US Navy, which was still mostly equipped with World War I era battleships.

There were other technological and industrial advances. Mitsubishi's A6M naval fighter, popularly called the Zero, went into mass production in 1940. It was the most advanced fighter design at the time. With features such as flush riveting and lightweight alloy components, it displayed a fine balance of speed, power, agility and range. The Zero would go on to outperform all Allied fighters until well into 1943.

British and American newspapers ignored these military advances, leaving their readers in the dark as to the real danger that Japan posed. Also because of the Depression, military spending was not a popular topic. Keeping tabs on Japan was simply not at the forefront.

Even so, by the early 1930s it became clearly evident that Japan had plans for further expansion in the Asia-Pacific region. An all out conquest of China seemed imminent, especially with the invasion of Manchuria in 1931, done under the pretext of protecting Japanese interests from so-called Chinese bandits. When Japan propped up the puppet empire of Manchukuo to give their occupation legitimacy, China officially protested this act to the League of Nations. In response, the League looked into what became known as the Manchurian Incident.

Having found Japan to be the aggressor in the Incident, the League thereafter demanded a withdrawal of all occupation troops from the Chinese mainland. By way of protest, Japan officially resigned from the League in 1933 and continued her military campaigns into China. Nothing was resolved. The conflicts continued as the ineffectual League watched on. Eventually, an open state of war erupted between Japan and China in 1937.

In 1940, the Japanese made clear their intentions by joining the Axis forces. Germany and Italy were by then the undeniable aggressors in Europe, the Mediterranean and North Africa. Japan would then become the same type of force in the Pacific. This was confirmed the moment France surrendered to Germany that same year. Japan immediately seized the opportunity to invade French Indochina, thus extending her influence into Southeast Asia. The primary purpose of this incursion was to prevent the American supplies and support from reaching the south of China. The secondary objective was to place the tin and rubber assets of British Malaya and Singapore—as well as the petroleum industry of Dutch East Indies—within Japan's reach. In response, the United States, backed by Great Britain, imposed an oil embargo on Japan. This did not quell the fire, but instead made the Japanese more resolute to seize all of the European Colonial assets in Southeast Asia and the Pacific for themselves. During this period, Japan began promoting the concept of a Greater East Asian Co-Prosperity Sphere, a propaganda which denounced Western colonialism of Asian lands. "Asia for Asians" was the mantra, portraying Japan as the rightful liberator of the native people. This propaganda fed the minds of more than a few in these colonies.

Unfortunately, four years of Japanese Occupation in these lands during the near future would prove that things weren't so bad under the European yoke after all.

In Singapore, the few who saw Japan as a potential threat had recognized the warning signs as early as 1920. However, it was

Japan's actions of the 1930s and especially the 1940 occupation of French Indochina that finally convinced the military leadership of the need to step things up. By this time though, it was not easy to play catch-up to the Japanese, who had been building up militarily for decades. With Britain under siege by Germany, resources were tied up, and what could be spared for their Far East Command was limited. Nevertheless, the British began to take more steps to fortify Malaya and Singapore.

True to tradition, they conducted the buildup in a steady manner, so as not to alarm the general population. By late 1941, the fortification of Singapore was complete, but only as far as artillery and manpower were concerned. Despite the considerable expense, there were some grievous inadequacies in Singapore's defense—products of poor planning as well as underestimating the enemy. Some of these became the subject of many misconceptions in the years after the war. One such myth was that the British had armed only the southern coast, ignoring Malaya to the north. This was not true. There were gun emplacements at various points along the west coast of Malaya as well as the north shores of Singapore. The real reason for their ineffectiveness was that these guns had become easily circumvented by a very mobile army. The British did not account for the speed of the Japanese conquest.

Another myth was that the south facing guns were never fired because they were incapable of turning to face the enemy in the north. This was also untrue. The brace of powerful fifteen inch coastal defense guns at Belakang Mati Island on the south end of Singapore were capable of rotating 360 degrees, giving full coverage to the entire island of Singapore and the southern tip of Malaya.

As a matter of fact, during the invasion the British defenders had turned these guns around and fired them, but they still proved ineffective. Not because of location, design or capability, but because of the wrong ammunition. The gunners had plenty of AP

(Armor Piercing) rounds that were capable of sinking any ship, but not much use in land warfare. What they really needed were HE (High Explosive) rounds, but there were very few of these in the battery. In any event, the fine Royal Artillery alone was not going to be able to save Singapore. British military planners had also underestimated Japan's Army and Navy aviation, and surprisingly enough, were not fully cognizant of the enemy's operating range and capabilities.

What had saved Britain from Germany's Luftwaffe and in turn prevented a land invasion was primarily the RAF's force of Supermarine Spitfire and Hawker Hurricane fighters. Singapore and Malaya, on the other hand, lacked an effective fighter cover in terms of number as well as quality of equipment. The infamous Brewster F2A Buffalo fighters assigned to the RAF and RAAF in Singapore and Malaya were slow, maneuvered poorly and lacked both firepower and range. Originally designed for US Navy and Marine aviators, who dubbed it the Flying Coffin or Flying Barrel, the F2A was already obsolete in 1938 when it rolled off American production lines. Nonetheless, the RAF's Air Chief Marshal Sir Robert Brooke Popham based in Singapore insisted that these were "quite sufficient," declaring that England needed the Spitfire and Hurricane fighters more. Unfortunately, this oversight ended up providing the Japanese with immediate air superiority when hostilities began, enabling their ground forces to mobilize quickly with the aid of close air support. When the RAF finally sent Hurricane fighters to Singapore, it was a case of too little, too late.

Singapore's naval defense was also severely lacking. All that was on hand were some ancient destroyers, gunboats and a few flat-bottomed river boats from China that could be armed. Realizing this deficiency, London authorized the deployment of a naval task force to bolster Singapore's defenses. Force Z's main star was the HMS Prince of Wales, the Royal Navy's top of the line battleship and one of the participants in the sinking of the notorious German battleship Bismarck. The other star was the HMS Repulse, a heavy cruiser by definition, but armed with the same lethal fifteen inch guns as the Prince of Wales. The rest of Force Z comprised of four destroyers.

While the task force could justifiably boast about having big guns and anti–submarine capabilities, it ultimately lacked aircraft carriers. Unfortunately, the course of World War II would prove that aircraft carriers, not battleships, were the key to victory in modern naval engagements.

There were yet other factors that undermined British defense capability. One was the lack of mobile armor. Tanks had proven their worth in Europe and North Africa, yet London failed to see their need in Malaya. They instead sent the requested tanks as aid to Soviet Russia—which turned out to be an unnecessary gesture, since the Russians were already manufacturing much better tanks on their own.

As such, Singapore and Malaya had no main battle tanks. The only equipment available to the British that could be loosely termed as armor were Bren carriers—lightly armored open top tracked vehicles armed with a single .303 caliber Bren light machine gun.

Other defense weaknesses included a fragmented command structure and overall inexperience of the troops. Under the British command were Scots, Australians, Indians, Gurkhas and Malays with extremely varying levels of experience, training and equipment. Most of the Indians were teenagers who had never seen tanks before and some had not even had a chance to fire their rifles before being sent to the front, as these had been rushed through training. Furthermore, India at the time was still struggling for independence from Britain. Many of these soldiers were not too keen to be fighting—essentially slaving—for their oppressor. The defense of Singapore, to the untrained eye, appeared bristling and formidable. Unfortunately for the defenders, the enemy was indeed very well trained, and had access to reliable information in Malaya and Singapore.

By the end of 1941, however, the military in Singapore and Malaya was at a state of alert, largely due to intelligence reports of Japanese military activity. For some time, the US Office of Naval Intelligence (ONI) had successfully been decrypting encoded Japanese diplomatic transcripts using a top secret process, codenamed MAGIC.

Honoring President Roosevelt's promise to Prime Minister Churchill on sharing vital technology, America had also provided Britain with the same decrypting machines that the ONI was using. Allied intercepts of Japanese transmissions were informing the British in Singapore that large troops and supply mobilizations of some sort were underway. Only, they were just not quite sure where the Japanese were headed, or what exactly they were up to.

War planners during the 1930s had agreed that an assault on the British colonies would present itself in one of two possibilities. One possibility, the popular one, was the idea of a force invading from the south of Singapore, hence the lethal fortifications established there. The other possibility was by landing forces in the north, on the narrow Kra Isthmus connecting Malaya to Thailand, thereby establishing a beach head.

Thailand, formerly known as Siam, is the only country in Southeast Asia to have never been colonized by Western powers. In the 1860s, King Mongkut knew his comparatively weak military could not hold out against the modern Europeans, so he played the French on his eastern border against the British in Burma to the west, and vice-versa. The outcome was a mutual decision from both European powers to leave Siam independent as a buffer state.

In the 1930s, the Thai military was still not strong enough to hold its own. Their government again wisely avoided confrontation by officially declaring neutrality.

Their unofficial stand was to see which way the wind blew.

The British knew that the Japanese would more than likely abuse the Thai declaration of neutrality, as they did not seem to care as much about world opinion. It was also common knowledge that there were already pro-Japanese factions within the Thai government. However, the British did not want to be the ones to create an international event by mobilizing forces on Thai soil, so their policy was to wait and see.

Nonetheless, in the event that their military intelligence should discover positive proof of a Japanese invasion, the British had already drawn up plans for a pre-emptive strike on the south of Thailand—Operation Matador.

On the evening of Thursday, December 4th 1941, two divisions of the Imperial Japanese Army set sail from Hainan Island in the South China Sea, where they had been consolidating their forces.

While the British knew that something was afoot—based on intercepted Japanese messages—they had no real idea where the enemy was, or that they had actually begun the attack. The weather had been extremely bad, creating poor visibility, and reconnaissance flights were grounded until further notice. The Japanese force steamed south toward Thailand and Malaya through the stormy swells, undetected.

The weather cleared up on Saturday morning; the reconnaissance patrols resumed. The RAF launched flights of Lockheed Hudson light patrol bombers. The Hudson was a twin engine aircraft based on the famous Lockheed Electra transport.

Around noon, one flight crew spotted the Japanese convoy in a heading of southwest. However, this still meant that the destination could be either Thailand or Malaya. Unwilling to commit the political faux pas of an unprovoked invasion of a neutral country, the British played it cautiously and ordered the reconnaissance patrols to tail the Japanese only, in order to ascertain their true intentions.

Unfortunately, the Hudsons—already low on fuel—were not able to shadow the convoy for long. But by the time they returned after refueling, the Japanese were nowhere in sight.

The British were truly in the dark at that point.

The next day was Sunday, December 7th. In Hawaii, and the rest of the United States on the other side of the International Dateline, it was still Saturday the 6th. While the date December 7th lives in infamy for Americans, in Singapore it was just a day of nervous tension for the defenders.

Where were the Japanese?

The RAF continued to patrol the South China Sea. For some time, one of their PBY Catalinas—long range twin-engine seaplanes built in the United States—had gone missing. Unknown to the British at the time, that Catalina had already been shot down by the enemy. The first casualties of the conflict.

Around evening, the crew of one of the Hudsons sighted and confirmed the enemy location. The Japanese were just off the east coast of Thailand, still heading south. There no longer remained any doubt as to their destination. The Japanese convoy also made their hostile intentions very clear by firing upon and damaging one of the Hudsons. At this point, it was more than obvious what the state of things were. But by then, the British had waited too long to mobilize. If there ever was a moment of advantage it was long gone.

In the early hours of December 8th, Japanese invasion forces landed on Kota Bahru in Malaya. Shortly thereafter, Singapore was bombed for the first time ever.

Britain was now at war with Japan.

THE BATTLE OF MALAYA

The British Indian Army and Australian defenders stationed at Kota Bahru fought fiercely through the night of December 8th, inflicting heavy damage on the Japanese, but the enemy was relentless. Detachments of the Japanese 25th Army dug in—literally tunneling under the complex of barbed wire barricades using shovels, their helmets or bare hands—and soon gained inroads. They then moved with blitzkrieg speed and tenacity, outflanking the defenders at multiple points and creating severe confusion, while Navy Mitsubishi Zero fighters provided ground support as well as fighter cover against the Australian Beaufort and Hudson bombers.

The Japanese had also successfully landed at Patani and Songkhla, just across the border, with no resistance from the Thai military. In fact, sympathizers had provided airstrips from which Imperial Japanese Army (IJA) could launch their Nakajima Ki-27 Nate and Ki-43 Oscar fighters.

The IJA bombed and strafed RAF fields in northern and central Malaya throughout that first day. By nightfall they had decimated the RAF by as much as fifty percent. Facing attacks from multiple directions, the defenders made hasty retreats, providing the Japanese with another fully functional airfield by that first evening. With the newly captured Kota Bahru airfield in their hands, the IJA was now able to launch even more land-based army fighters and bombers, with service ranges beyond Singapore. With their successes against the RAF earlier that day, the Japanese now had confirmed regional air superiority.

At one time or other, some of the defenders might have thought of the Japanese as a funny-looking lot, based on newspaper caricatures of "near-sighted yellow monkeys." Now, facing the intense enemy banzai charges, it certainly proved to be no laughing matter.

But what was proving to be equally worrying for the defenders were the constant air attacks and the clattering of enemy tanks, knowing that their own side lacked both air support and armor. Even the slow moving Nate fighters, with their obsolete fixed landing gear, were a concern for the RAF which now had nothing to throw back at them anyway.

The Japanese had another innovative idea regarding mobility. Having done their pre-attack homework, they knew that the locals moved around on bicycles mostly, and that there would be plenty of them available. As soon as they established control of an area, the Japanese then scouted around for bicycles and confiscated any that they found.

With these bicycles they were able to move even quicker than they would have conventionally. While this might perhaps conjure up funny images of the Japanese on a Tour de France, there is nothing humorous about a tank rumbling down a main road with an armed platoon ably keeping up with it. The Japanese invaders were on the move.

While all these were going on, the Royal Navy began stepping into action as well. Force Z, featuring the much flaunted HMS Prince of Wales and HMS Repulse, set sail from Singapore's naval base on the evening of the 8th in search of the enemy fleet. They sailed east around Singapore, past Ubin Island, before heading north into the South China Sea where the enemy lay.

By the next evening, Force Z was well on its way to Thailand when a pair of Japanese Navy Aichi E13A Jake reconnaissance floatplanes spotted the British warships. At the same time, Admiral Thomas Phillips on the Prince of Wales received reports of more Japanese landings at Kuantan, south of Kota Bahru. The Admiral then ordered Force Z to turn about and head south to Kuantan.

The Jake pilots observed their quarry from a distance in order to avoid being shot. Unfortunately for them, they lost the British convoy in the growing dark.

Then in the early hours of the next morning—Wednesday, December 10th—a Japanese submarine sighted Force Z and fired torpedoes at the Repulse, which was closely following the Prince of Wales. However, the British ships kept on moving rapidly and the torpedoes missed altogether, silently tunneling in the dark waters until they ran out of propellant. The crew had no idea of how close these torpedoes had come, or that they had even been spotted.

Later that morning, Japanese reconnaissance aircraft located the warships north of Kuantan. Now that they knew where to look, ninety-four Mitsubishi Nell and Betty bombers—carrying an array of bombs and torpedoes—took off from bases in Indochina.

The efficacy of aircraft against battleships was a source of contention among old-school Navy men. Admiral Phillips was of the conventional belief that battleships could not be sunk by aircraft, despite his own Fleet Air Arm's successful sinking of Italian battleships at Taranto, Italy, the previous year. He also had to have known about Pearl Harbor, even if that had only been two days earlier. Yet, he stubbornly held that air cover was unnecessary.

By that afternoon, December 10th, both ships were at the bottom of the South China Sea. Admiral Phillips went down with his ship, the Prince of Wales. Today—like the USS Arizona in Pearl Harbor—the Prince of Wales and the Repulse serve as war memorials, their hulls full of dead sailors.

On December 11th, Japanese forces in Thailand successfully overwhelmed the British task force which had gone north in execution of the old Matador plan. With that, they formed up with the Kota Bahru landing force, and the entire northern tip of Malaya came under Japanese control.

From the start of the campaign, the Japanese had carried out a routine bombing of Penang on the northwest coast. Now they were able to move overland to capture it, along with Butterworth, the mainland port.

Panic ensued, and an evacuation began of all Europeans from Penang to Singapore, including the military. Governor Thomas in Singapore called it a "very discreditable affair" when he learned how his countrymen had fled to their waiting ships, while their Asian friends and servants were kept away at gunpoint. Japanese troops walked into Penang on Wednesday the 17th. The local people were left to their mercy. Four hard years of the Japanese Occupation began that day for them.

In the post-war years, critics have portrayed the defending British, Indian and Australian forces as ineffectual, with some going so far as calling the troops cowardly. This accusation was far from true. There have also been some who described the campaign of Malaya as one constant advance for the Japanese and a constant retreat for the British. That, too, was an overtly simplistic description of events. While there were no doubt many loose ends in the defense structure, the ultimate failure lay in the chain of command and the timidity of the commanding officer, General Percival, and not in the brave men at the battlefront.

On the ground, the defenders were able to put up very stiff resistance in many cases, costing the enemy greatly. The Allied forces may not have had any tanks to boast of, but they were in possession of very effective artillery. For instance, on the evening of January 14th, Australian field gunners and infantry laid an ambush at the Gemencheh River with devastating results for the enemy and minimal losses on their side. There were yet other battles where the defenders caused the enemy to retreat. What came to be most disheartening for the defenders was fighting the enemy to a standstill, only to receive orders from command to withdraw, thus losing the very ground that they had paid for with their blood. This was the start of the breakdown.

With the loss of naval and air support, General Percival became increasingly worried that the Japanese could now easily land troops behind his men. Unfortunately, his timidity in this regard would only serve to undermine the morale of his men, as the campaign wore on. Once their morale began to diminish, it did so exponentially.

There began to be increased incidences of entire lines falling, with panicked Indian soldiers dropping their rifles and running for the jungles. For many, it really was not their fight in the first place. Most of the young Indians sent to Malaya had little training or experience and for some, it was their first time ever seeing a tank! It made more sense to ditch their uniforms and melt into the rubber plantations to hide among other Indian estate workers.

It was not only the Indians who gave in to fear or defeatism. After putting up a good fight in the first weeks, but then constantly being forced to retreat, some Australians asked out loud why they should be dying for their British cousins anyway. Accounts of officers shooting deserters made their way through the lines, yet men still continued to break ranks and run.

There were many reasons for the low morale. Their lack of coordination, armor and air support, along with the constant retreats, were strong reasons. But the British and Australians had encountered and overcome similar problems during the early days in North Africa. What seemed very different here was the ferocity and the unreasonableness of this new enemy.

The German military, even with the die-hard Nazis in its ranks, was made up of professional soldiers in the Western discipline concerning rules of engagement, as enforced by the Geneva Convention. They respected surrender treaties, and for the most part, did not abuse prisoners. The Japanese, on the other hand, lived by a different code of conduct. In their eyes, there was no honor in surrender; hence prisoners deserved no respect. If they captured you, the best thing that could happen was a quick bullet in the back of your head. All too often though, prisoners became the source of cruel, perverted amusement. Every once in a while, a prisoner would escape to tell horror stories of having watched Japanese soldiers practice their bayonet skills on tied up prisoners. Or having heard the screams of men being slowly cut to pieces.

It was not just prisoners-of-war that the Japanese soldiers abused freely. Australian artilleryman Russell Braddon, who endured the privations of prison camp life for almost four years himself, wrote an account in his book *The Naked Island* of a ghastly incident. Sometime after being captured, he witnessed a group of Japanese soldiers abusing an old Chinese man suffering from dementia. Braddon watched as things went from bad to worse.

At first, the soldiers simply pushed the old man around for a while. But tiring of this, they then doused his head with gasoline and set it on fire. As the man screamed in pain, the soldiers laughed and cheered. They then dumped a kettle of boiling water on the old man, which made him scream even more. The soldiers did this, over and over, until the old man finally stopped moving.

In this day and age of political correctness, it is not easy to discuss such shocking matters. Obviously, not all of the Japanese soldiers then behaved in such a heinous manner, nor are such actions representative of the Japanese people today.

But these things did happen then.

Ask anyone who lived through the Japanese Occupation of Singapore, Malaya, Hong Kong, the Philippines ... and the list goes on.

Ask them before they are all gone.

The bloody battles continued as the Japanese fought their way south. The January 5th Battle of Slim River was disastrous for the British, losing two entire Indian brigades to the enemy tanks. By Sunday, January 11th 1942—a month after landing on the beaches of Malaya—the Japanese marched into Kuala Lumpur, the capital city. Resistance was light.

The days leading up to that had been filled with panic, looting and anarchy as British residents abandoned their offices and businesses. For many of the locals, it was most disillusioning. After having watched newsreels of stalwart Londoners braving the Blitz, the last thing they expected was to see the *Tuan Besar* (a Malay term literally meaning "Grand Lords") run.

Three days later the Japanese reached Johor, the southernmost state of Malaya just above Singapore. As the defenders fought and retreated, they encountered heavy casualties, especially at the Muar River. It became increasingly difficult to transport the wounded, especially through the jungle terrain, and a tough decision had to be made. Despite all evidence to the contrary, the surviving Australian commander felt that perhaps the Japanese would have mercy on the wounded, and therefore ordered every man for himself.

There were an estimated 150 to 300 Australians and Indians left at Parit Sulong on January 23rd, men who were too badly wounded to move. The Japanese solution for these men was a systematic massacre. According to the handful of survivors, men of the Imperial Guards unit beat, kicked and stabbed the prisoners first. Then they shot some, others they poured gasoline on and burned to death.

So much for mercy.

Five days later—with the Japanese breathing down their necks—the British began evacuating the Malayan mainland for Singapore Island. By Saturday January 31st, the evacuation was complete. Army Engineers then laid explosives along the

Causeway that linked the island to the mainland, and blew it up. The Besiegement of Singapore had begun.

But how had the Japanese, armed with half as many men as the combined Allied defense forces of British, Indians and Australians, been able to move so rapidly toward victory?

A lot of it had to do with the tenacious leadership of one man, Lieutenant General Tomoyuki Yamashita—the famed Tiger of Malaya.

THE TIGER OF MALAYA

Tomoyuki Yamashita was born on November 8th 1885 in the rural village of Osugi in Shikoku, southern Japan, where his father was the local doctor. Academically, his older brother was the one to follow in their father's footsteps, but unlike their father, he moved to Tokyo to practice medicine, as he preferred life in the big city.

The younger Yamashita did not have the aptitude for medicine, but he was nonetheless very intelligent and a hard worker. His mother, a descendent of the famed samurai, was the one who recommended that he follow a martial career, having observed his strengths and weaknesses.

Thus, Tomoyuki Yamashita began attending military prep school as a boy, before attending Tokyo's prestigious Central Military Academy in 1904. During the course of his education, he learned German from the Prussian military instructors, as well as some French. As it turned out, he excelled at language, which would prove useful in his career later on.

Upon his graduation, the young Lieutenant Yamashita was stationed in Hiroshima, before working his way into the Staff Officer College. Proving his brilliance as well as diligence, Yamashita graduated from the College with awards in 1917. Two years later he became the assistant military attaché to the Japanese embassy in Berne, Switzerland. He returned to Tokyo after a three year stint abroad, with assignment to general staff. Again, he worked hard to prove himself, and made many recommendations to streamline and modernize Japan's military. A driven and direct man, Yamashita did not appreciate playing political games. Unfortunately, because of this trait he made himself unpopular with certain key figures. One of them was Hideki Tojo, who would later become Prime Minister.

In 1927, he again took the position of assistant military attaché, this time in Vienna, Austria. There, he became friendly with a certain German lady, and was very fond of her. He returned to Japan after three years of embassy service. Yamashita was now a Colonel, with a promising future.

In February of 1936 a group of Imperial Guard officers, dissatisfied with the corruption they saw, staged an unsuccessful *coup d'état*. Some of these officers had been friends of Yamashita. Although he was not a participant in the event, his old enemy, Tojo, saw this as an opportunity to discredit him. When Yamashita petitioned to the Emperor to allow the conspirators a chance to regain their honor by ritual suicide, it was denied. Furthermore, he earned the Emperor's displeasure and ended up banished to Korea, where he was to remain for eighteen months. Nevertheless, during this time he worked tirelessly to regain the Emperor's favor.

When Japan openly went to war with China in 1937, Yamashita received command of a division in Kwantung. Up to that point, all his experience had been in war planning and military bureaucracy. In China, he was to attain the field experience and the basis for his tactics in Malaya.

Brigadier-General Yamashita was an imposing figure on the battlefield. Standing nearly five feet ten (1.77 meters), tall for a Japanese man, with a large build and a stern countenance, one could say he looked like a *Sumo* wrestler. Yet, he moved swiftly, personally leading his men in fearsome battle charges.

By 1940 he was a Lieutenant-General on a mission to Germany and Italy to meet with Hitler and Mussolini. He had proven himself, and again his career was on the rise. The following year he received command of the 25th army and the task of taking Singapore.

THE BATTLE FOR SINGAPORE

February 1st 1942
Johor, Malaya

The British destruction of the causeway between Malaya and Singapore only succeeded in slowing the Japanese juggernaut for the moment. Unfortunately for the defenders, this same action had also cut them off from being able to observe their enemy's movements in Johor.

The Japanese, on the other hand, had no inadequacies in observation and aerial reconnaissance. Despite a shipment of RAF Hawker Hurricane fighters to Singapore's Kallang airfield via Dutch East Indies to the south, the Japanese still ruled the skies over Singapore. They carefully made plans for invasion, while amassing their forces.

After studying the layout of British enforcements, Yamashita decided that the main invasion force should approach from the west, landing on the Sarimbun Beach on the northwest stretch of Singapore. This would enable their forces to route the enemy stationed near the former causeway, and thereafter, they would march down the main road into the city via Woodlands and Bukit Timah in the center of the island. But first, they needed to create a diversionary attack—a feint—from the east.

Japanese artillery began shelling points east of the causeway on February 7th to begin the deception. Later that night, a unit of Imperial Guards crossed over from the mainland and landed on Ubin Island. There was no opposition; the British had already evacuated. Throughout the following day, Japanese artillery maintained a continuous bombardment of Singapore's northeastern shores, in order to perpetuate the idea that they would be coming from that direction. After dark, the main invasion began from the west.

February 8th 1942, approximately 2030 hours
Sarimbun Beach, Singapore

Amphibious landings tend to be an extremely dangerous prospect for the invaders. The defenders on dry land have the advantage of shooting from the cover of bunkers and pillboxes at relatively helpless open watercraft loaded down with troops. But for whatever reason, the Australians failed to raise the alarm before a large number of enemy troops were already on their shore and able to fire back.

This did not mean that the Japanese were simply able to walk over the defense lines. However, the defenders had now lost the position of advantage that they once held. Bitter fighting continued throughout the night. By midnight, the Australian 22nd Brigade was divided. With their communication severed, a haphazard order went out to retreat and regroup elsewhere.

Throughout the course of the night, more Japanese crossed the channel to reinforce the earlier landings. Since most of the defenders had already retreated, these men probably thought that they would land unmolested. This was not always the case. In one instance, a group of Australians who had become separated from their command were still defending a section of the beach. Having observed boats heading their way, they set a trap and lay in wait. As soon as the Japanese were almost ashore, the Australians ignited a sea of gasoline, killing many enemy soldiers. Unfortunately, a small success such as that was not enough to thwart the enemy.

In the early hours of morning, Imperial Guard units also began crossing over to Woodlands, near the site of the former causeway. Many of these too faced the horrors of a fiery sea, as the retreating British there detonated oil reserves. Still, this did not deter the Japanese invaders.

In the end, the Australian defenders never received reinforcements because British units were tied up on the east side of the island, waiting for an attack that never materialized. By the time Percival recovered from the confusion, the enemy had already amassed itself in the north and northwest of the island, and was now in position to head for the center. Yamashita's feint had succeeded.

Having secured the beachheads, Imperial Guard tanks began their crossing of the Johor Straits, floating on pontoons. Once across, the tanks rolled through Woodlands and Mandai down towards Bukit Timah, where they would have to face off with British artillery. By the morning of the 10th, however, the Japanese were past Bukit Timah and in control of Singapore's water supply. It was obvious who now had the upper hand.

Under heavy fire, local Malay regiments rushed to the west coast region to reinforce the Indian brigades that were stationed there. In the following days, fierce fighting broke out between these units and the Japanese. One unit heroically held the Japanese off at Pasir Panjang hill for two days before being completely overrun. The Japanese commended the few remaining survivors for their fighting skills, and then they executed them.

By this time, most of the civilian population knew that the end was near. Many of the European residents had already begun an exodus to Australia and India, but sadly, some would not make their destination, with Japanese aircraft patrols and a naval blockade in place. There was no amnesty for civilians. The Japanese ruthlessly sank any ship that they came across. Although the Japanese appeared unstoppable, the truth was that they too were starting to get stretched thin. Supplies were running low and they had lost many men during the month-long campaign through Malaya. Even though Yamashita knew that Percival was ultimately finished, the Japanese could ill afford an all-out counterattack, should the British find out their situation and decide to act upon it. He decided then to play a bluff on Percival.

On February 11th, Yamashita sent a flowery letter to Percival commending the gallant British defense. In this letter, he urged the British to nonetheless give up their "meaningless and desperate resistance" and surrender. The alternative was to face "annihilating attacks on Singapore." Percival remained uncertain.

In the meantime, combined Japanese forces continued to advance down Bukit Timah Road from the north, and also from Jurong in the west. Percival had no way of knowing the true nature of enemy strength—his Intelligence was too weak and unreliable. On top of that, the Japanese were bombing Singapore day and night, from the air and with artillery. By all appearances, Yamashita appeared to be able to carry out his threat of annihilation. In truth, he was rapidly using up everything that he had, in the hope of convincing Percival that surrender was inevitable. With airfields either in enemy hands or inoperable from damage, the RAF had by then evacuated all Allied aircraft and personnel to Dutch East Indies. IJA bombers continued to attack Singapore with impunity. Overall, the outlook for defense looked very dim. Regardless, the civilian evacuation continued to increase in intensity. Even up to that point, *The Straits Times* newspaper still featured optimistic "Singapore Shall Stand" pieces. Yet, everyone was fully aware of the bleakness of Singapore's situation.

Two days after Yamashita's letter, Percival's staff advised him to surrender. Even though he was ready to do so, he needed to hold out until he could receive the go-ahead from his superiors.

The following day, which was the 14th, survivors from the Malay regiments mentioned earlier were pulling out from Pasir Panjang and Kent Ridge. To cover the retreat, a rear guard set up machine guns near the Military Hospital on Alexandra Road and waited for the enemy. As they closed in, the advancing Japanese soldiers took out those gunners and then stormed through the hospital. What followed thereafter came to be known as the Alexandra Hospital Massacre—Japanese soldiers bayoneted some 200 patients and staff in this rampage, and forced another 400 more into a small room for three days. Most of them died of suffocation.

Although this atrocity happened without Yamashita's approval—he in fact had the responsible officer hanged and personally apologized to survivors—it still came to be one of the many crimes with which the victorious Allies would charge him after the war. As the commanding officer, he remained ultimately responsible for the actions of his men.

For now, Yamashita and his forces had successfully pushed the retreating Allies to their last line of defense. Hunkering down with dwindling supplies and rising casualty numbers, the defenders had to take stock of their options, and these were quickly running out.

The fall of Singapore was at hand. A period of terror known as the Japanese Occupation was about to begin. It was in this timeframe that a young Eurasian boy named Hans Schirmer learned about life.

One of Singapore's 15-inch coastal defense guns.

RAAF Lockheed Hudson patrol bomber.

Brewster F2A Buffalo fighter aircraft based at Sembawang airfield (1941).

Nakajima Ki27 "Nate"

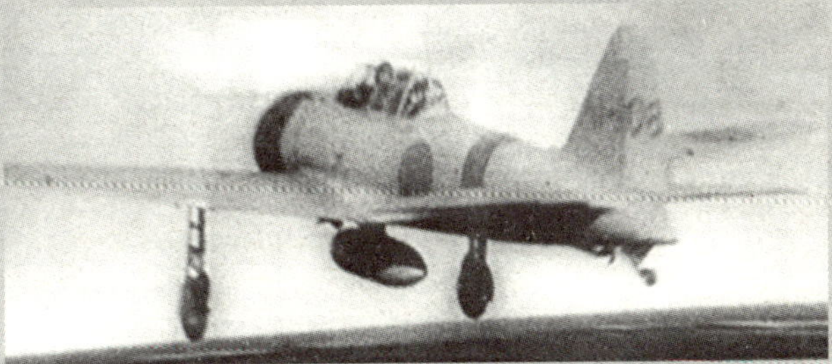

Mitsubishi A6M-2 "Zeke"

General Yamashita presents a sword to Field Marshal Walter von Brauchitch, Commander-in-Chief of the German army (1940).

1
CALM BEFORE THE STORM

In the middle of 1941, Edward Henry Schirmer contemplated taking the family back to Mauritius, at least until the threat of war had subsided. Florence, however, was dead set against it. Somehow, motherhood had dampened her desire to travel. Yet, it was ultimately Edward's duty as head of their household to ensure the overall safety of his family. It was a very difficult call. On one hand, the British seemed invincible. All throughout the arms buildup, there had been a certain air of assuredness—even cockiness—on their part. A common theme in *The Straits Times* daily newspaper editorials was that the Japanese would be foolish to take them on. So if nothing happened, Edward reasoned, all the loss of money involved in moving and closing the business would have simply been wasted. On the other hand, if the Japanese did attack and a state of war ensued, then it would be too late to do anything at that point.

But still, wouldn't the British just simply beat the Japanese back, as they say they will? Is it really worth it to uproot everything on the slim chance that the Japanese may succeed?

In the end, they stayed.

December 1st 1941
Singapore

Mondays could go either way, as far as business was concerned. On some days, Edward could hardly get a moment in to breathe, as customers—irate from having to wait for his shop to open after the weekend—would stream in one after another with repair demands or parts orders. Then on certain days, it could be strangely quiet, for no obvious reason. And it was not seasonal, either. In the tropics, boating takes place year around.

It was a good thing that this Monday was one of the quiet ones. Edward had hired Eng Guan for some remodeling work at his shop, and part of the work would render the repair end unusable for a couple of hours. Not that he couldn't work around Eng Guan if he had to, but it was much better not to be in each other's way. Besides, the slow day gave Edward some time to chat with his friend.

"So, the Royal Navy ships are supposed to be here any day now. What do you think of that?" Edward asked as he organized a stack of papers on his desk. He was referring to the news reports covering the arrival of Force Z from England.

Initially, the Royal Navy had kept the deployment under wraps. Then, as it became closer and secrecy was no longer essential, newspapers began announcing the arrival of the stars of the show—HMS Prince of Wales and HMS Repulse. In fact, because the arms buildup was largely meant to work as a visual deterrent against Japanese aggression, the timely advertising of Singapore's defense capability became part of that plan.

"Don't know, *lah*. I hope they whack the *Jipoon* bastards good and proper!" Eng Guan replied while sawing a board. Like many local Chinese, Eng Guan was not particularly interested in the news or politics of the day. However, the atrocities of the Japanese military in China—the 1937 Rape of Nanking being at the forefront—had gained everyone's attention. Normally easy-going in most regards, Eng Guan now had nothing good to say about the Japanese.

"Well, it may still come to that," Edward said, noncommittally. Personally, he hoped that war would not come to Singapore. There was too much to lose from the destructive nature of conflict, for either side involved.

Eng Guan remained focused on his work, but Edward could tell that something was still on his mind. Without looking up, Eng Guan voiced his thoughts after some time.

"Hokkien people like me come from different part of China ... more in the south," he said, referring to Nanking. "I myself never go to China before—I was born here. But I am still Chinese, and this kind of thing makes me angry! Japan has no right to attack my people, no right to kill women and children just like that! And our friends, America and England—hah! They all talk and talk, but never do anything. For what?"

Edward had listened to Eng Guan's bitter words before, and while he agreed with him up to a point, he was not sure what could really be done about an aggressive Japan. The last time nations stepped in because of the actions of other nations, a deadly four years of world war had ensued. Yet, if the news reports were to be believed, Japan was now perpetrating crimes against civilians in China on a scale that had never been heard of. Should not something be done?

The conversation ended on that note for the time being, as a customer had come in at that moment. Edward turned his attention to the customer, leaving Eng Guan to his work.

Dear God, please spare us this war. I just want to live in peace, take care of my family and be left alone. Is that too much to ask for?

In the days that followed, life for Edward and his family—the everyday people in general—continued on as it normally did. Since it was that time of year, everyone was busy, making preparations for Christmas and the New Year. The Raffles Hotel and other popular venues were fully booked with dinner and dance parties. Department stores such as Robinsons and John Little were busier than ever, as also were the grocers and butchers.

Whether one celebrated Christmas or not, it was indeed a jolly time of the year for everybody. Employees customarily received their year-end bonuses. In turn, they generously tipped their service staff, from house servants, to the gardener, to the men hauling refuse. On top of the festive mood, everyone felt a sense of security, knowing that His Majesty's armed forces were there to ensure it. Indeed, the buildup of men and equipment over the past few years was impossible to ignore.

Undoubtedly, most of the civilian population in Singapore was by then aware of some sort of Japanese convoy sailing in their general direction. Even so, the newspaper reports said that it was probably headed for Thailand, and nothing to worry about. In any event, they felt that it was the military and the politicians who were supposed to worry about that sort of thing. Blissfully unaware of a certain turn of events, the people of Singapore went to bed on the night of Sunday, December 7th, expecting nothing other than the normal workweek ahead. As darkness enveloped Ubin Island, the Schirmers were one of the many families in Singapore turning in for the night. Just like those many other families, they had no idea that their lives were about to change forever.

HMS Prince of Wales (*top*) and HMS Repulse (*below*)—stars of the Royal Navy's "Force Z."

2
WAR IN PARADISE

December 8th 1941, approximately 0015 hours
South China Sea

The Allies had code names for Japanese military aircraft: Male names were for fighters—Zeke, Oscar, Frank. Female names were for bombers—Betty, Mavis, Nell.

Innocuous sounding names for such lethal machines.

Shortly after midnight, thirty-two fully laden Imperial Navy Mitsubishi G3M Nell bombers took off from captured French airstrips in Indochina, rising slowly into the cloudy night.

Primary target: Singapore's Naval Base and Airfields in the north of the island.

Secondary target: Keppel Harbour and the downtown commercial and administrative district in the south.

Around the same time, divisions of the Imperial Japanese Army began landing on the beaches of Kota Bahru, in northeast Malaya.

The British Indian Army and Australian defenders stationed there rushed into position to repel the invaders, while their commander telephoned Lieutenant General A. E. Percival, the General Officer Commanding (GOC) in Singapore. The General in turn notified the Governor, Sir Shenton Thomas, that they were now undoubtedly at war with Japan.

On the other side of the world—at that same moment—the bombs were falling on American ships in Pearl Harbor.

The Japanese had orchestrated everything perfectly.

Around 0330—more than a half hour before the first bombs were to fall on Singapore—the RAF radar post in Mersing on the east coast of Malaya detected the Mitsubishis heading south. The radar operators on duty immediately notified their counterparts based in Singapore, per procedure.

Up to the moment of the first bomb explosions, virtually everyone in Singapore believed that they were living well outside the range of Japanese aircraft potentially flying from Indochina—based on RAF information available then. While the air force had been responsible for maintaining intelligence reports in this regard, and had let everyone down by not knowing the enemy's capabilities, it became the army that would ultimately drop the ball that morning.

This news about aircraft heading their way—along with the knowledge that the enemy had already landed on Malayan soil—should have spurred the army defense units into immediate action. They were responsible for the enforcing blackouts and taking anti-aircraft measures. Somehow, this did not happen, despite all the pre-war drills and training.

They even left the lights on.

December 8th 1941, approximately 0415 hours
Singapore

The Japanese bombers split into two separate flights upon approaching Singapore. Only seventeen had made it that far out of the initial thirty-two aircraft, the rest aborting due to weather and visibility.

The main group of twelve headed toward the northern tip of the island for Sembawang naval base and Seletar airfield. Despite flying through a spectacular display of anti-aircraft fire, none of the bombers were shot down. The jittery gunners on the ground were aiming wild. The remaining aircraft flew over the island, following the street lights to their secondary target and dropping their ordnance around 0430 local time. These bombs did not hit the harbor or any actual shipping, but instead fell loosely around Raffles Place and the nearby Chinatown. More than likely, the Japanese were anxious to turn around as quickly as possible, since they were already pushing the limit of their operating range.

General Percival would later admit that the British had been caught with their pants down, in spite of all the warnings. Although the air raid turned out to have limited tactical success—damage to the naval base and airfields had been negligible—it did effectively deal a blow to civilian confidence in the military. The death toll was around sixty, with hundreds more wounded. Most of them were local Chinese living in the protectorate.

With the exception of occasional hit-and-run strikes on RAF airfields, the Japanese did not follow up that pre-dawn air raid with more attacks on Singapore until a month later. Instead, they concentrated efforts throughout the month of December on a systematic campaign through the north—the Battle of Malaya.

For now, the residents of Singapore had their first taste of war. A taste that would only increase in bitterness in the following months.

December 8th 1941, approximately 0630 hours
Ubin Island, Singapore

Edward went back out on the porch to have a look around. The air raid sirens on the mainland were finally silent, signifying the "all clear." The Japanese were long gone.

"I'm going down to the *kampong* to see what I can find out," he called out to Florence. "See what you can find out on the wireless."

Hans ran alongside his father as the tall man strode toward the village. As they came closer, they could hear excited voices creating a buzz. One voice seemed to punch through intermittently.

Colonel Thomas Willoughby, some twenty-odd years retired from His Majesty's service in the Indian army, owned a bungalow on the north coast of Ubin, facing the Malayan jungle. He was a seventy-nine year-old who had first seen action along the Khyber Pass, as a young officer in 1879.

Edward had been to his place a few times to enjoy a beer and listen to some old war stories. They had gotten along well because, among other reasons, they both had some German ancestry.

Despite his age, the Colonel still drove around the island himself. This morning, he was dressed in his khakis and a well-worn campaign helmet, with his old .455 Webley service revolver concealed in a canvas cross-draw holster. He had come to the village to make sure everyone was alright, and to see if he could be of some assistance. People were scared. Yet, his authoritative voice represented an order that was familiar and comforting in times of distress.

"… important thing is to *remain calm*. Do not tie up communication lines at this time. If there is anything of urgency, we will hear it on the wireless. Of course you are worried about friends and family on the main island, but if we rushed over, we'd only get in the way. I urge you all to go home, make sure you have enough food and water stored up ... that sort of thing, you know."

The Colonel cleared his throat and repeated himself, this time in Malay. The people of Singapore at the time still had a sense of awe about the British *Tuan Besar*. By taking charge of things and speaking in both languages, Willoughby provided the necessary reassurance that Britannia would prevail, as it always had. As far as he was concerned, that was unquestionable.

The crowd dispersed slowly at first, then more rapidly as they realized how much there was still to be done by way of emergency preparations. Edward waved at the Colonel.

"Ah, Edward! And a Good Morning to you too, little Hans! Looks like the blighters want a fight, what? Dirty fellows! Not a word, too. Simply pop out of the skies, drop their bombs and run away. No formal declaration of war, whatsoever. Bloody cowards!" Colonel Willoughby said as he walked over.

Edward shook the old Colonel's hand. "I had rather hoped that this would not have happened. You know, I was quite hopeful for the diplomatic process. But it's obviously too late for that now."

"Quite so. Well, as you know I've seen my share of war up close, and it isn't pretty. But that was a long time ago. We had no tanks or aeroplanes, or any such rubbish then. Between you and me, I am rather worried about things. Not that we can't beat back the yellow bastards, mind you, but what it will cost our young men here. It was bad enough in the last war; how much worse will it be this time? Our old friends the Germans have already shown us over there what we can expect."

Edward nodded in agreement. "Colonel, what have you heard so far?" he asked, in a quiet voice.

"Well, it would appear that the Nips hit Sembawang and some parts downtown. Not very hard, but there are some civilian casualties. That's all I've heard, I'm afraid."

Edward shook his head slowly. "I suppose I should be getting home and making sure we have everything we need for a while. Thank you, Colonel. You are a pillar for us all."

They shook hands grimly, then the old Colonel walked back to his car. Edward patted Hans on the shoulder and smiled at him, to reassure the young boy.

For all the "what if" scenarios that Edward had played in his mind over the past year, as war seemed more and more probable, he now found himself at a loss about what to do first.

As they walked back to the house, Hans observed his father's serious face and instinctively remained quiet. Edward looked down now and again to make sure his son was able to keep up, but otherwise, his mind kept racing.

They reached the house. Edward opened the door.

"Florence, the Japanese have bombed the navy shipyard and downtown," he said. "I don't know what will happen next, but let's make sure we have extra food and water."

"*Aiyah*, I'm sure there's plenty! You have been buying all those tins of food for months," she replied, rolling her eyes. "But do you really think they will come here?"

"You mean land on our shores? I don't know. The old Colonel was at the village. He seemed to think that we will be fine fighting the Japanese off, should they try to invade."

"I hope so," Florence said, but her face expressed pessimism.

Radio broadcasts later that morning confirmed their fears of a Japanese invasion. News bulletins reported that large enemy forces had landed at Kota Bahru earlier that morning. However, the announcer cheerfully assured listeners that the army and the RAF were gallantly beating the invaders back into the sea at that very moment.

That was not really what was happening.

While it was true that the defenders had indeed fought gallantly throughout the night, what was not being reported was the Japanese breakthrough of the British defense lines at Kota Bahru by that time. The Battle of Malaya had already begun, and the enemy was on the move.

When Edward Schirmer chose to remain in Singapore earlier that year, he knew that it was a gamble, but the odds then seemed very much in British favor. How else could it not be? Now, he was not the only one stunned by the rapid turn of events. Just two days after the Kota Bahru landings, the Royal Navy's much vaunted HMS Prince of Wales and the Repulse were at the bottom of the South China Sea. Every day, it seemed that the Japanese were getting closer. For all their bluster, the British defense of Malaya had turned to shambles in a few short weeks.

When British forces abandoned Penang to the enemy on December 17th, morale sank as quickly as the two principle ships. By the end of the year, most of Malaya was in Japanese hands. The proverbial writing was on the wall.

Before the Japanese closed in on Johor in early January, the British had already begun evacuating civilians from Ubin Island. Around Christmas, Edward brought the family to the main island and they moved in to the small apartment above the shop. His mother-in-law went to stay with relatives during this period, as there was just not enough room for all of them.

Apart from the initial bombing on the morning of December 8th and some sporadic raids on airbases in Singapore, the Japanese were up to that time concentrating their aerial efforts mainly in Malaya.

Then as they got closer to Johor and more airbases fell into their control, the Japanese turned their focus on Singapore again. The end of December saw the beginning of a nightly bombing campaign.

Mitsubishi G3M "Nell"

Mitsubishi G4M "Betty"

Downtown Singapore, with smoke billowing from the naval base in the north.

3
AIR BATTLES

Hans had a fascination for aircraft, even as a toddler. He distinctly remembered when his father would take him to the Kallang airfield before the war, to watch the different aircraft taking off and landing. When he first saw the F2A Buffalo, he thought it looked a bit like a bumble bee. It looked nothing like the sleek RAF Spitfires and Hurricanes, or even the German Messerschmitts that he saw in the newsreels. He wondered then what the Japanese flew. Before long, he would see for himself.

December 29th 1941, sometime before midnight
Changi, Singapore

Hans awoke to the drone of air raid sirens in the distance. It was pitch dark outside, and he had no idea what time it was. All he knew was that it had not been very long since he went to bed, and he was still tired.

Edward came into the room. "Keep the curtain closed. No lights. Stay away from the windows and keep low," he said quietly.

The family sat in the dark, trying to make sense of what was going on from the sounds they could hear. They made out the sound of many aircraft in the distance, but these seemed to be actually going farther away. The faint rumble of many explosions came soon after. Again, these sounded as if they were very far away.

This was the first of a series of nightly bombings. Edward naturally took all precautions necessary, as he had no idea what the targets might be, or if they were in the line of fire. After a few nights, it became obvious that the Japanese were only targeting military installations as well as the downtown area. Although there was an army base in Changi, at the Selarang barracks, the enemy did not seem to be targeting it. They were in no immediate danger where they were staying.

After that point, Hans looked forward to the nightly arrival of Japanese bombers. Being barely four, it all seemed to him more like an exciting show, even though his father had explained the seriousness of the matter. Nevertheless, he still wanted to be able to see the airplanes, not just hear them.

That would happen soon enough.

January 12th 1942, early morning

After breakfast, Edward headed downstairs to the shop to tinker around. Business had, for all intents and purposes, come to a stop by then. Still, it gave him something to do.

The shop stood by itself off a dirt road. While there were a few similar buildings in the area, separated by other dirt roads, most of the surrounding terrain was flat. Tall *lalang* grass grew in fields between the roads. Farther off in the distance, the land sloped into a few gentle hills.

Hans was off wandering nearby in the brush, looking for birds. He had with him the slingshot his Papa had given him last birthday, and was quite a marksman with it. The *croo-croo* sound of a dove caught his attention. The bird was on the ground somewhere ahead, hidden by the tall grass. He advanced silently, searching for it.

His concentration was broken by the droning wail of air raid sirens in the distance. Immediately, he looked up to see if there were any aircraft in sight.

Edward had observed that Hans, even at an early age, had been endowed with amazing long distance vision. The boy had always been able to see birds flying in the distance when no-one else could. Now he scanned the skies in search of anything flying.

Then he saw it.

To the north he could see the dots of many aircraft flying in formation toward Singapore. It had to be the Japanese! Then there came the roaring sound of low-flying aircraft from the west, gradually increasing in volume. A flight of Brewster F2As had just scrambled from Kallang to intercept the incoming bombers.

From where he stood, Hans could see the Buffalos climbing slowly. He did not know much about the fighter; all he knew was that these were what the British flew. What he did not know at the time was that the aircraft had been plagued with a multitude of design flaws, and it stood no chance against anything the Japanese had. To begin, the F2A was obsolete from the second it rolled off the assembly line. Compared to other frontline fighters of the day, it maneuvered poorly, was slow and had a poor rate of climb. On top of that, it possessed a faulty oxygen system that prevented effective operation above 10,000 feet. An overweight weapons system also forced armorers to replace a fairly effective gun platform of four

.50 Browning heavy machineguns to an ineffective platform of four .303 light machineguns. In comparison, the Japanese Navy A6M Zero had a pair of 7.7 millimeter machineguns—similar to the .303—in the nose, but in the wings were the very deadly 20 millimeter cannons. Although the Army Nakajima Ki-43 Oscar did not have these cannons and was somewhat similar in armament to the F2A, it still remained vastly superior in all other aspects.

Hans watched intently for the air battle to begin. Before the flight of F2A interceptors could halfway reach the altitude of the incoming bombers, a flight of Ki-43 escort fighters swooped down on them with guns blazing. One of the F2As shuddered and burst into flames. It flipped over and spiraled to the ground, trailing smoke. No parachute emerged.

Panicking, the remaining Buffalo pilots broke formation and dived to gain speed. It was to no avail, as the Ki-43s simply chased them and picked them off one by one. A couple of survivors managed to turn back towards Kallang, but these too were trailing smoke and it was clear they would barely make it back, if they did at all.

Hans ran all the way back to the shop, where he found his father standing outside, watching the dogfight as well. "Papa! Papa! Did you see that?" he called out.

"Yes, son. I did."

"Wasn't that exciting?"

"Son, I know it looked exciting from here, but there are people, real men, in those aeroplanes. They are probably dead, you know," Edward said quietly.

Hans became silent. He knew that his father was serious, but he had yet to see a dead person, and was still trying to make the connection.

It would not be long before he saw his first body.

That had been the first of many daylight raids. From that day on until the fall of Singapore a month later, the Japanese came back to bomb day and night, increasing in frequency and intensity as the days wore on. It was part of Yamashita's display to the British of just what they were capable. In the meantime, civilian casualties in the city were increasing at an alarming rate. This became one of the main reasons why General Percival and his staff wanted an end to hostilities as soon as possible.

January 20th 1942, late morning

The air raid sirens were wailing in the distance. Hans ran out the door of the shop to watch the planes again. This time he saw a new player in the skies—the Hawker Hurricane Mk II.

Every time he had gone to the cinema, they always ran a newsreel before the actual show. Hans was familiar with footage from the Battle of Britain, showing the Hurricanes. When he saw them flying in the skies overhead that morning, he knew right away what they were.

The RAF had sent fifty-one Hurricanes to Singapore at the beginning of the month to replace the F2As. By the 20th, operational squadrons were in place, ready to challenge the Japanese. The Hurricane was an all-around improvement over the F2A, but would still prove to be no match against the Japanese, even though they were deploying army fighters only by that time, and not the navy's superior A6M Zero. But because the army's Ki-43s were flown by battle-experienced pilots, they could still outperform the Hurricanes. The Japanese also retained the upper hand in terms of number.

The British Hurricanes were better suited to close support roles, that is to say, strafing missions or to cover ground troops. That was its main role in North Africa. During the Battle of Britain, Hurricane squadrons primarily went after the slower bombers, while the faster, more agile Spitfires tangled with the Messerschmitt Bf-109 fighters.

Singapore did not have the luxury to choose which fighter was going to do what—all they had was whatever they had on hand, and even then, it was clearly not going to be enough. In any event, it was a case of too little, too late.

Hans watched the new fighters climb at a much more impressive rate than their predecessors. But the odds were still against them—they were about a dozen fighters against a combined force of more than four times as many aircraft. Still, they attacked the incoming aircraft with ferocity. Hans could see them turn and bank with the enemy fighters, firing their eight machineguns in short, rapid bursts. Aircraft from both sides exploded in the air, their wreckages twisting down to earth while spewing smoke. The four year-old found it to be like watching a sporting event.

Then he noticed that one of the Hurricanes was flying in his direction. Unlike the other aircraft that were constantly maneuvering to evade enemy fire, this one seemed to be flying in a straight line and a shallow dive. It took almost a minute for the aircraft to fly overhead. All the while, it continued the shallow dive until it crashed into one of the small hills nearby with a loud, dragged out bang.

The wreckage lay within sight, perhaps a quarter mile (about a half kilometer) away. Hans began running toward it with excitement. Maybe the pilot would say "Hello!"

Edward, who had also heard the noise, came out of the shop to see his son running in the direction of the wreckage. Immediately, he ran after the boy and shouted, "Stop! Don't get too close! It may still explode!"

Hans stopped, turned around and smiled.

"Come, Papa! Let's go see. Maybe the pilot needs help."

Edward thought about it.

My God! What if the pilot is badly hurt? Or worse? I don't want the boy to have to see that! But he is right—we should try to offer some help.

Finally, Edward nodded and said, "You're right. Let's take a look. But slowly, understand?"

As they came closer, Edward put a hand on his son's shoulder. Having observed the wreckage for a while, he saw that there was no sign of fire, and felt that it was safe to approach. He decided to do so from astern. Hans carefully followed.

The Hurricane was in bad shape. The starboard wing had folded upwards and the propeller blades were twisted and bent back. The entire engine section had crumpled rearwards into the cockpit section of the fuselage. Crumpled and shattered, the canopy had come off and lay beside the tail section. Edward could see blood dripping from the twisted framework and broken Plexiglas. He stopped and held Hans back.

"Don't look! It's not good."

"What's wrong, Papa?"

"The pilot's dead, son."

"Are you sure? I want to see. Maybe we can still help him."

Hans looked up at his father. Edward knew that the war was not going well for the British. Even if their propaganda was to be believed—that they would ultimately beat the Japanese back—he remained convinced it was only a matter of time before the battles took place on the streets of Singapore.

I cannot hide everything from him. Poor boy. I wish he didn't have to learn about these things, ever. But he will see this sometime, the way things are going.

Edward loosened his grip on his son and allowed him to approach the aircraft. When Hans came to the cockpit, he gasped loudly and pointed. He could not say a word. The impact of the crash had forced the engine backwards through the firewall, crushing the pilot. The man's body had burst like a fruit.

"Hansel, that is what dead means," Edward said quietly as he picked up his son and turned him away. "The man is gone. He will never fly, or walk, or smile, or do anything ever again. Do you understand?"

"B-b-but I wanted to help him, Papa," Hans sobbed, his face buried in his father's chest.

"I know. I know. You're a good boy. Sometimes, in life, there are things we cannot fix. But he was probably already dead before he crashed. We can be grateful that he did not feel much pain."

Aerial battles continued for another two weeks. The last defense sortie was flown on the morning of February 8th, against the IJA fighters that were supporting the invasion of Singapore.

Ten Hurricanes rose to the skies that day. Only four survived, but they were unable to land at Kallang due to all the runway damage. Instead, they flew on to Sumatra in Dutch East Indies. Two days later, all remaining Allied aircraft and personnel followed suit, flying to bases in Dutch East Indies. Any equipment that could not be salvaged, non-flying aircraft, were all destroyed on the ground, removing the last vestige of Singapore's air defense.

For the following week, the Japanese bombed Singapore's city center day and night without any challenge. At one time, the RAF (British), RAAF (Australian) and RNZAF (New Zealand) squadrons proudly flew the skies over Singapore. By February 14th 1942, they were no more than a distant memory.

Nakajima Ki-43 "Oscar"

The old and the new. Antiquated Brewster F2A Buffalos (*above*) made way for the marginally superior Hawker Hurricane (*below*).

4

COMING UNDER FIRE

It was not just the constant aerial bombing that served to weaken General Percival's resolve in defending Singapore. Artillery bombardment from guns based in Johor came around the clock as well, prior to the Japanese crossing. The death toll among civilians was rising at an alarming rate, something that weighed heavily on his conscience. He knew they could not hold out much longer.

Being where they were, the artillery campaign had not directly affected Edward and his family, up until the time Yamashita's forces were getting ready to cross the straits for the invasion of Singapore on the night of February 8th.

Then—for a twenty-four hour period prior to the invasion—the Japanese concentrated their efforts on shelling the areas east of the Causeway, as part of Yamashita's ploy to distract Percival and his forces from the actual attack at Sarimbun, in the west. During this time, Changi began to come under fire.

February 8th 1942, sometime after midnight
Changi, Singapore

Each time Edward heard the screech of artillery shells flying overhead, he clenched every muscle, anticipating an explosion all around. So far, that had not happened yet. Nevertheless, it was the waiting, the terror, not knowing how much longer it would go on. All these things were wearing him down, fraying his nerves.

He lost track of how long the barrage had been going on—all he knew was that it started sometime around sundown. His watch told him it was now past midnight.

Had it been that long? Part of him knew that it could be worse. Unlike the poor devils in the city center and some other places, Edward and his family had been spared the bombings until now because of the lack of enemy interest in the area at the time. For whatever reason, that had now changed. But no matter how he rationalized things, it remained terrifying to come under fire. There was no way of knowing if the next shell would actually land on the shop where they were taking cover.

When Edward was a young man, he could only imagine what other young men his age were experiencing on the battlefields at Flanders or Gallipoli. Now he knew firsthand the terror they must have felt as the shells screeched over their heads.

He looked at his family, feeling helpless. Despite what was going on, the children appeared to be alright. After the first hour or so, the two younger boys no longer paid any attention to the noise. They quietly played on the floor as though nothing was wrong. Hans also seemed to be holding up well, but was quiet and still in the corner. Perhaps he was trying to make himself invisible, Edward thought. He had noticed a slight change in the boy since the incident with the Hurricane pilot, as if Hans was beginning to understand the seriousness of what was going on. As long as the boys stayed inside the building, Edward knew that they were doing everything that they could. What was the point of them being worried, the way he was worrying?

Florence no longer looked scared, either. In fact, she was scowling quietly. After a while, she turned her glare toward Edward. "I am so sick and tired of all this!" she snapped.

Edward nodded. What was there to say? He moved toward her, to try and hold her. She held her hands up, palms out.

"What, you think you can hold me and that will stop the bombs? Now you want to play the hero?" she said.

"You think that this is my fault? What, I told the Japanese to bomb us here?" Edward flared up.

This is ridiculous! He knew her nerves were also frayed, but come on! How was this helping anything?

They both said nothing for a few, very long seconds. Florence spoke first. "We should have left this bloody place weeks, months ago! Now we are stuck here, with no place to go. Any second now, a bomb will come crashing through the roof and kill us all!"

"Florence! Not in front of the boys!"

"What do I care? We are all going to die, anyway!"

"That's enough of that! We are not going to die!"

"What, you are God that you should know these things? Edward Henry Schirmer—God of Heaven and Earth—has proclaimed that we shall not die! Well, dear Heavenly Father, why don't you just make it all stop right now?"

"Enough, Florence! You are blaspheming!"

"Hah! That's a laugh! What do you care about such things, huh, Mister Never-Goes-To-Church? If you were a real man, you would have taken us away before it became too late!"

"Where the hell do you think we should have gone, then?"

"I don't care! Anywhere! Didn't you say your family had a place in the Mauritius? I bet you the Japanese aren't bombing there!"

Edward was stunned into a moment of silence.

"What, nothing to say, Mister Hero?" Florence continued.

"Florence, this is not even funny. *I* was the one who suggested that we try going there even before the war began. *You* were the one dead set against the idea!"

"Well, I don't remember that!" she said, after a moment.

"How convenient! Well, it is pointless to fight about it now…"

Another screech went overhead. Edward and Florence both clenched their bodies and crouched. The explosion sounded near—as near as it had ever been. Florence came apart, screaming.

"I hate you, you bastard! I hate you! You have no balls! It's all your fault! You…"

Edward gripped Florence's flailing hands. "Stop it!" he shouted, his face inches from hers.

She spat at him.

He raised his hand.

She stopped moving and glared at him.

He lowered his hand, ashamed.

She nodded her head, slow and full of contempt.

"I knew it. You men are all alike," she said, almost a whisper.

What could he say?

Meanwhile, the shells continued to fly overhead. The children watched as their parents finally gave in to the terrible stress that they had been under. While bombs had not terrified Carl and Eugene into crying, the fight had. They wept, seeking maternal comfort, but receiving none. As Edward held them, cooing to them, Hans stood by his Papa. He had no tears. He just glared at his mother silently.

In the hours that followed, Japanese invasion forces battled Australian defenders on the other side of the island. By dawn, the Japanese were well established in the north and northwest of

Singapore, and the Australians were retreating to regroup. The Battle of Singapore, which would last a week, was well under way.

As the skirmishes were taking place down the core of Singapore, some civilians, Asians as well as Europeans, took up arms and made their stand against the enemy. Unfortunately, such ones were even less organized than the retreating professional army, and many of these civilians lost their lives in a meaningless way, without even a fight. Then there was also the problem of recognition. Unfortunately, Chinese men with rifles were all too often being mistaken for Japanese soldiers.

At the end of January, Colonel Willoughby made it across from Ubin with the last of the evacuees. True to form, he had offered his services to the very end. He was dismayed at the way the campaign had turned out, but he was especially shocked to witness the manner in which the distraught Allied forces came apart before his very eyes, the moment the enemy crossed over to Singapore.

During the retreat down Bukit Timah Road, Willoughby watched as a group of four or five Australians broke rank and ran down a residential side street. Despite his age, he still moved with purpose, crossing the road and following the men from a distance.

They appeared to be looking for any form of transportation available. By then, vehicles of any sort were getting harder to come by. Many had been destroyed in the fighting, and the ones used by civilians fleeing south were usually abandoned at the dockyards. Most of these ended up being unceremoniously pushed into the sea, to make way for other vehicles.

Upon seeing a family loading their car further up the road, the men rushed up, pointing their rifles and shouting at the family to get out of their way. Instead of complying, the owner of the car stood in between the soldiers and his family, firmly standing up to the rabble. A loud shouting match began, but it promptly ended with one of the soldiers shooting the civilian, his screaming family watching on as he crumpled to the ground.

Willoughby already had his revolver out as he approached the scene. Aiming at the soldiers, he shouted, "Stand down, the lot of you! Put down your weapons!"

The soldiers spun around to face him. The one who had shot the civilian worked the action of his .303 Lee-Enfield as he turned around. He had just managed to eject the spent cartridge casing when Willoughby shot him in the face, the .455 Webley resounding loudly between the rows of houses.

Colonel Thomas Willoughby went down with three .303 British bullets in his chest. As he lay in the middle of the road, his lungs felt as if they were on fire. Just before his last breath, he could see the Australian soldiers driving off in the car, while the man's family wailed around his body.

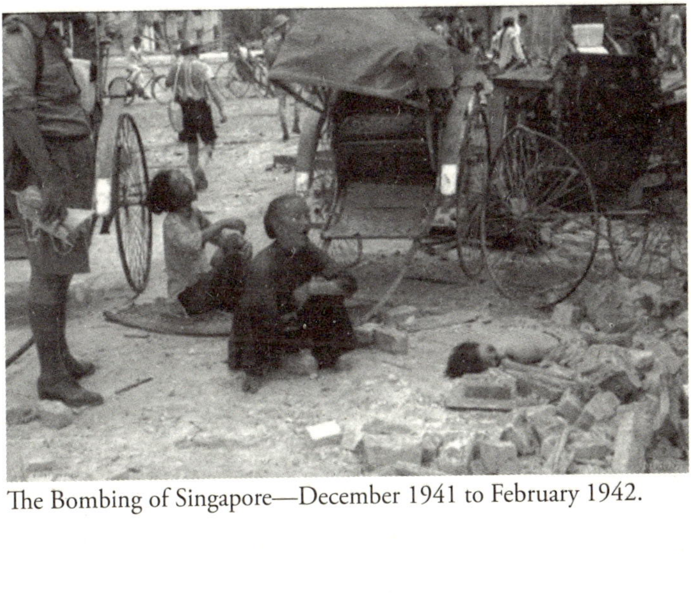

The Bombing of Singapore—December 1941 to February 1942.

5
THE SURRENDER

February 15th 1942, 0930 hours
Command Post – Malaya Command Fort Canning, Singapore

Lieutenant General Arthur Ernest Percival paced the underground bunker room with his hands folded behind his back, deep in thought. Lieutenant General Sir Lewis Heath, Australian Major General Gordon Bennett, and their staff watched silently. His pacing in the silent concrete room was unnerving.

Finally, he cleared his throat and spoke. His voice was steady, but soft. "Gentlemen, I thank you for gathering here today. I realize there have been words going round about a certain communiqué I received yesterday evening. I will now confirm for you that at this time I have been authorized by General Wavell to surrender our forces to the Japanese. He thanks us for our dedication thus far, but leaves the final discretion to us."

Percival was referring to General Sir Archibald Wavell, the Commander-in-Chief of India. Up to that point, Percival had been under pressure from him, who in turn was under pressure from Prime Minister Churchill, to stand firm to the bitter end.

Murmurs broke out. Some were visibly relieved—ones who had been pushing some time for the surrender. The men discussed details over the next hour. The majority was in favor of accepting surrender terms immediately, but there remained some on Bennett's staff who were proposing a counterattack to regain Bukit Timah and the water supply. These options were weighed out, but in the end, they all came to the conclusion that the counterattack was not feasible. Once this unanimous decision was made, they moved forward to face the enemy again, but this time under truce of the white flag.

Later that morning, Brigadier General Terrence Newbigging of Percival's staff crossed over to Japanese lines carrying the Union Jack and a white flag of truce. After listening to the enemy dictate terms through a translator, he then returned to convey these demands to General Percival.

Should Percival agree to meet and formalize the surrender at the Ford Motor Factory that afternoon, then the British were to fly a Japanese flag from the tallest building in Singapore, the Cathay Building. The captured Factory had become the operational headquarters for the Japanese Army.

The flag of the Rising Sun flew over the Cathay Building for a ten minute period, signifying agreement. Later that evening it was raised again, after the official surrender had taken place. It would continue to fly for another three and a half years over Singapore.

February 15th 1942, 1630 hours
Ford Motor Factory, Upper Bukit Timah Road, Singapore

Lieutenant General Percival and his staff officers walked up the curved driveway to the Ford Motor Factory, where his adversary Lieutenant General Yamashita was waiting. Wearing the "tin hat" helmets and short trousers standard to British army personnel in the tropics, they marched behind a Japanese officer, who wore a sword on his hip. One of Percival's men carried the Union Jack, while another carried a white flag.

Once inside, another officer ushered them into the board room, which had been furnished with a table and chairs. On one side of the table, with Yamashita in the middle, the Japanese delegation was seated. Empty seats on the other side awaited the British delegation. After exchanging formalities, Percival and his men proceeded to sit down in their designated places.

Yamashita sat on his side of the table, glowering at his vanquished opponents while an interpreter presented the Japanese terms for unconditional surrender.

After the war, the Allies recovered a captured Japanese film of the event. Because of the difference between film and projector speeds, when one views the footage, there appears to be an increase in motion speed—similar to the comical effect of the old Charlie Chaplin or Harold Lloyd shows.

Unfortunately for Percival, this effect makes him appear to be blinking nervously throughout the parley, with a dumbfounded expression fixed on his face. One can see him nodding rapidly and occasionally resting his fist against his mouth in thought. He looked weak and insipid.

Percival, in his soft and steady voice, replied to the demands of the Japanese, stating terms on behalf of his people. A brief exchange ensued, only to be cut off by Yamashita slamming his powerful hand on the table. "Surrender, or no surrender! There is no debate! Yes, or no?" his heavily accented voice punched through the silent air.

Percival folded. There was no more discussion. He quietly signed the surrender documents shortly after 1715 hours.

Thereafter, Singapore received a new name from the new masters—*Syonanto*—"Light of the South." It was the first of many changes for Singapore. As part of Japanese efficiency, clocks also had to be changed to match Tokyo time.

The Occupation force wasted no time in removing all vestiges of British rule. Schools were to convert to Japanese. Currency of the Straits Settlement would be replaced by the Japanese Occupation dollars. All European persons, civilian or military, were to be interned.

The Occupation had officially begun.

When Percival capitulated, he was not just surrendering his armed forces. He was surrendering the liberties, the hopes and dreams of the people who had trusted in him for deliverance.

He had even surrendered their culture.

Beaten and resigned, General Percival and his staff approach the Ford Motor Factory on the evening of February 15th 1942 to sign surrender documents

The Opponents—Lieutenant General Arthur Ernest Percival (*left*) and Lieutenant General Tomoyuki Yamashita (*right*).

Surrender formalities at the Ford Motor Factory—February 15th 1942.

6
MEETING THE TIGER

February 17th 1942
Changi District, Singapore

It was Tuesday morning, two days after the British surrender. Edward was riding with a neighbor to the Padang, a large parade field facing Municipal Building (today known as City Hall) in the downtown area. Shortly after the surrender on Sunday evening, the Japanese Occupation administration had ordered all Europeans in Singapore, including men, women and children, to report there for a registration.

Edward knew that this had to be bad news. He decided to report alone, having reasoned that his wife, being a Straits-born Chinese, should be exempt from the registration. By the same reasoning, the children should be exempted as well. In any event, the further he could keep them out of the picture, the better. He would not mention them at all, if he could.

The Padang was filling up with bewildered-looking Europeans. They showed up with suitcases in one hand, children in the other. The Japanese had set up makeshift desks at the edge of the grass, each one manned by an army clerk. There were also interpreters present who spoke French or Dutch. Armed soldiers stood behind them, watching the civilians with contempt.

The head of each family had to come forward, identify himself first, and then his family. In many cases, there were unaccompanied women who had to represent themselves. These were ones whose husbands had either been killed in action or were being interned separately as military Prisoners-of-War.

When it came to be Edward's turn, he stepped up to the nearest desk and waited for instructions.

"Your name?" the Japanese clerk said in English.

"Schirmer. Edward Henry Schirmer."

The clerk frowned. "How do you spell that?" he asked.

Edward proceeded to spell his surname.

"Funny name! Does not sound English," the clerk said.

"It's German."

The clerk looked up, his eyes widening. "You are German?"

Edward nodded.

The clerk turned and spoke with the overseeing officer, who was walking from desk to desk. After a brief exchange, the officer walked off. The clerk turned to Edward.

"Wait one moment. Over here." It was an order, but the clerk had said it politely. He nodded his head in a small bow at Edward.

Edward stepped to the side of the makeshift desk, wondering what was going on.

The officer returned, accompanying a large Japanese officer. Edward did not understand their rank insignias at the time, but he could tell that this man was a very senior officer—perhaps even a general—from his mannerisms. All Imperial Japanese Army officers had stars on their collar badges. What distinguished the ranks were the color of the star, or stars, as well as the color of the background and stripes.

The large man moved with determination. As he came closer, soldiers immediately came to attention. The crowd grew silent. He stood before Edward, sizing him up. Edward met his eyes. Firmly, but with respect; not belligerent in any way.

After a moment, the large Japanese officer spoke. "*Entschuldigen Sie bitte, aber wie heißen Sie?*" he said, in fluent German. It was the formal way to inquire someone's name.

Edward was surprised. The officer had spoken German proficiently, and with a hint of a Prussian accent, something he had not heard in a while. Edward decided to address him as "General."

"*Ich heiße Edouard Henri Schirmer, mein General,*" he replied, bowing slightly at the waist in the Japanese custom.

The large Japanese general had a severe countenance, made even more intense by his scowling mouth and shaved head. Suddenly he smiled, bowed and continued speaking in German.

"I am called Yamashita. You are surprised that I speak German, aren't you?" he said.

"I must confess that I am. You speak most proficiently, General," Edward replied.

"Thank you. I have spent some time in Germany, Austria and Switzerland. But even before that, my instructors at the Academy were Prussian. You speak as they did, Herr Schirmer. Is that where you are from, perhaps?"

"My family did originally come from Prussia."

"But you were not born there?"

Edward shook his head. "I was born in the Mauritius Islands."

"Interesting! Come with me, Herr Schirmer. Tell me more."

Yamashita began walking toward the large Municipal Building. Edward followed him. As soon as they were gone, murmurs arose from the crowd which had gone silent in the presence of the famous Tiger of Malaya, as the newspapers had begun calling him.

General Tomoyuki Yamashita ushered Edward Schirmer into an unoccupied office inside of Municipal Building. "Sit, sit. Would you like some tea?" he offered.

"Yes, please. Thank you, sir," Edward replied. He was still feeling wary about the kind treatment, but decided the best thing for him was to be polite and see where it went.

Yamashita barked out an order in Japanese. A young soldier came running in and stood at attention. Yamashita spoke to the soldier, who bowed and replied, "*Hai!*"

The young soldier returned with a pot of green tea and two small cups. Having poured some steaming hot tea into the cups, he bowed and backed out of the room.

"Come, drink!" Yamashita urged, picking up his cup of tea.

After standing in the hot sun for hours, Edward welcomed the drink. "Thank you, sir. You are most kind," he said, raising his cup.

Yamashita raised his cup in return. They both drank the hot green tea in silence. Edward was impressed by the flavor and the quality.

"I say, this tea is very good!" he said, after a moment. It seemed inane to make small talk at a time like that, but Edward did not know what else to say.

The General smiled broadly. "You like it? Good! I am somewhat fussy about my tea, so my wife personally packed some of this for me. You know, I believe it has brought me good luck."

Edward smiled back. "This is very fine tea. It is good to have a wife who cares for you," he replied.

"You are married, then?"

Edward hesitated momentarily, but then he nodded.

"Children?"

"Yes, sir. Three boys."

Yamashita smiled and made a pleased grunting sound. "The gods have blessed you with sons!" Then his smile faded. He continued, "I myself do not have the fortune of having children, much less sons. I envy you, Herr Schirmer."

"Perhaps you may still have children in the future, General. I became a father some years after I turned forty," Edward said. Again, it seemed a pathetic thing to say, but really, what does one say, given the situation?

Yamashita looked at Edward and burst out in loud raucous laughter. For a moment, Edward felt alarm. Did he say the wrong thing? But the general's laughter was that of amusement, not contempt.

"I am fifty-six years old! Can you imagine me becoming a Papa at this age? Although Mrs Yamashita is younger than me, she is not about to have children anytime soon, I regret to inform you. I know that in your Bible there is a story about a very old couple named Zechariah and Elizabeth having a son. Unfortunately, I don't believe that sort of miracle will happen for us. But I thank you for your optimism!"

Edward began laughing as well. It was most surreal.

"But enough of that," Yamashita said, with a wave of his hand. "If you are German, you are entitled to protection from the Japanese government, since our nations have signed a pact of co-operation. Is that what you want then, Herr Schirmer?"

Edward remained at a complete loss as to what he should say. *If the Japanese actually ask for my papers, they will know that I am not a German national! On the other hand, if I play this right, I may be able to protect my family. But if I accept their protection, isn't that a form of treason? What do I do here? What do I do?*

Knowing that he would be blowing his chances if he was to take too long, Edward replied "Yes, sir," before he was really able to think matters over.

"Fine. You don't have to go back out there with those other people. You are a friend of the Empire."

Yamashita held out his meaty hand. Edward shook it.

What am I getting into?

Meanwhile, the registration process continued on, for many more hours. When it was done, Japanese soldiers were to round up the European residents of Singapore—the once venerable *Tuan Besars*—like so much cattle, and march them off to the makeshift civilian camp located in Changi for indefinite internment. Later, the civilians would be moved to another camp on Sime Road. They would end up staying in captivity for almost four years, not leaving these camps until September 1945—after the Japanese surrender.

Some would never leave.

The Municipal Building, with the Padang in front.

7
A FRIEND OF THE EMPIRE

As Edward left the Padang area to return to the apartment in Changi, he glanced over at the droves of Europeans standing about, still waiting to be registered for their internment.

Men, women and children with dirty, doleful faces. *I should be among these people, yet I am not. But really, why should any of them have to be there? And if any of them were given a chance to leave as a free man, who would not take it?*

Inwardly, Edward cursed the callous British administration, who had let everyone down despite such a show of pomp and circumstance before the invasion. But that was now neither here nor there. It was up to everyone to do their best to survive the enemy occupation.

While walking, he scanned the crowd for the neighbor who had given him a ride to the Padang earlier that morning. So many faces. Edward failed to find him.

Despite all the rationalization, Edward still felt a sense of guilt that he was going home, and these ones were not. Nobody here had asked for the tragedy that was war. Yet it had affected everyone differently. Some were dead. Some had been maimed for life—either physically, mentally, or both. Everyone had lost something; some had lost everything. But by a strange stroke of fortune, Edward was now going home.

They never asked for my papers...

General Yamashita had even arranged for one of his men to drive Edward back to Changi, as the buses were still not running.

The young Japanese lieutenant was a friendly man who spoke, surprisingly enough, some French. As they drove, they exchanged small talk at first, but the conversation dwindled after a while. Then the lieutenant loosened his collar and began humming a tune. Edward did not know what the tune was, but it definitely sounded Japanese to him. After offering Edward a cigarette, which he declined, the lieutenant lit one for himself and contentedly smoked and hummed his tune, smiling all the while.

The elation of a victor. The elation of a man who could breathe once again, after having faced death up close. Edward could certainly identify with that feeling.

The car, an older Vauxhall Cadet, drove away with the young lieutenant at the wheel, waving goodbye. Edward turned to walk up to his shop when Hans and Carl ran to him, hugging his legs and crying out, "Papa! Papa!"

Tears welled up in Edward's eyes. He absolutely knew then that he had made the right decision.

I will do anything for these boys—for my family.

"Yes, Papa is home. Everything is alright."

They walked up to the apartment. Florence stood at the door carrying Eugene. She put him down and folded her arms. Eugene wobbled over to his Papa. Edward picked up the toddler.

They're still babies...

Edward and Florence had come to a truce, cooling off after the moment of tension caused by the bombing had subsided. But the fight had essentially snuffed out the already smoldering embers of their relationship. There was no real love between them—there had not been for a long time, if there ever was any in the first place—but they knew it was important to pull together and learn to co-exist.

"You're back!" she said, almost a whisper. "I didn't know what to think. People everywhere are saying all sorts of horrible things. I thought the Japanese had ... I just didn't know if you would be coming back."

"I know. I wasn't so sure myself. I thought I was done for. All the other Europeans are being taken someplace. Don't know where, though."

"Then how come you are here?"

"It's most strange," Edward began. He narrated to Florence the events of that morning.

When he finished, Florence was silent for a moment. Then she spoke slowly, "I'm still worried. I don't trust these people. What happens now?"

"Well, for now we carry on with our lives. General Yamashita told me we can go back to Ubin in the next few days, as soon as things settle down and they can restore order."

"And do you trust this General? You don't think you are being naïve?"

"Florence, don't start a fight again. You have any better ideas?"

"I don't like it. Are we co-operating with the enemy?"

"I know ... I know ... it feels wrong. But I don't see that we have any choice. Besides, the Japanese are the new government. They became that legally, as soon as General Percival signed the surrender and told his men to lay down their arms."

"But what about becoming a so-called friend of the Empire? What will happen if the British come back? Besides, you're not really German. Or I should say, a German citizen."

"I know, I've thought about that. We'll cross that bridge when we get to it. Or if we get to it. As far as my citizenship … the General never asked to see any of my papers this morning. As long as they don't ask for them, I don't intend to say anything about it either."

"I don't know..."

Edward nodded and gently put his hand on Florence's arm. She did not pull away. "I don't, either. Let's just see how things go for now," he said.

It was more than a week before they could move back to Ubin as a family. Old Mrs Chia joined them a few days after that. The Japanese allowed all families who had lived there to return, and they did so as soon as they could.

It seemed strange to be back. In some ways, it seemed as if nothing had happened—all the fighting had taken place elsewhere, so there was no noticeable damage. But it was not the same. For one thing, there was now a small garrison of soldiers on the island. When one saw a soldier, one had to stop what they were doing and bow until the soldier had passed by. Even then, the soldier could, at his whim, strike anyone whom he pleased. However, by not bowing, it was a guarantee of a beating, and occasionally a beheading. When that happened, the soldier would then order everyone to leave the decapitated body alone, where it would lay for days as a lesson to all. Only when the maggots appeared and the stench became unbearable could they remove the body.

The other noticeable difference was that not all the families had returned. For instance, Edward no longer saw the old Colonel out on his daily walks. Nobody knew what had happened to these ones specifically, but it was more than obvious what had become of them.

A few days after they had moved back, General Yamashita came to the island to visit Edward, much to his surprise.

"You thought perhaps I had forgotten about you, yes? How are you today, then?" the General said, speaking in German.

"General Yamashita! What a surprise! Do come in, and meet my family," Edward replied, ushering him inside. Noticing that the General's forehead was covered in perspiration, he added, "I'm sorry I only have water to offer you, but would you care for some, anyway?"

"Yes, thank you," the General said. He ordered his men to wait outside, and then he entered the house. When he saw Edward's sons, he exclaimed, "Handsome boys! Handsome boys!" He patted them on the head and gently pinched their cheeks.

In the meantime, Florence had rushed to the kitchen to get a glass of water. She returned, held it up to Yamashita, but never made eye contact. He took it without a word, and she left the room.

"Please sit down, sir," Edward invited.

Yamashita sat and drained his glass. "Ahhh! Much better. Too hot around here, don't you think?" he said.

"Oh, I don't notice it too much anymore. Been here for ten straight years now," Edward said.

"Ten years! What did you do here for ten years?"

"I sold boat engines, among other things. Marine equipment, that sort of thing."

"Boat engines? Big or small?"

"Actually, they were the small outboard type. Seagulls."

"Seagulls? Ah! Very good engines. We found some in Johor and used them to cross over to Singapore. Must have been some of your engines!" Yamashita said, laughing.

Edward smiled uneasily. "Perhaps," he said.

Yamashita looked around and continued, "You have a very nice house. Life is good for you, no?"

Edward smiled again. "It has been a little rough of late, but no, I can't really complain," he said.

Yamashita nodded quietly. "I apologize for your inconvenience. War is unfortunately necessary sometimes. Although I am a soldier, I am glad that it is over," he said.

Edward nodded. "As do I. Now we start picking up the pieces again, I suppose."

Yamashita nodded again. Then, changing the subject, he said, "Your wife is also very beautiful. Chinese?" He said it more as a statement than a question.

"Yes. Straits-born Chinese, as a matter of fact," Edward replied warily.

"Ah, so! That's good, they are a very friendly people. Much friendlier than their relatives in China. Those ones seem predisposed to be Communists. Very vicious! The Kuomintang under Chiang Kai Shek is just as bad."

Edward shrugged. "Well, I can offer no comment, sir. I have never been to China."

"Don't worry, you did not miss much. Yes, there are some beautiful places there, but the people are either vicious Communists or filthy peasants. At least, that seemed to be my experience."

It was awkward for Edward. To change the subject, he said, "Tell me about your time in Germany, General."

The General's face took on a peaceful expression as he remembered his time in Europe. "Beautiful country, beautiful people. Very beautiful people," he commented. He smiled as he thought about a certain beautiful woman whom he had met during his tenure in Austria. "I do hope to return to Germany someday soon. I have dear friends there," he added.

As their conversation continued, Yamashita softened further and Edward began to feel more at ease. He actually found himself liking the powerful Japanese man. Despite his forbidding—perhaps even brutish—countenance, Yamashita was a deep thinker, with surprisingly gentle manners when he was comfortable.

If it was not for this war, or foolish nationalism, I might like to have been friends with this man.

Before Yamashita was to leave Singapore, Edward and he were to become friends. Perhaps it was not a close friendship, but it was one born out of mutual respect.

Florence was in the kitchen during the conversation and had overheard bits and pieces of it. She had heard the General's compliment of her and, despite her initial misgivings, was flattered. Maybe it wasn't so bad after all. She began to soften toward their situation. It could definitely have been worse.

When it became time for the General to leave, he stood up and straightened his uniform. Edward stood up, as well.

"One more thing before I leave, Herr Schirmer. I know how fond the German people are of the hunting sport. It would therefore be reasonable to assume that you are in possession of hunting firearms. I regret to inform you that you must turn any such items over to the *Kempeitai*, the military police. That is Occupation Law, even for friendly nationals," Yamashita said. Sincere regret was apparent on his face.

Edward was devastated inside, even though he knew something like this was going to happen sooner or later. "I understand, General. Let me get it, then," he said.

He returned with the Drilling—the breech was open, to show the empty chambers—along with ammunition for it, all of which he had hidden under a false floor board.

Yamashita took the gun and appreciatively examined the fine engraving. His eyes finally rested on the name etched in the receiver. "This belonged to a relative? Your father?" Yamashita asked.

Edward nodded.

Yamashita looked at him and then nodded sadly. "I understand these things. We Japanese are that way with our swords, especially those of samurai heritage. Herr Schirmer, please allow me the honor of safekeeping this, your family heirloom. You have my word; I will return it to you as soon as it is possible to do so," he said.

Edward nodded silently, and then bowed to the General.

General Yamashita returned the bow. Cradling the Drilling in his arms, he turned to leave.

It was the last time Edward or Hans were to see it ever.

For the residents of Singapore, returning to their lives would not prove to be as easy as it had been for the Schirmers. Although they were not being interned the way the Europeans had been, the locals still faced various challenges. Food and housing shortages affected everyone. Then there were social and racial issues as well.

The Japanese Occupation created an atmosphere of unease and distrust among the people. Informants and malicious individuals plied the *Kempeitai* military police with all sorts of tales to better their positions or take revenge on former rivals. In turn, the *Kempeitai* men were very skillful in using this to their advantage. By creating distrust amongst neighbors, classes and races, they had effectively divided and conquered.

The Japanese had courted the Indians, even before the war, as their friends in the fight against British imperialism. Now, many Indians openly sided with the new government. Burly Sikh policemen and former soldiers could now be seen guarding the military and civilian prison camps, and some began taking a perverse pleasure in abusing the *Tuan Besars* in their charge.

The Malays received special recognition as the indigenous people of that region. Even before the invasion, the Japanese attempted to court their favor, saying that they recognized the Malays as the rightful owners of the land. They promised that *Nippon* would help them in their struggle to shake off the White Man's yoke, and give them back what was rightfully theirs. Some fell for these words, and co-operated freely with the new government, much to the expense of the other races.

As time went on, all would begin to realize that the Japanese were friends to nobody.

The Chinese, on the other hand, received the short end of the stick from the very beginning. For generations, the two races had warred with each other off and on, both sides viewing the other as racially inferior. Now the Japanese had the excuse of the ongoing Sino-Japanese war to persecute the Chinese in their conquered territory.

While it was true that many of the Chinese had been sending money to the different organizations in China, not all of it was for the war effort. Most of it was for humanitarian relief. Nevertheless, the Japanese viewed it all as aiding the enemy. Furthermore, they simply labeled anyone whom they chose as Communists, or agitators. This led to a series of violent purges. After the war, these purges became known as the Sook Ching massacre.

8

SOOK CHING

The Japanese occupation administration wasted no time in getting down to business. In the first two days following the British surrender, there was a period of establishing order.

During the first twenty-four hour period, 1000 Allied servicemen were allowed to retain their weapons, for assisting the Japanese in police work. The following day, the Japanese themselves dealt with the former Colonial masters. All servicemen were disarmed and remanded to the notorious Changi prison, with the overflow being sent to the nearby Selarang barracks. European civilians were also being interned, at first in the Changi area, and later at a new makeshift camp on Sime Road.

On the third day, the Japanese turned their full attention to the Chinese population.

February 18th 1942
Singapore

General Yamashita, even before arriving in Singapore, had his orders to "clean up the undesirable element." This no doubt referred primarily to ethnic Chinese, especially ones who were born in China and had gone overseas anytime during the Sino-Japanese War period.

Three days after the fall of Singapore, all Chinese males between the ages of eighteen and fifty were to present themselves at local "screening centers" for an inspection. The *Kempeitai* "screeners" were primarily targeting persons who were (1) suspected of Communist affiliation, (2) triad members—tattoos were a dead giveaway—and (3) former civil servants, who may still be loyal to the British.

Anyone even remotely suspected of falling in these target groups was also in danger. In harsh times like that, the worst in human nature emerged and people did all they could to save themselves. There were many who panicked and even furnished the *Kempeitai* with names of friends and relatives, in order to deflect any attention from themselves.

During the course of the "screening" the *Kempeitai* separated the men into two groups. When they were satisfied that an individual was of no potential danger to the Japanese cause—obviously this was a very subjective process—they would issue him a certificate or put a stamp on his body, and send him on to the first group for further processing and eventual release.

Those who did not pass the "screening" had to wait with the second group in a separate secure holding area. They did not know what to expect, but whatever it was, they knew it could not be good.

The next day, the *Kempeitai* tied these men up and drove them in truckloads to remote areas such as Punggol beach in the northeast, or Changi and Tanah Merah beach in the east. They then lined the men up at the edge of the water, or in some cases, made them dig a slit trench first, and then lined them up in front of it.

By then, the young Chinese men knew what to expect next, so some of them closed their eyes and waited for the impact of bullets. Others tried to escape, while some attempted to fight back, knowing that they were dead either way. As expected, their fate was no different from the ones who had stood still. After the smoke cleared, Japanese privates went around inspecting the fallen men. If anyone still moved, they stabbed them with their bayonets.

This systematic massacre went on over the next two weeks throughout Singapore as well as in the more populated areas of Malaya. While the ostensible purpose was the removal of "dangerous" or "undesirable" men who could pose opposition to the Japanese government, it clearly was a thinly veiled form of ethnic cleansing. Even though the target group was supposed to have only been males in a certain age range, the killings were actually extending to other groups—men, women and children—more often than not. Typically, there were very few survivors from these killings. One young man from a Chinese village in Malaya who survived the ordeal awoke to find that the Japanese had bayoneted his entire family, including the women and children.

After the war, the local Chinese communities tallied the death toll to be between 50,000 to 100,000. Naturally, this number includes the other men, women and children also killed in these purges, aside from the so-called target group.

The Japanese government today, while acknowledging the purges, insists that only "less than 5,000" Singaporean and Malayan Chinese men were killed in the process. This is similar to the argument that the post-war Nazi sympathizers have put forth, justifying that Hitler could not have really killed six million Jews in Europe. Perhaps one or two million, but definitely not six.

As if the number made all the difference. Murder is murder.

Although the Sook Ching massacre mainly took place between February 18th and March 3rd, it did not mean that those who went home with a certificate of inspection were safe after that period. The Japanese could still arrest and summarily execute anyone at their discretion, especially when someone accused another, even falsely, of being subversive. That kind of thing happened all too often during the Occupation.

9

FAREWELL TO THE TIGER

As Edward walked about on Ubin Island, he was constantly reminded of the fact that it was not really the same anymore. Every time he saw a familiar face, he would greet that one as he always had, and try to make the usual small talk. But what he got in return was not the same as it had been.

It was not that people were being rude, or even shunning him. It was something else. The nervous smiles ... the restless eyes...

They are afraid of me. What, because of Yamashita's visits? What would they have me do, throw the General out on his face and sing "Rule Britannia?"

If, for one moment, Edward thought that this preferential treatment was causing someone else to be imprisoned in his place, or that it was costing anyone anything, he would not accept it at all. Or if the Japanese had asked him to betray anyone in Singapore—whether British or Asian—he would not have done it. That much he knew.

I know there is a fine line between peaceable co-operation with the occupying authorities—in order to ensure one's safety—and that of total collaboration. But I don't think I have crossed that line by allowing the General into my home and having a friendly discussion, have I? Is it any different than a café owner in occupied France serving beer to German soldiers? Do these people not see that?

Nonetheless, there could no longer be any closeness between Edward and his neighbors. They simply did not trust him, and he really could not do anything about that.

Whenever Yamashita was on the island, he made it a point to stop by at Edward's for a visit. The General always brought his favorite tea, and they would sit on the porch, exchanging ideas while enjoying the fragrant brew. Florence began warming up to this arrangement, but she knew her place. She was friendly, but otherwise let her husband do the talking.

Despite the pleasantness of these visits, Edward found them very difficult initially. Something was always looming at the back of his head. He had heard about the massacre of Chinese men, as well as some of the other brutalities that the Japanese had perpetrated during the course of the campaign. Whether Yamashita had personally ordered these things or not, he still remained the Commander-In-Chief of Japanese forces in the area, and therefore had to have some culpability. Knowing about these things made it difficult for Edward as he sat before the General.

Yet, he saw the human side of Yamashita. The man who was gentle with his children. The lover of art and poetry. The student of history. Edward accepted that these were facets of the same man who was also ruthless in battle, who would fearlessly charge through a fusillade of fire. The true descendent of samurai.

Edward respected and feared him, both at the same time. The main thing though, was that Edward was not in a camp someplace, unable to take care of his family. If sharing tea with the General would preserve that peace and freedom, then it was what he would do willingly.

Wouldn't anyone?

Yamashita's tenure in Singapore did not last long. There still remained too much animosity between him and Prime Minister Tojo, who was not happy with how the Japanese press had been referring to Yamashita as "The Tiger of Malaya" since his victorious descent on the former British colonies.

Tojo felt that his rival was receiving more than his fair share of publicity, and when that happened, he knew Yamashita would then be able to fully redeem himself in the Emperor's eyes. So Tojo promptly found a way to send Yamashita out to the sticks. In July 1942, he ordered Yamashita to proceed directly from Singapore to Manchuria, to take over the Army garrisoned in Manchukuo. While it sounded on one hand like a promotion, it was clearly a stonewalling tactic on Tojo's part—Yamashita's orders clearly stated that he was not to stop in Tokyo to see the Emperor.

July 15th 1942
Upper Thomson Road, Singapore

"Edward-*san*, I appreciate you indulging me this way," General Yamashita said, in German.

"General, it is I who should be grateful for your kind hospitality. And so is Hans here. Lunch was most delicious," Edward replied. Turning to his son, he said in English, "Hansel, say 'thank you' to the General."

"Thank you, sir General," Hans said, a shy smile on his face.

Yamashita smiled broadly and bent over to the boy's height. "You are welcome," he said in halting English.

He stood up to his full height. Returning to German, he said, "And now, one more item. There is a photographic studio nearby. I would like to have our picture taken together."

"Certainly, General. May I ask—is there a special occasion?"

Yamashita grimaced. "I would like to have a reminder that there still are better people in the world, after I leave this island," he said. "Edward-*san*, in two days I have to go to Manchuria. I very much doubt if I will be returning."

"Oh," Edward said. He was not sure what to say. Despite the awkwardness in the beginning, he had come to like the General, and enjoyed their talks. He did not really want to say goodbye.

After a moment, Edward spoke again. "That is ... too bad, General. I take it that you are not altogether pleased with the assignment?"

Yamashita curled his lips in a sneer. "Politics!" he said, emphasizing the filthiness of the word. "But what can a soldier do?" Then he softened his tone. "Edward-*san*, I have one more favor to ask of you. Please call me Tomo. We are friends, are we not?"

Edward was honored that this powerful man was lowering himself in this manner. "Certainly we are, Tomo. Thank you," he said, with sincerity.

The owner of the photographic studio was not unaccustomed to Japanese soldiers at his business—these days they made up most of his customers. But here was General Yamashita himself! The photographer quickly set up the portrait stool and the backdrop.

"Edward-*san*, you sit on the stool, your son stands in front of you, and I will stand behind," Yamashita said, motioning them.

When they were in position, he turned to the photographer. "This is good?" he said in English.

"Yes, sir! Looks very nice, sir!" the photographer said. "Alright, hold still now.

After the pictures, Yamashita motioned for Edward to step aside for a few words. They went to a quiet corner of the studio.

"I will not be seeing you again before I leave, Edward-*san*. I wanted to say goodbye to you properly."

"Tomo, I have greatly enjoyed our time together. It has been an honor and a privilege to get to know you. I hope we will see each other again."

"I certainly hope so, as well. Edward-*san*, I don't want you to think I have forgotten my promise."

"Promise?"

"Your hunting firearm. I cannot return it to you at this time, and I do not want to leave it in the armory here. It is too fine for that; someone will take it for themselves. I will bring it with me and treasure it, as I do my own sword. When this war is over—as soon as I am able to—I will return it to you. On my honor, I will do this."

Edward was touched. "Friends need not offer pledges on their honor. I understand why I cannot have it back at this time. Thank you for taking care of it, all the same."

Yamashita nodded and shook Edward's hand. "There is one more thing," the General said. "There is the delicate matter regarding the place of your birth. I know that it was in a British colony. That also explains how you have been able to reside in another British colony for so many years."

Edward felt tightness in his chest. He said nothing.

"I never did ask to see your papers when we met," Yamashita continued. "I do not wish to see them now. As far as I am concerned, you are German. That is good enough for me. Do not show your papers to anyone, Edward-*san*. Before I leave, I will issue the orders that you are to be left alone, that you are a friend of the Empire. We will see each other after the war, my friend. Under better circumstances."

Edward's eyes watered. He stepped back, bowed deeply to the General, and spoke slowly, "*Arigatou gozaimashita, Tomo-san. Sayonara*, my friend."

For Edward, life returned to normal—or at least, as close to normal as possible under the circumstances. His business days were over. Survival became the most important thing. Fortunately, there was room to grow food crops around his home. This kept him and his family from starving.

With Yamashita's edict in place, Edward became the only European in Singapore at the time who was allowed to live in his own home, without harassment. He knew how fortunate he had been, and thanked God for it. He only hoped it would last.

The *Kempeitai* left him alone, but so did his neighbors. And there was really nothing he could do about that. The only person whom he could still call a friend was Eng Guan, who treated him the same as before. True friendship is like that. It transcends changes. Unfortunately, the two friends were seldom able to see each other, with the fuel rationing and transportation shortages in place. Still, they thought about each other and waited for better days.

Tomoyuki Yamashita—
The Tiger of Malaya

10
ENG GUAN

August 5th 1943
Joo Chiat Road, Singapore

Lee Eng Guan sat on a rattan chair straddling the walkway outside his shophouse, watching the sky change color as the evening approached. Behind him was his carpentry shop, above him was the apartment where he and his wife lived. It was, all things considered, a very pleasant evening.

Just before the war, he and his wife had saved enough money for him to start his own business, and so they bought the shophouse with great plans for the future.

Then the war began.

Then the Japanese came.

For years, they had been trying to have children of their own, but they were not successful. Now, in view of the war, perhaps it was better that they had remained childless. Food was becoming more and more scarce—imagine if there were more mouths to feed.

"And so now, I have become a farmer," he said to himself sadly. He thought of the small plot of garden in the backyard that barely kept him and his wife fed. But it was better than nothing, and it was also in compliance with the Japanese campaign encouraging the residents of Singapore to grow more food.

As Eng Guan sat there on his stoop wool gathering, he heard the sound of Japanese voices coming from farther up the street. His heart jumped. Every time he saw the Japanese come by, he became filled with anxiety. He still thought of the day, a year and a half before, when he had gone before the *Kempeitai* for inspection. That evening, he went home a free man. But he knew what happened to those who had not.

About a dozen soldiers and a *Kempeitai* officer marched up, coming to a halt in front of his shop. They pointed their rifles at Eng Guan. He quickly stood up, knocking the chair over, and put his hands above his head.

"This is your house? Who are you?" the officer asked.

"My name is Lee Eng Guan. Yes, sir—I live here."

"Then you are a dealer in black market goods!"

"What? No, sir! I am a carpenter!"

"You lie! It has been reported that you are moving stolen goods through your business!"

Panic coursed through Eng Guan. The accusation was obviously false, but he knew that it would not matter to the *Kempeitai*. Who would say such a thing? He and Su Ling were on good terms with all their neighbors.

Then it came to him out of the blue.

"That dirty lying bastard!" Eng Guan shouted.

Not two days before, Eng Guan had been upstairs when he heard some sounds coming from behind the shophouse. Upon investigation, he found an old Chinese man trying to hide some vegetables in his trousers. Vegetables that he had stolen from Eng Guan's garden, the nerve of it all.

He did not recognize the old man as anyone from their neighborhood. Nevertheless, if the stranger had come asking for help, Eng Guan would have done what he could—he was just that sort of person. But stealing was a different matter altogether.

In fact, had he reported the incident to the *Kempeitai*, they would have come and beheaded the man on the spot, without a trial. Eng Guan did not want the old man's death on his conscience. So instead, he ran the man off, warning him not to try it again. Instead of being remorseful, or even remotely grateful, the old man spat at Eng Guan and cursed him vehemently before leaving.

He did not think much of the incident—people did things like that when they were desperate—and went back to minding his own business. The old man was probably not right in the head, anyway.

Eng Guan never imagined anyone could be that malicious.

The *Kempeitai* officer pushed his way past Eng Guan and entered the shop. The soldier nearest Eng Guan grabbed his arm and pushed him into the shop as well, while another three followed with their bayoneted rifles at the ready. The remainder of the detachment stayed on guard outside, for a crowd had appeared to see what was going on.

As curious as they were, the crowd of neighbors did not dare challenge the Japanese soldiers. They kept their distance, watching what went on from across the street. Inside the shophouse, the officer barked orders. Two of the soldiers slung their rifles and proceeded to tear the place apart. The other two soldiers kept their rifles pointed at Eng Guan.

He thought of Su ling, and hoped that she would not come downstairs, no matter what she heard. Maybe he could distract them somehow...

Meanwhile, Su Ling was upstairs preparing supper. When she heard the sounds below, she immediately came running down the stairs, filled with dread. She stopped mid-way, as soon as she could see what was happening.

At the sight of her, the two ransacking soldiers stopped what they were doing. They snapped their rifles to their shoulders and aimed at her.

The officer looked at her with interest, and then he beckoned for her to come down. She hesitatingly obeyed, coming down the stairs slowly with her hands up above her head.

Su Ling was thirty-three, slim and attractive. Because she worked as a manual laborer, she dressed very plainly and had never worn make-up, even before the war. Nevertheless, her good looks still showed.

At their officer's command, the two soldiers pushed her to the floor and held her down. She screamed. From that moment, everything seemed to pass in slow motion for Eng Guan. He charged, pushing past the guards and rushing toward Su Ling. He had to save her somehow, but how exactly, he did not know.

As he charged, he felt a sharp blow to his head. He lost his balance and stumbled forward. With the ground rushing toward his face, he suddenly felt an excruciating sharpness on his left side, above his waist, through the kidney. Then his face hit the floor, the impact breaking his nose and jarring his brain. Another terrible piercing, this time from behind, through his right kidney.

Another one ... yet another one…

Eng Guan could not see; everything was black. It was also getting harder and more painful to breathe. The last thing he heard was the sound of his wife shrieking horribly.

I'm coming, Su...

Outside, the growing crowd of people could hear the shrieking and were becoming agitated. The senior ranking soldier among the ones standing outside the door, a non-commissioned officer, issued orders to his men. The soldiers immediately took positions with their rifles—four knelt in a firing position, while the other four stood behind them, aiming their rifles at the crowd as well.

One of the standing soldiers and the non-commissioned officer ordered the crowd to go home. They did not move. He then repeated himself and fired a round in the air to make a point.

That single shot gained the attention of the crowd, and they rapidly dispersed.

The soldiers outside remained on the alert. From inside the shophouse, the terrible shrieking went on for a while longer before the short, sharp bark of a Japanese officer's Nambu pistol sounded once, then twice.

The shrieking stopped.

Not long after the soldiers left, a strange old Chinese man went into the backyard and helped himself to some vegetables. He knew there was nobody in the house who would need them anyway.

11
BETRAYAL

December 30th 1943, 1200 hours
Ubin Island, Singapore

Ang Poh Yin felt an immediate pang of alarm upon the sight of her uncle standing outside her house, when she came home. The old man lived on the main island and it was very difficult for him to travel. If he was here, it could not be good news.

"Uncle, li ho bo? Simi tai ji?" she greeted him, apprehension on her face. How are you, Uncle? What's the matter?

The old man's face was chagrined.

"Aiyah, wa ka li kong, bo ho lah..." I'll tell you, but the news is not good.

He continued speaking in Hokkien. "The *Kempeitai* has your son, Ah Chun! They picked him up this morning. He is being held at the Outram Road jail!"

Poh Yin's heart fell. The Outram Road jail was where the dreaded Japanese military police detained and interrogated political and military prisoners. Very few came out of there alive. Even if one survived, it was not without having endured excruciating torture.

The Japanese were very good at extracting information. They had found very few individuals who were able to keep quiet with bamboo spikes rammed under their fingernails. Or while being pumped full of water to the point of bursting, and then having their abdomens jumped on. There also seemed to be many *Kempeitai* officers who were more than willing to practice their kendo skills, with the bamboo sword, on prisoners.

Oftentimes, just the mention of any of these methods had the detainees singing for their lives.

Tears streaming down her face, Poh Yin ran into the house to gather all the money she could find, and to pack some essentials. Her uncle had a boat waiting for them, and he walked as quickly as he could back to the jetty while she collected her things.

December 30th 1943, late afternoon
Outram Road, Singapore

It was a long trip to the jail, which was located near Chinatown in the south part of Singapore. Reeling with fear and exhaustion, Poh Yin could barely make it up the few steps to the main entrance. Her old uncle—who already had trouble holding himself up on a good day—needed to catch and steady her more than once.

Before the war, the Outram Road jail housed a regular police station. Also called the Pearl Hill Prison, the place had already gained certain notoriety during British rule for having been the location where Indian mutineers were lined up and shot after a summary trial in 1915.

During the Japanese Occupation, the name simply spelled terror.

There even seemed to be a smell of terror about the place. Standing in front of the main entrance, Poh Yin thought she could hear muffled shrieks coming from beyond the walls. It was more than she could bear, but she steeled herself up, forcing from her mind all the horrible thoughts.

She explained the purpose of her visit to the sentry. After looking her up and down, he did the same to her uncle. Silently, he motioned for them to pass.

The *Kempeitai* clerk sitting behind the booking counter glared at her and began shouting in Japanese, which she did not understand.

"Please, sir. I come to see my son..." she said in halting English, staring at the floor.

The clerk sneered at her. "Why you speak the Engrish, *baka-yero! Ni jiang hua-yu?*"

He was asking if she spoke Mandarin. Apparently, this one must have served some time in China.

Poh Yin's Mandarin was not very fluent, and it was heavily accented, but at least now she could communicate with him. "Please, sir. My son is in there. There must be a mistake—he is a good citizen," she said.

The clerk glared at her in silence. After a long, terrifying minute of staring at the ground, Poh Yin heard him speak, "*Nippon* does not make mistakes. If he is in there, then he has done something wrong and will be punished!"

"Please, please, I beg you! His name is Ang Seng Chun. Could you please review his case? Please!" Poh Yin said, placing, as discreetly as she could, a wad of British currency on the counter.

Upon taking over the administration of captured territories, the Japanese had replaced the colonial currencies with Japanese

Occupation notes. The locals called them "banana notes" partly for the picture of a banana tree on the paper, but mainly because of the lack of value. By 1944, with Japan not doing too well in the war, the notes were worth even less. The hard-to-come-by US dollars, even the old British currency, were certainly more desirable.

The *Kempeitai* clerk jumped up in feigned indignation. Pocketing the notes, he screamed at her. "Do you want to die? I can shoot you for such an outrage! *Baka-yero!*"

Poh Yin cringed and got on her knees. "I mean no disrespect, master..."

"Well, you can go home. Your money is no good here. Go!"

Poh Yin wailed, despair mounting. "Please! I give you anything!"

The clerk laughed. "You disgust me, old woman! What can an old hag like you give me? Get out of here before I shoot you!"

Poh Yin had no idea what prompted her next words, except that a desperate mother would say or do anything for her son. "I know where you can find a British spy!"

"What? Repeat yourself!"

It was too late to recant. "I know where you can find a British spy. Please, release my son and I will take you to him!"

The clerk was quiet for a moment. "Well, if this is true, it is your duty to report it anyway. No bargaining. Now you better tell me everything, or I shoot you!"

"Please, please! I will tell you everything, but let my son go. I beg of you!"

With his eyes fixed on Poh Yin, the clerk turned his head slightly and shouted something in Japanese. An orderly came out of an adjoining room, bowed, and came to attention. After a quick exchange the orderly marched off and returned accompanying a tall, austere looking *Kempeitai* officer.

The clerk bowed profusely to his officer, and a rapid-fire conversation ensued. The officer then turned to look at Poh Yin.

"So, you know the whereabouts of a British spy?" he asked in a conversational manner. The *Kempeitai* officer had spoken in fluent English, the accent a mark of his education at Cambridge. "How very interesting! Get up. Do tell me more."

Poh Yin swallowed the terror she was feeling—she knew that it was crucial for her to do so. "Please, sir. Can you let my son go?"

Ignoring her, the officer opened an ornate cigarette case. He took out a stick and tapped it. His orderly snapped open a gold-plated Dunhill lighter and held it out with his head bowed. A few puffs later, the officer spoke.

"You want to bargain for your son's life, I see. You do realize—I can have you shot for harboring a spy. Why then should I have to bargain for this information?"

"Sir, you have children?" Poh Yin stammered.

"No."

Her heart sank. "I beg you, kind sir. He is my only son."

The officer seemed to be thinking things over. He then turned and barked a command to the orderly, who bowed and marched off. He returned with a badly bruised young Chinese man, one who seemed barely able to walk on his own.

Yin gasped.

"I take it that you recognize this man?" the officer said.

She nodded, too shocked to speak.

"He is a communist agitator. The charge, therefore, is treason. Surely you know the punishment."

"Please, sir ... there must be mistake. My son work at shipyard, never join any party..."

"So you say. Alright then, let's talk. Tell me all about this spy. If your information is of any good, then you can take your son home with you."

With tears streaming down her face, Poh Yin blurted out, "His name is Schirmer. He lives on Ubin Island."

"Schirmer? European man with a house on Ubin Island?"

Poh Yin nodded.

"What rubbish! I know of this man. He is the only European left on the island. General Yamashita gave orders to leave him alone as he is our friend, a German!"

"But I know he is British. I worked for him. I see his passport before..." Yin faded away, guilt and horror eating her up.

"This is most interesting. Very well, we shall look into it. Your co-operation is most appreciated, Mrs Ang."

With a guttural shout the *Kempeitai* officer drew his sword, sliced it through Ah Chun's neck and then returned it smoothly to the scabbard, in one fluid motion. For a moment, the Chinese man stood with a shocked look on his face. Then he crumpled to the ground. His head rolled away.

Poh Yin tried to scream, but no sound would come out of her mouth. She stood trembling, her mouth wide open and her eyes rolled back. Her uncle, who had been quietly standing behind her throughout the exchange, fell to the floor in shock.

"Do please clean up this mess, before you take your son home with you," the tall officer said as he turned and walked toward his office.

Major Minoru, the *Kempeitai* officer, now had to organize an investigation into the Chinese woman's allegations. He did not mind. It gave him something to do, after all. Things had become fairly quiet for him, since the mopping up activity of Allied personnel and Chinese agitators was, for the most part, over and done with for some time now.

But more than just having something to do, he actually took personal pleasure in being able to exert *Nippon*'s greatness over other races, especially over Europeans. He had been unhappy to find out that there was one European remaining, who was not behind bars. As far as he was concerned, Minoru believed that man belonged in a camp, just for being a white man, even if he was allegedly a member of a friendly nation. But out of deference to one of the last standing orders of General Yamashita, the *Kempeitai* had left the German on Ubin alone.

Things were different now. For one thing, he had this charwoman's words of allegation. But also, he knew that the General had fallen out of political favor in Tokyo. Minoru feared no repercussions for what he was about to do.'

Japanese Occupation currency, informally known as "Banana Notes," were printed and distributed by the Japanese government from 1942 to 1945.

12
EVERYTHING FALLS APART

January 2nd 1944
Ubin Island, Singapore

Edward Schirmer sat down for breakfast with his family. Although supplies were scarce, he did his best to make sure the children never went hungry. All things said, that endeavor was becoming harder as the war went on.

Their meal for that morning was one that they had not had in a while—watery rice porridge. A small amount of rice cooked in a large amount of water made a somewhat satisfying dish, although it was also one that was severely lacking in nutrients. To remedy this deficiency, one could add eggs or boil bones in it, if one was able to get hold of such things.

While this may not sound like much of a treat, it was a welcome change. They hardly ever had rice anymore, as it had become an increasingly rare commodity due to the rationing.

It was a new year. Edward hoped it would be a good one.

Maybe the war will end and we can all start to rebuild this crazy world again.

He had barely taken his first spoonful when things began to happen. It started with loud shouting in Japanese from outside, followed by a violent banging on the door.

"Florence, take your mother and the children into the bedroom. Now!" Edward whispered. As soon as they left the table, he moved to the door and opened it cautiously.

The Japanese infantryman banging on the door was not a very big man—the Arisaka rifle with bayonet attached came up to his eyes—but he was pounding the door with a ferocity that made up for his size. As the door opened, he stepped back and stood ready to lunge with the bayonet.

Edward held his hands up in surrender. From a group of six or seven more soldiers standing in front of the house, a *Kempeitai* officer strode forward and stepped onto the porch. He was tall for a Japanese man—almost five feet ten (1.77 meters)—and was dressed in full field uniform, complete with black riding boots.

"You are Edward Schirmer?" he said, more statement than question.

"Yes. How may I help you, sir?"

"Your passport. I would like to see it."

Edward felt a chill of alarm crawl up his back. Up until that moment, the Japanese had left him alone, and had never requested his papers. He was at a loss.

"I'm sorry, Major…?" he said, trying to buy time.

"Minoru."

"Major Minoru, I regret to say that I have no idea where it is. You see, I have been a resident in Singapore for so long, and I have never needed it. I did clear this up with General Yamashita when he was here."

"Unfortunately Mr Schirmer, the General is still in Manchuria, I believe. You say that you have been here for how long?"

"Eleven ... no, twelve years. Since 1932," Edward replied.

What is this all about?

Major Minoru thought about that. "You are saying that you have not returned to Germany or used your passport since then?"

"That is correct. May I ask...?"

"As you know, the present German government—your Third Reich—has been in power since 1933. Therefore, the passport you possess must be invalid. Which is an offence, you know. However, if you can produce your old passport, I will take care of matters for you in honor of your relationship with the General. You will receive a current passport, and everything will be straightened out."

Oh my God! What do I do?

"Major, I really don't know where to start..."

"Perhaps you require some assistance, Mr Schirmer. My men are most happy to search the house for you."

Minoru's smile appeared sincere, yet somehow menacing.

Edward feigned indignation despite the shrinking feeling inside. Rising to his full height, he replied, "That will not be necessary, Major. General Yamashita assured me that there would be absolutely no problems of this sort."

"*Herr* Schirmer, as you well know the good General is no longer here. It is said that Prime Minister Tojo himself ordered him to Manchuria. So you see, I don't expect him back any time soon."

Another menacing smile.

Edward knew there was no alternative. Like the maître d' of a restaurant, Edward bowed slightly and ushered the Major into his house, with an outstretched arm.

The men accompanying Major Minoru were regular infantry thugs. This was a very common occurrence, as the army regularly augmented the *Kempeitai* with manpower. Seeing that their officer had made no effort to restrain them, they moved through the house, pulling drawers open roughly and dumping contents out.

Edward could hear the children crying. Controlling himself, he turned to the *Kempeitai* officer.

"Please, Major! There is no need for all this. The children are frightened!"

"Then you come up with the passport, *Herr* Schirmer."

Before Edward could reply, one of the soldiers rushed out of the bedroom, holding a booklet. He smiled and held it up, before thrusting it in Minoru's hand.

"I see. 'Subject of His Majesty the King.' How very interesting!" Minoru said, raising one eyebrow. "Well, well ... 'Occupation: Commissioned Agent.' You are a British spy, then!"

"No, I am not! It means that I make a living on my commissions, as a sales agent. Really now, would a spy have his occupation listed right in the open?"

"So you say. In any event, this is treason! You lied about being a German national!"

"I never said I was..."

"Well, *Herr* Schirmer. It really doesn't quite matter, does it? You still are a citizen of an enemy nation residing in occupied territory. Therefore, you will be interned for the duration of the war. In the meantime, we will find out if you truly are an enemy agent!"

Minoru barked orders to his men. They pushed Edward up against a wall while one of them tied his hands behind his back. He could hear his family screaming in fear. The desperation in him rose.

"Please, Major! I will go quietly with you. Just leave my family alone and stop frightening them!"

"Don't try and tell me what to do! You are in no position for that! You know, I can shoot them all on the spot for harboring a spy. Although, maybe not your wife—she would be more valuable working in a comfort station, don't you think?" Minoru sneered.

The Japanese military staffed their "comfort stations" with young women abducted from occupied territories, to serve as sex slaves for the soldiers. These women—mercilessly raped and beaten, sometimes to death—came to be known as the "Comfort Women" after the war. For the Japanese people, this remains a controversy to this day, as their government still denies culpability.

Edward had heard of these military brothels. Horror welled up inside him, but he knew he had to keep his head straight. He chose his words carefully. "Please, Major. I meant no disrespect. I know that any act of mercy on your part would be most undeserved. However, I do appeal to your honor as an officer, as a warrior gentleman. Please do not harm my family, sir."

Minoru smiled. "Very good! You know how it works then. Alright, as a gentleman I assure you that your family will be left alone ... although you had better make some arrangements for them," he said.

"May I speak with them, sir?"

Minoru nodded. Although he could be brutal, ruthlessly so when he wanted to be, he felt it was unnecessary at this juncture. Perhaps it would even prove advantageous to let out the line a little, before reeling it in. He ordered his men to untie Edward.

"Florence, I have to go with them now," Edward said to his wife privately, allowing for his words to sink in. He looked in her eyes and held her hands. She nodded understanding—he did not think he would be coming back this time. Even though the love between them had cooled, tears welled up in her eyes. This was finally it.

"You need to get in touch with Eng Guan. He will take care of you and the boys," he continued. "Can your mother go and stay with someone else for the time being?"

Florence thought about it. She nodded. "I have an aunt I can ask. I'm sure she can stay with her. But where is Eng Guan these days? We haven't seen him in months."

"I don't know. I hope he's alright. But we have to start someplace."

With that, Edward hugged her, smiled, and then he knelt before Hans. "Alright, Hans. You are the big man of the house now. Think you can take care of things while I'm gone?" he said.

Hans nodded and tried to smile back, to look brave. Papa had always been there, he had always taken care of everything. However, this was all very different now. Hans knew it was serious. Where were the soldiers taking his father? But deep inside, he believed Papa was going to be fine.

Papa had always been able to fix things, somehow.

Edward then turned to Carl and Eugene, who were crying, and held them tight. "Papa has to go with the soldiers now. Mama will take you to see some relatives. Don't cry—it will be alright. I'm sure I won't be gone long," he said.

He knew it was a lie, but he didn't know what else to say.

Edward stood up and looked at Minoru. "Major, will you transport my family to the main island?"

Minoru nodded. "They are to be ready in the morning. I will send a launch for them."

Edward looked one last time at his family and smiled at them. "I love you all. Always," he said.

"Come," Minoru said.

Edward nodded and followed the *Kempeitai* officer as the soldiers prodded him on with their rifles.

13
WHERE DO WE GO FROM HERE?

When the soldiers left with her husband, they also took with them the sense of security that Florence had allowed herself to believe in for almost two years. She stood staring at the door, the hollowness in the pit of her stomach expanding outward, like ripples in a pond.

Her sons looked at her for a response, some sort of reassurance. Seeing none, the oldest one turned to his brothers and said, "Come, want to go and play outside?"

Children are always very good at finding something to distract themselves with. Florence thought she heard Hans say something like, "Come, I'll show you something really funny with the chickens. Hurry up—Papa may be back soon..."

January 3rd 1944, morning
Ubin Island, Singapore

Florence had been up all night. Not because she still had things left to do but because she just could not fall asleep. As soon as the Japanese had left with her husband, she immediately started making plans and packing efficiently everything she and the boys would need.

Now dawn was approaching. With that, the Japanese would be coming back for them any time soon. Only now, her eyes felt heavy. Frustrating...

When the *Kempeitai* left with Edward the day before, Florence had felt momentarily paralyzed. However, she quickly snapped herself out of it, knowing that their time to get a move on was short. Years of living with a demanding, unreasonable father had trained her to move quickly and not feel sorry for herself. She had to make plans.

After thinking things over, Florence knew that they could not all squeeze into Eng Guan's tiny shophouse in Joo Chiat. Neither could they impose on her aunt that way. She then decided the best thing to do was to split up—Hans would be the one to stay with Eng Guan. Her mother would go to the aunt's, and she would take Carl and Eugene to another relative.

Florence splashed cold water on her face and went to wake the boys, to prepare everyone for travel. In the tropics, one never worries about having warm clothing. One or two changes of clothing were usually sufficient for a stretch. She had a small suitcase containing her clothes, as well as those of the two younger boys, while Hans had a small satchel containing his things.

Mrs Chia moved about in a trance-like state. More upheaval in her life. She did not want to think about things, so she had shut down mentally. Florence was exasperated but there was nothing she could do about it. She had packed for her mother the night before and now she ordered her to sit by the front door and wait.

A small detail of soldiers came to their door shortly after 0700 hours. While it was apparent that they did not speak English, they seemed to know their orders, nonetheless. They led the family to the small wooden jetty, where a thirty-foot diesel fishing boat lay moored with the engine idling.

Florence and her family sat on benches facing each other. The pilot, an old Malay man, cast off the moorings and returned to the helm. The boat slowly chugged toward Changi.

As ferocious as the Japanese soldiers were in battle, one thing Hans had noticed was that most of them seemed to be very fond of children. He observed now that the one sitting across the way was smiling at him.

The soldier, a private, looked at the nervous faces before him. Smiling, he reached in his chest pocket and began to dig. Out came a few dried sour plums, and he offered one each to the boys. They accepted the treat. Another soldier looked on, smiled and shook his head as if to say, "You fool! Now you'll go hungry."

The private smiled back at his friend and shrugged.

Hans would learn later that their gift had been an extremely generous one indeed. A Japanese army private at the time typically received about a handful of rice each day with a few dried plums, and some bean paste soup if he was fortunate.

War generally brings out the worst in people. Yet, there are numerous accounts about singular acts of kindness in the midst of all the madness. Perhaps there is still hope for mankind, as long as these individuals do not allow the world to snuff out their inner flames.

Upon arriving at Changi, the soldiers herded them to the back of an open truck. There, a *Kempeitai* officer spoke to Florence in

English. He wanted to know where they needed to go. Florence gave him the addresses.

Again, the soldiers displayed kindness by picking the boys up and swinging them playfully on to the truck bed. They also helped the women up, although somewhat impatiently.

They traveled along the winding Changi roads, heading west in the direction of Punggol. Hans lay on his back, watching the canopy of tree boughs passing overhead.

The truck slowed down on a narrow road in Tampines and turned off onto a bumpy dirt track. Hans had no idea where he was, but he could tell that it had to be a farm of some sort, from the smell of the place—the thick steamy pong of mud and manure was rich in the humid air.

As the truck came to a stop in front of a run-down *attap* house, Florence stood up. She then climbed down from the truck and went into the house. After a while she came out and nodded at the Japanese officer. She had with her an older Chinese woman dressed in the garb of a manual laborer—thin cotton tunic without buttons and thin baggy cotton trousers, called a *samfoo*.

The old woman looked worried, but she smiled nonetheless at Mrs Chia. She then walked around to the back of the truck and helped her down.

"Mum, Aunty Chu over here will take care of you now, alright?" Florence said, holding her mother's hands.

"Hmm? Where are we, *Sayang*?" Mrs Chia asked, looking around as if she had just noticed her surroundings for the first time.

"*Aiyah*, Mum! You know where we are! This is your cousin, Aunty Chu."

Aunty Chu smiled patiently.

"Hah? Ah Chu, is it? *Alamak*, when was the last time I saw you?" Mrs Chia said, her eyes widening. For the first time in a long while, she almost seemed her old self. Almost.

"Many years, dear. Even before the war," the old woman replied. "Come, *lah*. Let's go inside. We'll catch up." She took Mrs Chia by the arm and guided her up the porch, into the house. Before going in, she turned around to look at Florence and nodded once at her. Florence nodded back.

"Come! No more wasting time," the Japanese officer called out. Florence nodded at him and got in the back of the truck. The truck lurched forward, and rolled down the driveway back to the main road.

The truck had been moving for some distance along the shady, winding country roads, when the dense foliage overhead gave way to a more open terrain. Here and there, they passed through small villages, where people stopped their work and stared, and then the roads would become empty again. The truck came to a stop on Teo Kim Eng Road, near the Bedok area.

Florence got up and sat next to Hans. "Hansel, you need to stay with the soldiers. They will bring you to Uncle Eng Guan's place, alright? He will take care of you until we can sort things out. Your brothers will stay here with me," she said.

Hans looked around. "Where is this place, Mum? Who are you staying with?" he asked.

"Never mind, I don't think you know these people. You just stay with Uncle until we can come for you. Be a good boy for these soldiers. They will take you there, alright?"

Hans nodded. He did not hug his mother or feel sad at seeing her go. The truth was, they were not very close as mother and child. He was still thinking more of his Papa.

Florence climbed down from the truck, and the soldiers handed Carl and Eugene to her. She set the boys down and picked up the small suitcase. "Come with me," she said to the boys. "Carl, make sure your brother doesn't run away. Say goodbye to Hansel."

The boys waved at Hans and he waved back. His mother cast a quick glance at him and tried to smile.

The image of his family standing by the roadside—waving to him as the truck rolled away with him in it—was etched into his mind.

14
WHERE IS EVERYBODY?

January 3rd 1944, 1200 hours
Joo Chiat Road, Singapore

Hans could already recognize where he was even before the truck turned onto Joo Chiat Road. He had been to Uncle Eng Guan's place with his father many times before the war. The truck came to a stop outside Eng Guan's shophouse. There were a few people sitting outside their own shophouses, but as soon as they saw a truck with soldiers pulling up, they discreetly disappeared indoors.

The *Kempeitai* officer opened his door and walked around to the back. Hans was already standing up. "You come down, boy. You go there," the officer said, pointing at Eng Guan's door.

Hans jumped down from the truck. One of the soldiers called out to him. At first he did not know what the soldier was saying, but it became evident as the soldier picked up a small satchel from the bench and held it out. Hans had almost forgotten his bag. The soldier tossed it at him, grinning.

Hans watched the officer get back in the truck. As soon as it drove away, he turned to face Eng Guan's door. Nobody had come out, so he knocked on the door. No response. He knocked again.

After waiting for a while, he decided to try the doorknob. It was unlocked. He let himself in.

"Uncle! Aunty! Hello!" he called out, poking his head in the door.

There was still no response. It was dark inside, with the windows shuttered, and it took a while for his eyes to become accustomed. Looking around, he noticed that the place was bare.

That did not seem right. *Where's all the furniture?* he wondered.

The air was also very musty—it smelt as if something had rotted some time ago. Hans knew that was very unlike Uncle and Aunty to leave the place that way. Despite all this, Hans was not really worried at first. He just did not know what to make of things, actually. Leaving the door open to let in some light, he walked around to see what he could find.

"Uncle Eng Guan! It's Hans," he called again.

It was obvious by then that nobody was home. The thick dust told him that nobody had been home for a while, in fact. That was when Hans began to worry. He ran up the stairs to the living area. Again, he found that the furniture was all gone, except for a few broken items. With a sense of panic coursing through him, he ran down the stairs.

Somehow, something had escaped him earlier. As he came down the stairs, he noticed for the first time two large dark stains in the hardwood floor. The six year-old boy's mind suddenly flashed back to the dead Hurricane pilot, and his blood that seemed to cover the entire cockpit. Hans had not thought about the incident for a while. He began to whimper. The realization of what might have happened at the shophouse began to hit him.

"Uncle ... Aunty..." he called out in a small voice, between sobs.

Then a series of thoughts hit him.

What about Papa? Where were the soldiers taking him? And what did they want him for? Was Papa going to die?

With those thoughts, Hans burst out in tears and wailed for his father. He knew then and there that he had to go and find him. But he had no idea where or how to even begin! His feelings of inadequacy were compounded by hunger—it had been a long time since breakfast. There was obviously nothing to eat in the house, and he had not brought any food with him.

The dark and musty shophouse was starting to get to him as well. Hans rushed through the door into the bright sunlight. People had come back out again, to go about their business, the moment the Japanese had driven away. They stared at the crying boy coming out of the former carpenter's shop, shook their heads and carried on their way. Hans sat on the curbside, feeling alone in the crowd.

An elderly *Nyonya* lady across the street had come out of her shophouse about that time. What she saw was a strange, small boy sitting on the curbside, crying. She crossed over to him quickly.

"*Ala, Sayang*! What happened to you?" she said, holding his hand with tenderness.

Hans looked up at her. She reminded him of his grandmother.

"I'm supposed to meet Uncle Eng Guan here," he said.

Dismay flashed across the lady's face. "*Aiyoh*, you poor thing, *lah*! You don't know what happened here?" she said.

Hans nodded slowly at first, but then he shook his head.

"That one was your uncle, *is it*?" she asked, nodding her head at Eng Guan's place.

"He is my Papa's friend."

Sadness filled the lady's face. She looked around. "You better come with me, boy. What is your name?" she inquired.

"Hans Schirmer."

"You can call me Aunty Rose. Come, let's cross the road."

Hans followed the *Nyonya* lady to her shophouse across the street. As he entered, he could smell something edible. His mouth watered. Rose looked at him.

"Boy, are you hungry? Want to *makan*?" she asked.

He nodded.

"Come into the kitchen. Got not much to *makan*—nobody does any more. But I made some *ubi kayu* porridge this morning. Still got some left in the pot. You want?" she offered.

"Yes please, Aunty. Thank you."

"*Wah*, so polite, this one! Your Mummy and Daddy taught you good manners," she said with a toothy smile. Hans sat down to eat the porridge.

Ubi kayu was the Malay name for the tuberous root of the tapioca plant, also known as cassava or yucca. During the Japanese Occupation, food shortage was at critical levels. The tapioca plant, which grew like a weed in the tropics, was a common staple because of its abundance. If you cut off a shoot and stuck it in the ground, it would develop an edible tuberous root in no time. It was much easier to cultivate than rice, which needed vast amounts of land and water, or even potatoes.

As with other starches, tapioca could fill the stomach, but it was not very nutritious. However, people then did not have much choice about what they ate. All the same, tapioca had helped to save many lives during the war. As Hans would exclaim later on in his life, "Did you know I ate these almost every day during the Japanese Occupation?"

Rose moved about the kitchen, tidying up. While working, she spoke to Hans. "Actually, I know your grandmother. We went to school together, many, many years ago," she said. "I also met your father once or twice. Very tall *angmoh*, correct?"

Hans nodded and continued eating.

"I remember seeing him at Eng Guan's place. Now that I think about it, you must be the little boy who was with him at times."

"Aunty, where is Uncle Eng Guan and Aunty Su Ling?"

Rose stopped moving and became silent for a moment. With a sigh, she said, "The Japanese killed them a few months ago. I'm so sorry."

Hans started to cry. "Why did they kill them?" he asked.

"Don't know *lah*. From what I heard, some crazy fellow accused your uncle of something, so the *Kempeitai* came. They were supposed to question him only. But instead, they shot both your uncle and aunty in their own house. Terrible!"

Rose sat by Hans and held him as he wept. Tears filled her eyes, and she began to sob as well.

"I have to find my Papa! I must tell him about this, but I don't know where they took him," he said, after a while.

"Who took your Papa? The *Kempeitai*?"

"Yes."

"*Aiyoh*, this is terrible! Then, where is your Mummy?"

"She is staying with some people. But I don't know who they are—I didn't recognize the place. Then after that, the soldiers brought me in a lorry and dropped me off here."

"*Sayang*, I don't know what to do with you! Don't you have a place to stay?"

Hans shook his head. "Uncle Eng Guan was supposed to help me. I don't know anyone else."

Rose stood up. "This is terrible," she said again.

"Can you help me find my Papa?"

"*Ala Sayang*, I don't know where in the world is he! How can I help you, then?"

"Where do the soldiers go?"

"*Aiyoh*, little boy! They go so many places. How would I know which one?"

Hans gave in to the feelings of helplessness that coursed through his core. He sobbed uncontrollably. Rose felt his anguish, and began to weep again.

"What did the soldiers say? When they came for your Papa?" she said, after catching her breath.

Hans could not speak; he was sobbing too hard. Finally, he too caught his breath. "They called him a spy or something," he said.

Rose gasped. "That is not good. They might have taken him to Outram Road jail then."

"Where is that, Aunty?"

"Very, very far from here. You cannot just walk there, you know. Also ... I don't know how to say this... If they took him there, surely *habis* already." *Habis* is the Malay word for "finished, the end."

"No!" Hans screamed.

Rose had regretted her words as soon as she said them. She tried to recant. "I'm so sorry. Don't know why I said that. It's not true ... it's not true. Maybe he's answering questions only," she said.

"You think so, Aunty?" Hans said, a glimmer of hope on his face.

The old lady hated lying to the boy, but she nodded anyway.

"I want to go see him!"

"*Sayang*, it's very, very far away..."

"It's alright. I like to walk a lot. Tell me which way to go."

Rose saw the determination on the boy's face. She sighed, took him outside and gave him a general idea of which way to go. It was going to be very difficult for someone unfamiliar with the street layout to remember the directions to the jail—there were many different roads to take. An adult would have had a hard time of it.

Rose felt certain that the little boy would become lost along the way. But she knew that she could not talk him out of it, nor could she keep him anyway, had she been successful, so she just said, "You take care of yourself, boy. Look out for danger, and always bow to the soldiers. You can ask people for directions, if you think you are lost."

"I will. Thank you, Aunty."

15
CARL AND EUGENE

January 3rd 1944, 1200 hours
Teo Kim Eng Road, Singapore

This was going to be difficult.

Florence knew that she was showing up at her cousin's home without any forewarning. But how was she expected to call ahead anyway, under the circumstances?

To make things more awkward, she had not spoken to this relative since before her father's funeral and truth be told, they had never been close anyway. However, Florence knew that her cousin was still living in her own home, unlike many others. She had to try. It was a long shot, she realized, but she never quite expected to be received the way in which she was.

Agatha Chia opened the door to see her younger cousin standing there, with two small boys. She had not seen Florence in years. Now here she was, with a suitcase in hand, and children, no less.

"What do you want? You can't stay here," Agatha said, frowning.

"You're not even going to say hello?" Florence asked sarcastically.

"Eh, look—let us not pretend we are all that *cheng* with each other. You never even liked me in school! Your father was a rude bastard who treated my father like shit, and to tell you the truth, you were not much better either."

Florence was aghast. Hot tears of humiliation streamed down her cheeks. She forced herself to speak without choking. "If I could go anywhere else, I would go. If I didn't have to take care of the children, I would jump off a bridge rather than come here, believe me!" she said, glaring at her cousin in fury.

Agatha glared back at her. Then she looked at the boys standing with her—mere toddlers.

"Where's your husband? What happened to you all?" Agatha asked, in a softer tone.

"The *Kempeitai* took him yesterday. They agreed to take us to a relative's place. The oldest boy is staying with a friend in Joo Chiat. My mother is staying at her cousin's place near Punggol. I simply have no place left to go," Florence said.

Agatha shook her head in sympathy. "I'm sorry about Edward. How horrible for you all! Look, if I could help, I would—given these circumstances. But I already have other relatives staying here and we have no more room. I can put you up for the night, but you need to think of something else tomorrow," she said.

Florence nodded and said, "Thank you."

Agatha stepped aside to let her cousin and the boys in.

While the boys were busy playing in the backyard, Florence and Agatha sat down at the dinner table to discuss options.

"I heard that they are still accepting single young women who have been displaced down at the YWCA. That might be your only hope. The thing is—what do we do about your boys?" Agatha said.

"I don't know! I don't know! I cannot think anymore! Everything was just fine, but then I don't know why this is happening. I thought the Japanese had agreed to leave Edward alone."

Agatha nodded slowly. "You cannot just sit around and think everything will be alright—there's a war going on, after all. You always need to be thinking of something," she said.

Florence closed her eyes. The emotional weight of her situation—which she had managed to keep under control for the last twenty-four hours—finally erupted and coupled itself with her exhaustion. She collapsed back into the chair and wept uncontrollably.

Agatha, despite herself, reached over and held Florence. No matter what, it was heartbreaking to see anyone that way. She sat quietly, letting her cousin cry.

After a while, Agatha spoke. "Come, let me ask around, alright? Maybe one of my neighbors can help us, or at least suggest something. You never know."

The next morning, Agatha had some news for Florence. "I think we have a solution. One of my neighbors said he can help. He has daughters about our age who can take in your boys. I know this may be hard to do, but I don't see any other choice *lah*. Florence, don't worry—I know these people. They are very good-hearted. The boys will be fine with them," she said.

Florence nodded. Secretly, it really was not a difficult choice. She had been feeling overwhelmed with the responsibility of the two boys, and felt inadequate to take care of them. Here were some good Samaritans offering to help—she would be foolish not to accept. Florence knew that they could do a better job providing for Carl and Eugene than she ever could.

Agatha's neighbor, Tan Teck Imm, had been a junior clerk for a Dutch East Indies-based bank before the war. When the Japanese took over Singapore and, within months, the Dutch East Indies as well, they immediately liquidated all European holdings in the region, and transferred these assets to Japanese banks.

Naturally, this put many people out of jobs. Fortunately for Mr Tan, the Japanese still had the need for some clerical workers, and being good at what he did, he managed to stay employed. This was very helpful, as he had six daughters and three sons, some of whom were still quite young.

Agatha and Florence brought Carl and Eugene to meet the Tan family later that morning. Despite their own meager situation, the Tans received the boys warmly, assuring Florence that they would do their best for them.

"Young lady, take heart. These times cannot last much longer. I'm sure that you will be reunited with your whole family soon. You go and take care of yourself, try and find your husband. Don't worry about these young men. My daughters will love to have them," Mr Tan reassured Florence.

Florence gave a weak smile. "Uncle, I cannot thank you enough..." she began.

Mr Tan held up his hand and smiled kindly. "Times like these, we all need to help each other out the best we can. Otherwise, the enemy truly will have won," he said. "Go and take care of your affairs. Everything will be alright."

16
THE JOURNEY BEGINS

January 3rd 1944, around sundown
Kallang Road (west of Lavender Street), Singapore

Hans had been walking since he left Aunty Rose's that afternoon, stopping briefly to rest only when he could no longer stand. He no longer had any real concept of how far he had traveled and how much further he had to go. All he knew was that he *had* to find his Papa.

He was also extremely hungry. As he passed by shophouses along the way, people would look at the strange Eurasian boy. But when he approached them for help, they quickly closed their doors. Nobody wanted to help him, for fear that if they did so, he would not go away.

Darkness was quickly encroaching, and Hans knew he could not go on much further. He had just gone past a strange neighborhood, where men were constantly going in and out of the shophouses there. Shophouses where young women sat on the balconies, watching the street below. Hans did not understand what was going on, but he also did not like the looks of some of the men. He kept moving on, following the setting sun.

As night fell, the streets became emptier. As Hans looked about, he could see the dim glow of lights emanating from certain windows above him, but it was not enough to illuminate the stretch of road where he was.

Fear built up in him, causing the hair on his neck to stand. Every sound was starting to frighten him. He forced all thoughts from his head and moved slowly with his back up against the wall that connected the row of shophouses. Then the wall ended, and he found himself in an open lot. A dim glow seemed to be coming from up ahead.

Hans stood still. "I wonder what that is?" he said aloud, to bolster himself.

He swallowed the lump in his throat and walked cautiously towards the light. The glow turned out to be a small kerosene lamp inside a ramshackle wooden shed. As Hans approached the shed, a booming voice startled him.

"*Oi! Siapa tu?*" the voice bellowed in Malay. Who is it?

Hans screamed and fell backwards, landing on his bottom.

A large Sikh man came forward. All Hans could make out was this giant of a turbaned man, with thick eyebrows and a very full beard, made even more ominous-looking by the dull light that was casting shadows everywhere.

He screamed again and tried to scramble backwards.

The man stopped. "*Eh? Mari kichi, mari kichi. Jangan takut,*" he said, gently lowering his voice and holding his palms out. Little one, come. Don't be afraid.

"*Mahu makan, kichi*?" the man asked, pointing to his mouth. Want some food, little one?

Hans remained afraid. Chinese boys in the village were always making fun of Sikh men, saying how scary they were. Until then, he had never actually seen one up close—there were no Sikhs living on Ubin during the time he was there.

Yet, here was one right before him. With the big beard and bushy eyebrows, he actually looked more like a dark-haired Santa Claus. There really was nothing scary about him at all.

Hans then realized that his fear had more likely come from his shock at having been startled. He decided to trust his instincts that said everything was safe. Standing up, he smiled cautiously.

The man went into the shed and returned with a stale piece of flat bread, holding it out. Hans took it and ate quickly. The bread was hard and dry, but he did not care. When the man turned to go, Hans decided to follow him.

The man walked back into the shed, where he sat on a wooden cot called a *chapoy*. He poured some milk into a jar and offered it to Hans. It was warm and it smelt funny to him. But again, Hans did not care. As he drank the milk, he heard a strange sound from outside the shed. He furrowed his brow, trying to make out the source of the sound. The man noticed the look on his face and smiled.

"*Kambing*," he said, pointing backwards with his thumb. Goats.

Just then, one of the goats bleated clearly. That explained the source of the milk. Hans smiled. Goats were funny.

The Sikh man then pointed to a corner of the shed, where some burlap sacks lay in a pile. "*Tidur*," he said, flattening his palms together and placing them to the side of his face, signifying sleep.

Because of his Peranakan grandmother, Hans had some Malay words in him. "*Terima kasih, Encik*," he said. Thank you, sir.

As Hans lay on the rough burlap sacks, his mind raced through the events of the day. Worry for his father was still at the forefront.

After some time, exhaustion took over his body. Hans finally fell into a deep sleep. Then he dreamt...

He was seated on the back of a tiger, which was walking along the narrow roads of Ubin. For some reason or other, the tiger was explaining the defense structure of Singapore and Malaya in a crisp English accent.

Sounds just like Colonel Willoughby...

Every now and again, the tiger turned to look at him, continually speaking as he did. Hans watched in fascination as the tiger's mouth articulated in a very human fashion.

Then the tiger raised a finger *(claw?)* to his mouth and pursed his lips *(do tigers actually have lips?)*, a serious frown showing on his face.

"Shhh! But just between me and thee—you can keep a secret, can't you, boy?—we have a slight problem," the tiger whispered.

"What is it?" Hans replied.

"I have your word, then? You mustn't tell a soul! The Japs have their spies *everywhere*," the tiger said, stretching out the last word. To emphasize his point, he glanced from side to side, squinting as he did.

"I promise, Mr Tiger."

The tiger stopped and sniffed the air. He looked all around. "Aeroplanes!" he growled, startling the boy. Just as he said that, a Japanese fighter aircraft roared directly over their heads, the big angry red ball insignias clearly standing out from the mottled camouflage pattern. The tiger sprang forward, galloping along under the fighter. Hans nearly fell off, but he grabbed the tiger's coarse mane in time.

After some time, he realized that he was no longer on the tiger, but it was his own legs that were propelling him forward at the same speed as the fighter above. It took a while to slow down from the momentum. When he finally managed to stop, he took a look around. The tiger was nowhere in sight. Where had it gone?

Just then, more aircraft—both British and Japanese—appeared overhead and a dogfight ensued. Hans stood and watched the sight. As the battle went on, a Hurricane fighter trailing smoke soared over and crashed into a hill up ahead.

Hans ran over to the wreckage. It all seemed so familiar. Just like the one he had seen two years before, this one was also mangled in the same way. He did not want to see the crushed pilot again, but something was compelling him to keep going.

To his horror, Papa was in the cockpit! His body may have been smashed, but his face remained unmistakable.

"PAPA!"

His father's body lay unmoving, as he approached the fuselage. But just as he was climbing onto the wing root below the cockpit, his father's cold gray eyes opened and his head swiveled toward him. Hans screamed in terror.

"So sorry about all this, Son. I tried to fight them off, but there were too many. So sorry ... so sorry," Papa said.

He sounded so weak and wheezy! Hans had never heard his father's voice sounded like that. His own voice came out barely above a squeak.

"Oh, Papa! I have to help you!"

"Hansel, there is nothing you can do for me now. You have to take care of your Mum and your brothers, understand?"

"Papa, I want to stay here with you."

"I know. I wish we could have had more time, Son. There just ... wasn't enough time."

A rumbling sound caught their attention.

"You have to go now. The petrol is going to explode!" Papa urged, his eyes widening.

"I don't want to go, Papa!"

"GO!"

Hans awoke to a rasping, growling noise. He looked up from the floor to see the Sikh man flat on his back in his *chapoy*, snoring loudly. He wiped the tears from his eyes and sat up.

He attempted to wake the man before he left, but was not successful. Since there remained a little more milk in the bottle, Hans poured some into the same glass jar that he had drunk from the night before. He was hungry again.

After drinking the milk, he tried once more to wake the man. He wanted to thank him again, but the man snored on. Hans thanked him in his mind and exited the shed.

The sun was just on the horizon. There were two goats tied to the shed. "Bye-bye, goats," Hans said. They ignored him and maintained a steady chewing. He turned south and continued his journey to find Outram Road jail. There was still a long way to go.

17
INTERROGATION

January 4th 1944, dawn
Outram Road jail, Singapore

Dried blood crusted over his eyes, making them difficult to open. Edward no longer had any concept of time. Every now and again, one of several burly Japanese men would come into his cell to hit him. Some were short, some were tall, but all of them were muscular. This had been going on since the moment they brought him there two days before.

He had not slept all that time—he never had a chance.

Sometimes it was only minutes between beatings, sometimes it was hours. The beatings ranged from a single slap on the face, to a full punch and kick session. All that time, the Japanese had not said anything to him, nor had they asked any questions of him. Yet.

The cell door opened with a loud clang. One of the big apes, as Edward thought of them, pulled him to his feet while yelling something in Japanese. Edward stood as straight as he could.

Major Minoru stepped into the cell, smoking a cigarette. He offered it to Edward, who shook his head—no. Minoru shrugged and sat on the bunk. He motioned for Edward to do the same.

"Are you ready to talk?" Minoru asked.

"Sir, I was ready all this time. There was never any need for the rough treatment."

Minoru smiled and rapped his knuckles on the cell wall.

"I am sure you have been listening to the lovely screams of others coming through these walls. Trust me, *they* are the ones who have had the rough treatment. I see you still have all your fingernails with you. I really wouldn't complain too much, if I were you," he said nonchalantly, as if he were talking about houseplants or the weather.

But what Minoru said was true. Edward knew about the various forms of torture that the *Kempeitai* had perfected. They had only been softening him up.

"What can I do for you, Major?"

"Why don't we start at the top, *Herr* Schirmer?"

"My name is Edward Henry Schirmer. I was born in the Mauritius Islands in 1894..."

"I know that part—your papers tell me as much. But why are you here, in Singapore?"

"After 1929, our sugarcane business in the islands failed. The economy there was also ruined. So I came here in 1932, to start over. I began selling outboard motors, and that's how I made my living."

"What if I don't believe you?"

"Then ask around, Major! I am not a spy! I have never worked for the British government! I am a private businessman. Or at least I was, before the war started. I don't know anything about the military!"

Minoru stared at Edward for a while. "Tell me about Ivan Lyon," he said.

"I'm sorry, but who?"

The beatings resumed after that.

The previous year, in October of 1943, a British officer who had been stationed in Singapore before the war devised a daring commando raid on Japanese vessels in Singapore's harbor. Although the damage to shipping was limited, the mission was considered highly successful, with all participants escaping to safety.

The officer's name was Major Ivan Lyon, of the Gordon Highlanders.

Lyon trained with his men in Australia before sailing for Singapore in an old Malay fishing trawler named the *Krait*. A mixed group of Australian and British commandos, they wore body paint to appear dark-skinned, in case they were spotted. In the hold of the boat were rubberized folding kayaks, or canoes, and a supply of limpet mines. That was the crux of Operation Jaywick.

As soon as the trawler reached one of the Dutch East Indies islands close to Singapore, they lowered their kayaks and paddled in the cover of night to the Japanese ships in the harbor. This was not a short distance, about fifty kilometers. The commandos then attached limpet mines to the hulls of the Japanese ships, before paddling back to the trawler. Lyon and his crew sailed back to Australia in high spirits, having sunk 39,000 tons of shipping. Bolstered by the success of the mission, Lyon immediately sat down to plan a follow-up raid.

Unfortunately for the residents of Singapore, this expedition came to be a major loss of face to the Japanese. As expected, the *Kempeitai* conducted so-called investigations and commenced immediate reprisals upon the local Chinese, assuming first that the saboteurs had to have been the Communists. Leaving no stone unturned, the *Kempeitai* also tortured Allied POWs in the process, just to see if anyone knew about the raid.

Sometime later, Japanese intelligence sources discovered who was actually responsible for the attack, but not before the *Kempeitai* had already tortured and killed many who never even had any knowledge of the mission, or the perpetrators. This came to be known as the "Double Tenth Massacre," for it occurred on October 10th 1943.

Edward came about with water splashed on his face. He found himself lying on the floor. Sometime during that thrashing session, he had passed out.

Minoru was sitting on the bunk again, smoking a cigarette.

"Alright, so you don't know anything of importance. Why then did you lie about being German?" he asked.

It was difficult to reply; Edward's face was badly swollen and bruised. He swallowed blood and gathered his strength.

"I did not lie—I am German. Alright, so I'm not an actual citizen of Germany, but I am a German, by race. That is not a lie," he said. After a moment he added, "And yes, it is also true that I am a British Subject, since I was born in a British colony. I admit that I did not disclose that part to General Yamashita. But he never asked for my papers, so I did not show them."

"So you lied to him, then!"

"Major, I did not lie to him. At the registration, they asked me if I was German, I said 'yes.' They reported to the General that I was German. I let him ... make his own assumption, I suppose."

"Well, isn't that the same thing as lying about it? You should die for such treason!"

Edward closed his eyes. "Major, my life is in your hands. Do with me what you will. I admit that I may have left out certain facts at the time, but by not saying too much, I gained my freedom. Would you have done it any differently?"

Minoru laughed. Softly at first, and then cracking up altogether, as if it was a very funny story.

"In the end, it all comes to the same. Here you are, behind bars, anyway! Would you like to know how this came about?" he said, chuckling.

Edward nodded reluctantly.

"Your faithful housekeeper sold you out in order to save her pathetic son! You know, there is a saying that one should always be careful of the help. That, my friend, is a universal truth."

Minoru departed the cell, still laughing, leaving Edward to think about his turn in fortune.

January 4th 1944, 1200 hours
Teo Kim Eng Road, Singapore

Mr Tan had arranged for a friend to give Florence a ride into town that day. When she saw that her sons were playing with his daughters, she decided that it was better to go without disturbing the boys. The less anxiety, the better, she reasoned.

The family friend drove a truck for the Japanese, transporting supplies around the island for them. He picked Florence up shortly after noon.

The journey was uneventful, at first. However, as they neared the Kallang area, Japanese soldiers manning a routine checkpoint stopped them. The friend got out of his truck, bowed and held out his pass. A soldier walked up and took the pass. He did not look at it because his eyes were fixed on Florence, who was still sitting in the truck cab.

"You! You come here!" the soldier demanded, pointing at her.

Florence fumbled with the door handle in panic. With no small amount of difficulty, she opened the door and stepped out. As soon as she was able to, she bowed to the soldiers, keeping her eyes to the road.

"Where you go?" the soldier asked.

"To the YWCA, sir."

"The YW...?"

"The Young Women's Christian Association hostel, sir. I need to find a place to stay."

"To stay?" He seemed to be thinking about that one. "Where is your home?"

"On Ubin Island, sir."

"Why you no stay there?"

Florence was scared to tell him more, but there really was no alternative. "My husband is gone," she said simply.

"Gone? Go where?"

Florence hesitated. "*Kempeitai* took him two days ago."

At this, the soldier's eyes widened and he raised his rifle at Florence. She shrieked in terror, covering her face. The soldier called out to the other soldiers. They rushed up with their rifles at the ready. The first soldier then walked over to the driver of the truck, glaring at him. With the butt of his rifle, the soldier struck the driver across the face, shouting as he did so. The driver fell to the ground, clutching at his bleeding face.

The soldier then walked back to Florence. "You come!" he said. He turned and marched toward a convertible civilian car. She followed him, tears streaming down her cheeks. As she climbed in the back seat with him, two more soldiers appeared—one to drive and one to guard.

January 4th 1944, late afternoon
YMCA Building on Stamford Road, Singapore

In 1942, the *Kempeitai* had taken over the once hospitable YMCA building on Stamford Road, turning it into a house of horrors. It served as their East District branch, where they carried out the torturous interrogation and imprisonment of civilians suspected of anti-Japanese activities.

Upon arrival, the soldiers pushed Florence up the stairs, into the main lobby. The arresting soldier reported to the officer on duty, explaining the situation. After an exchange of salutes, the officer dismissed the soldiers, who returned to their car outside.

Turning his attention to Florence, the officer spoke. "Who are you? And what is your husband's name? You better tell me everything. I don't want to have to force you to speak."

Florence wanted to break down and cry, but she forced herself to speak calmly. "Sir, my name is Florence Chia. My husband's name is Edward Schirmer..."

She then proceeded to explain how she came to be there, starting from the beginning. She spoke of General Yamashita's arrangement with them in 1942, and ended up with her husband's arrest.

"I don't know why they took him. The Major called him a spy, but that is not true! He was a private businessman—he never worked for the British government," she tried to explain. "It must be a misunderstanding, sir."

The officer took it all in, nodding his head. "We shall look into this. You will stay here until further notice," he said.

Details surrounding the rest of this episode are hazy, but the main thing was that Florence had to remain there for the duration of the Japanese occupation. During that time, the *Kempeitai* would not release her to see her husband or her children, for some reason or other.

Florence never talked much of her wartime experience, other than to say that the Japanese had put her to work in the kitchen during her time at the YMCA building, feeding both the prisoners and their jailors. For whatever reason, she was not free to go home, but she never spoke of being abused during her internment.

In that regard, she was much more fortunate than one Elizabeth Choy, who was also interned at the YMCA building around the same time. Like Florence, Elizabeth Choy had gone in search for her husband, whom the *Kempeitai* had taken for interrogation. When she went to the YMCA building to enquire his whereabouts, they arrested her as well, for acts of treason against the Japanese.

Unlike Edward and Florence, who really had no involvement in anything of importance, both Elizabeth and her husband were actually responsible for smuggling food and other forms of aid to the British prisoners-of-war in Changi. The K*empeitai* found out all the details of their activities in short order.

The Japanese tortured Elizabeth repeatedly but she endured the treatment, refusing to be broken. After the war, she and her husband were both honored with the Order of the British Empire (OBE) for their heroic acts in assisting the British prisoners-of-war.

Elizabeth Choy is regarded as a heroine of Singapore, and her amazing tale of perseverance is still being talked about today.

Major Ivan Lyon (*center, rear*) and the men of Operation Jaywick aboard the vessel Krait.

18
THE OUTRAM ROAD JAIL

January 4th 1944, afternoon
Eu Tong Sen Street (Chinatown), Singapore

Hans knew by then that he had to be close to his destination, based on the directions that different people had given him. But he was also finding it more and more difficult to take yet another step. He had been walking since dawn with nothing in his stomach—apart from the bit of goat milk that morning, and some small pieces of baked tapioca that an old Malay man had shared with him around noon.

The cramping in his stomach from hunger had grown more acute as the day wore on. As much as he wanted to sit down and cry, he forced himself to remember that he was a big boy and that he still needed to find Papa. Although he was only six, he had a survival instinct that would later propel him throughout his life.

After allowing himself a moment of respite—he had found a grassy patch and lay down to rest his entire body—Hans stood up and continued walking in the direction which he believed would lead him to the Outram Road jail. He stopped here and there to ask directions from several people, to make sure he was still on track. It had taken a few inquiries to get the information he needed. Some people had stared at him and shaken their head as if he was crazy. Others had scolded him and told him to stay away from the place.

It was not easy obtaining help. To begin with, there was the language barrier. Although life on the street would later teach him to be conversant in all the dialects of Singapore, he only spoke English and some Malay at that time. Furthermore, he knew that some of the people whom he had spoken with actually understood English but had pretended not to, possibly for fear of association with the British.

After many unsuccessful queries, he chanced upon a young Chinese man who not only spoke English, but also was willing to help.

"Eh, why you want to go there?" the man asked, in response to the request for directions. He sounded genuinely bewildered.

"My Papa is there. They took him away a few days ago."

The young man shook his head in sympathy. "Little boy, that is terrible. I don't know if they will let you in to see him, you know," he said, frowning.

"Uncle, I have to find him."

The man shook his head again. After a moment, he said, "Alright *lah*. I will take you there. Come."

It turned out to be quite a distance yet from where they had met. The Chinese man, who identified himself simply as Ah Boon, was certainly going out of his way to help Hans.

The Outram Road jail was a squat, ugly series of buildings arranged to form a perimeter. The walls had not been whitewashed in a while, and a black mildew—the kind which grows readily on exterior walls in the tropics—had taken over large sections. Barbed wire crowned the fences connecting the buildings.

Ah Boon brought Hans as far as he dared to go. It was not a good idea to even be there in the first place; loitering near the doors was really asking for trouble. He wished the boy good luck, and quickly disappeared after that.

The sentry outside the main door frowned when he saw the boy cautiously approaching him. "Go home, foolish boy. This is not a place for you to play games," he said in Japanese.

Hans did not understand the soldier but he could tell that the soldier was feeling irritable from the tone of his words. He spoke as politely as he could to him. "Please sir, I would like to see my Papa inside," he said, pointing at the prison.

The soldier did not speak much English, but he picked up on the word "Papa." He frowned again, this time in curiosity. Keeping his eyes on the boy, he called out to someone inside the prison.

Another soldier came out. They conferred briefly and the second soldier went back inside. Hans recognized the tall Japanese officer who came out a few minutes later. Apparently, the officer recognized Hans as well. "You! What are you doing here?" he said, his eyes widening in amazement.

"Please sir, you know who my Papa is. I would like to see him, please."

"But how did you get here, boy?" Major Minoru said, still in amazement.

"I walked here."

"But aren't you supposed to be with your mother?"

Hans carefully explained what had happened to him since the *Kempeitai* had taken his father, up to what he found at Eng Guan's place. He added that he did not know where the rest of his family was, either.

"So you came here, then? How did you know where to find us?" Minoru said.

"A lady said this is where she thought my Papa could be. Some other people gave me directions, too."

"You walked here from where?"

"Joo Chiat Road, sir."

Minoru remained speechless. He was simply astounded with what the young boy standing in front of him had done, the perseverance he had shown.

Takashi Minoru was considered to be very young for having attained the rank of a *Kempeitai* Major. The reason for his rapid promotion was simply that he was very good at what he did—his interrogations always yielded results. To a certain degree, he took a perverse pleasure in watching men break down before him—especially the once haughty Europeans. He did not have any compunction about torturing women either, in his quest for information. They were also easy to break down, but in different ways than men. It all came down to exploiting a person's fears.

Children, however, were another case altogether. While Minoru had no problems with killing children if it served to make a point—he had done so on a number of occasions—he did not find any pleasure in it. They were too weak. Although one could argue that women were also physically weaker than he was, he knew that many were capable of viciousness beyond men. It was why he almost enjoyed hurting them.

Children, on the other hand, were not the same. He felt it was pathetic to hurt them unless absolutely necessary. Above all that, the European man's son standing before him had shown a determination that was most impressive, and Minoru reluctantly admired him for it. As such, he did not want the boy to have to see his father in his current condition.

"Alright then, boy. You will see your father, but not right now. You come back later," Minoru said.

"When can I see him?"

Minoru thought about it. "You wait here, then. I will tell you when you can come in," he said. He turned to speak in Japanese to a nearby soldier before disappearing down a dark hallway. The soldier bowed when he received his orders, and left. He returned shortly with some tea and a few sticky rice balls for Hans.

Thanking the soldier, Hans accepted the food and bowed before him, in imitation of what he had seen other Japanese doing. The soldier broke into a wide grin and bowed back.

Edward's cell door opened. Two soldiers came in and, without a word, helped him to his feet. They brought him to a shower stall down the hallway. Using signs and gestures, they instructed him to take off his clothes and to enter the shower.

In Singapore, water straight from the faucet is not really that cold, due to the tropical temperature. Although it did shock Edward at first, the cool shower felt refreshing on his bruises. Then the sharp pain from places where his skin had split began to set in. He winced initially, but after a while, the pain became a dull sensation. The dried blood dissolved and washed away as well.

After the shower, the soldiers brought Edward back to the cell. There was a set of baggy cotton pajamas on the bunk. Shrugging in wonder, he put them on.

A Japanese man in his thirties came in, wearing a different uniform. Apparently he was a medic or even a doctor of some sort, as he began to treat Edward's wounds. After dressing the last wound, he stood up, looked at his patient over to make sure that he had not missed anything, and then turned to leave.

"*Arigatou*, doctor," Edward said. He bowed from his shoulders up, as he was still seated on the bunk. The doctor or medic returned the bow and smiled. Just after he left, Major Minoru stepped into the cell. He regarded Edward approvingly.

"You certainly look much better, Mr Schirmer."

"Thank you, Major. I do not mean to look a gift horse in the mouth, but why the change of heart?"

Minoru smiled. "Let's just say you have a guardian angel, Mr Schirmer," he said.

"I don't understand."

"Your son. He is quite a remarkable boy."

Edward's stomach tightened. "What do you mean?"

"Your oldest boy walked all by himself from the eastern part of this island to see you."

"Hans?"

"I didn't ask him his name—how rude of me! Anyhow, he is here to see you. This is how it works, then. I have no further use for you. I know when a man is lying, and I can see that you really do not have any information that I can use. However, you are British, and as such you will remain in captivity. We will try and transfer you and your son to one of the civilian camps on the island, but for now, you are not to leave this jail. I will let you see your son occasionally at my discretion, while you are here. But he cannot stay here with you. Do you understand?"

Edward's eyes filled with tears. He nodded and said, "Thank you, Major. Thank you."

Hans stepped into the cell. Everything smelt musty—a combination of concrete, dust, mildew and body odor.

"Hansel!" Papa's voice called out.

Hans looked and saw his father sitting on a narrow bed. "Papa!" he replied, rushing to hug him.

They held each other tight. "You silly boy! How in the world did you get here? Where is everybody else?" Papa said.

"I don't know where they went. Mum took me to..." Hans began to say. Then he remembered the bad news. *Papa still doesn't know!*

"Papa, the soldiers have killed Uncle Eng Guan and Aunty Su Ling!" he said in a small voice.

Papa made a strange noise in his throat. That was when Hans noticed that his father had bandages on, and his face was badly bruised. Hans gasped at the sight.

"Oh no, Papa! They beat you up!"

"I'm alright, son. Don't worry about me. Come, sit here next to me and tell me what happened after I left."

Hans sat down and told Papa everything. After that, they held each other and cried some more.

19
LIFE ON THE STREETS

The tall *Kempeitai* Major would not allow Hans to stay with his father, even though Hans had begged.

"This is not a place for young boys. You can come back tomorrow, around noon, for a short visit, but you cannot stay. Do you understand?" the Major said.

Hans reluctantly agreed to the terms, and slowly walked away. Now he had to think about where he was going. As he left the Outram Road jail behind him, Hans noticed that shadows were starting to get longer. Earlier, he had promised Papa that he was alright, but the truth was that he had no idea where to go or what to do.

Sleeping outside the prison was not an option—the Major had made that quite clear. Neither could he simply sleep out in the open field. He had tried that once on Ubin and had woken up shivering, cold from the morning dew. Then there was also the possibility of rain, which sometimes came down without much warning.

Hans walked away from Outram Road, following the setting sun. After a short distance he came across some shophouses and walk-up apartments off Tiong Bahru Road. Similar to the concept of council flats in England, the Singapore Improvement Trust (SIT) had begun building these apartment buildings to accommodate the growing population in the 1930s.

Hans walked around the buildings looking for any kind soul who might offer some form of help. Most of the people he encountered simply ignored him, but one or two rudely chased him away. These were hard times and nobody wanted to share what little they had with a strange boy.

There were other boys, apparently homeless as well, on the streets. Some congregated in gangs, squatting by the roadside and staring down anyone who walked by. Others stood by themselves. Hans did not fully understand these things at the time, but he quickly recognized that there was some form of pecking order in place.

Resigned to the fact that he was going hungry that night, Hans decided that there was nothing much else he could do but find a covered place to lay down until morning. The cold cement pad under a flight of stairs was not a comfortable place, but it sheltered him from the weather. He put on his extra clothes to keep warm, rolled up the satchel to form a pillow, and lay down to get some sleep.

January 5th 1944, morning
Seng Poh Road (near Tiong Bahru Road), Singapore

A thin sliver of light broke through the needle-like leaves of a Casuarina tree growing near where Hans lay, landing on his face and waking him.

He sat up, and was immediately aware of two things—that his body was aching from having slept all night on the cold cement, and that his stomach was cramping from hunger. As he stood up and looked around, he became aware of activities going on nearby—he could hear the scraping sound of someone sweeping with a coconut leaf broom, and also voices conversing in Hokkien. Despite the reception he had received the day before, Hans felt that he still had to at least try to get some food from anyone that would help.

He approached two old Chinese men who were engaged in loud conversation while they worked, sweeping leaves in a drain. They glanced at him momentarily, but otherwise ignored him in order to continue with their talking.

"Hello, uncle," Hans said, smiling. He mimed eating with his hand, looking at the men with hopeful eyes.

"*Aiyah! Gia, gia*!" one of the men said, shooing him off with one hand. The message was perfectly clear—go away, kid. He moved on to see what else he could find.

The rest of the morning slipped away, with one unsuccessful attempt after another at obtaining food. Again, while most of the people only yelled at him, there were some who chased him with brooms or even threw rocks at him.

It came as a rude shock to the young boy. This sort of thing had never happened to him in his life and he realized then that he had lived a rather sheltered one under Papa's wing. Hans gave in to his tears, frustrated and miserable.

He became desperate. Even digging about in garbage cans did not yield anything edible. People were so short of food that if they threw anything away, you could bet that it was not even worth looking at. It was a miserable situation altogether, but there was nothing he could do about it.

When the sun was almost straight up in the sky, Hans knew that it was time to go and see Papa. He traced his steps back to the Outram Road jail.

Upon seeing Hans approach, the sentry outside the prison reported to Major Minoru that the boy was back. The Major came out and nodded at Hans. "Have you had anything to eat?" he asked.

Hans shook his head.

"Come," Minoru said.

He led Hans to a kitchen. A Korean cook was stirring a large steaming pot. Minoru spoke with the cook, who bowed and proceeded to put some scraps of food in a steel plate for Hans.

"When you are done, you come back and look for me. Do not wander around here by yourself. Understand, boy?" Minoru instructed.

Hans nodded. "Thank you, sir," he said. He did not take long to eat what was in front of him.

After that, he did as he was told, and sought Major Minoru, who brought him to his father's cell. Papa looked a little more rested, but his smile still appeared painful. Hans sat beside him on the bunk and held him tight. As soon as the soldiers left, they began to talk. They talked about everything; they also talked about nothing in particular. All they could do was talk. Time was on their side. Nobody was going anywhere soon.

Papa was by nature not too much of a talker. Hans had followed him about as a young boy, quietly observing and learning. Here and there, Papa would explain things to him, but for the most part, Hans learned more from his father by listening to his interactions with other adults.

Sitting together in the jail cell with nowhere to go, Papa began to talk about his younger years. He told Hans about their family history, about growing up in the Mauritius Islands and Singapore, about his time in Europe. He spoke of his happiness, but also of his regrets with candor.

When it became the time for him to leave, Hans walked back to thc Tiong Bahru neighborhood. The next morning, he wandered about looking for scraps until noon, essentially wasting time, before heading back to the jail to visit Papa. That was the way it was for the next few days.

Apart from being able to spend time with Papa, the one other thing Hans looked forward to during those visits was a chance at food scraps from the prison kitchen. Unfortunately, there was no guarantee of this always. Some days the tall Major offered him food, some days he did not. As such, the quest for sustenance remained a constant challenge.

One day, Hans discovered that a resident in the area owned chickens. As discreetly as he could manage, the boy observed the man's yard for a while, to see if there were eggs lying about. There did not appear to be any, to his disappointment. But there was, however, one lone chicken wandering not far from where Hans lay in the tall grass, pecking at the ground in oblivion.

Hans had not had meat in a very long time. He could barely remember what chicken tasted like. Right then and there, he hatched a plan to nab himself some chicken. He quietly emptied his satchel and stuffed the contents either in pockets or down his shorts—there really was not much in the bag—and began making chirping noise like a cricket.

Hans was quite talented at making animal sounds. The chicken perked its head at the strange noise, and curiosity got the better of it. It came strutting toward him. As soon as the bird was within reach, Hans used the satchel as a sack and covered the chicken's head and as much of the body as would fit in the satchel.

At first the bird squawked and struggled, but then the darkness and the soft constraint of the bag seemed to comfort it. It settled down and clucked occasionally. The stupid bird must have thought it was roosting time.

Hans carefully picked up the bundle and crept away. When he felt he was a safe distance off, in an open field, he stopped walking and thought about how he should prepare the bird.

It was at that moment he realized that he had no idea what to do. He now had a live chicken in his grasp that would, without a doubt in his mind, scratch and peck him to death as soon as the bag was removed from its head.

"I suppose I could break the neck inside the bag. Then it can't hurt me," he reasoned.

The more he thought about it however, the more he realized that he just did not have the heart to do that. Besides, what was he supposed to do after that? He was not sure how one slaughtered a chicken, and even if he did, he did not have a knife anyway. Eating raw chicken with feathers just did not sound appealing, no matter how hungry he was.

He had to take it back.

Reluctantly, Hans walked back to the house from which he stole the chicken. There, he found an older Chinese man standing in the yard. Hans swallowed the lump in his throat, and carefully approached the man.

"Uncle, I think this belongs to you," he said, holding out the bagged chicken.

The man turned to Hans with surprise. When he saw the bag with feet sticking out, he laughed. He took the bag and freed the chicken, which ran away clucking.

"Thank you! Thank you! That one likes to go here and there. I always worry that someone will steal it! Thank you, little boy," the man said, still laughing.

Hans did not know what to say by way of reply, so he smiled, mostly out of embarrassment.

"Wait, boy. I have a present for you," the man said, as he walked away.

He returned carrying two eggs, saying, "*Nah*, take. Thank you for bringing back my chicken."

Now Hans felt even more embarrassed, but he accepted the eggs, nonetheless. "Thank you, Uncle," he said and quickly left.

Hans had mixed feelings about the eggs. He finally had something to eat, but he also felt dishonest about how it came about. It felt worse than stealing the eggs—the man was actually grateful to him for returning the stolen bird. He felt full of shame.

As he cracked one egg and swallowed it raw, he had a hard time making it go down. Not because of the taste—he had eaten raw eggs before—but because of the guilt he was feeling. But as soon as the egg settled in his stomach, that guilty feeling subsided. He was much too hungry to feel bad for long.

The second egg went down as quickly as the first.

20
I WILL ALWAYS BE WITH YOU

As the days dragged on in prison, Edward began to feel weaker. It was not just because of the lack of food; he knew something else was wrong.

During the first five days, he did not have any bowel movement. That was not unexpected, given the shock he was undergoing, as well as the meager rations. However, the first time he went, there was dark blood, almost black, in the pan. Something must have ruptured from all the beating. It was not fresh blood. The bleeding continued, and it remained difficult to move his bowels. Then one day, he could not hold anything in. He could feel his life slipping away, every time he rushed for the pan.

Outbreaks of dysentery were common in the prisons at Outram, Changi and other places of confinement. Physical abuse, coupled with the lack of medication, nutrition and sanitation quickly added up to these illnesses that were oftentimes fatal.

January 10th 1944, around noon
Outram Road Jail, Singapore

Papa was lying on his bunk when Hans arrived. He seemed to be having difficulty sitting up.

"Poor Papa, you look so tired!" Hans exclaimed.

"Hansel, sit over there. Don't get too close. I haven't been feeling so well. I don't want you to get sick, too. Might be the flu."

"Alright, Papa."

Hans noticed that the cell smelt worse than it usually did. After the first day or so, he had gotten used to the place, but now it smelt like a toilet. He knew that Papa was feeling worse than he had let on, but he did not know what he could do for him. He sat up against a wall, across from his father.

"How now, Son? What have you been up to?"

Hans told Papa about the things he had seen outside the jail. He was by then quite familiar with the area around Outram and Tiong Bahru, and so he described it all to his father, even where he slept. As he spoke, Papa smiled and nodded but did not say much.

After a while, Hans noticed that Papa was sweating profusely, and that he was quite pale. "Are you alright, Papa?" he asked, concerned.

Papa nodded. "I'm alright, son. I think you had better go now. I need to use the toilet. Maybe Major Minoru will let you back in later," he said.

The Major looked at Hans in a strange way when the boy told him what had just happened.

"Your father is not feeling well. Perhaps you should not come back for a few days. Let him rest. You don't want to get sick either, do you?" Minoru said.

"No, sir."

"Two or three days. Come back then."

"Yes, sir."

January 12th 1944, noon

Hans wanted to cry as soon as he entered the cell. The smell was worse than ever—a rotten, sour, fecal odor. Horrible!

Papa lay there on his bunk, seemingly unable to move. His eyes opened at the sound of the steel door. A weak smile crossed his face as Hans approached him.

"Very tired, Son. Still not feeling well. You alright, though?" he said.

"Yes Papa, I'm alright," Hans replied, fighting back the tears. What he wanted to say was, "Oh, Papa! What is wrong with you?" but decided it was best to keep his thoughts to himself.

"Come, but don't sit too close. Tell me a story."

"I don't know any stories, Papa."

"Make something up."

For a moment, Hans could not think of what to say. Then he began to make up a story about a baby goat, based loosely on one of *Aesop's Fables*, something that he had heard as a little child. Papa closed his eyes and smiled.

After a while, Hans stopped. Papa was not moving, but there was a gentle snoring coming from his nose, indicating his breathing. Hans stayed for as long as the Major allowed but Papa did not wake up the whole time.

January 14th 1944, morning

Edward knew it would not be long. He could no longer get up from his bunk, so he just lay there in his filth.

So this is how it comes down, then. What a way to die!

His mind drifted in and out of consciousness, from lucidity to delirium. Not for the first time, he wondered what had become of the rest of the family. Images of Florence and the boys—especially of them huddled together that last time he saw them—darted through his mind.

He was especially grateful that he had been able to spend some time with Hansel the past two weeks. The boy made him very proud; Edward felt confident that he would turn out all right. It was just too bad that he would not be around to see him or the other two grow up.

How had it all come down to this? The best laid plans and all that, to paraphrase Steinbeck.

I suppose I shouldn't complain. Had a rather good run of things, for the most. I just wish...

It seemed so pointless to say "I wish" or "I should have," even though everyone is guilty of saying it at some point in time or another. One could go crazy thinking about such things, Edward knew as much.

Still...

That morning, he woke up knowing that he would be gone before the end of that day, or at the most, by the very next. He refused to let that happen before he could see his son one more time. He mustered up strength to call for Major Minoru.

Minoru shook his head when he saw Edward, a somber look on his face. "It will be over soon," he said.

"I know. Last request, sir ... My son ... please find him for me," Edward whispered.

Hans had been wandering around Tiong Bahru Road looking for scraps that morning, when he noticed two Japanese soldiers walking in his direction. As they approached, he bowed to them. The soldiers looked at each other. One nodded his head at his partner.

"You ... come. You ... Papa ... very sick," the other soldier said.

Hans followed the soldiers back to the jail. Upon arrival, they reported to Major Minoru, who came out and escorted Hans to his father's cell.

Papa's face was ashen-gray and he smelt bad. Really bad. Hans carefully approached him.

"Hansel ... thank God they found you."

"I'm here, Papa. I won't leave you."

Papa smiled. "I'm sorry ... wish things had turned out differently," he said. "Promise me something, Son."

"What, Papa?"

"Never give up, do you understand? Even when life gets hard. You ... go on and become a man. A good man."

"I promise."

"I will always be with you, Hansel. Remember that, Son. I know that I will be gone soon, but I will still be watching over you. Do you believe this?"

"I do, Papa. But please don't go!"

"Can't be helped, Son. I wish ... I wish we had more time. Hansel ... very proud of you, my son. Remember me ... always..."

Papa seemed to run out of strength at that point. He lay back and closed his eyes.

"Papa!"

Papa smiled weakly. "Go … Love you always," he whispered. Hans lay his head on his father's chest and sobbed. He could feel the breathing weaken.

"Come, boy. It is not good luck to watch your father die," a voice behind him said. Hans turned to see Major Minoru standing at the doorway, his hand held out.

He turned to look at his father one last time. "Goodbye, Papa. I love you too. Always," he said. A faint smile showed on Papa's face.

Major Minoru gently took Hans by the hand and walked him out of the cell. Without a word, he placed a small package containing some rice balls and sour plums in the boy's satchel. Then he led him outside.

Hans looked up through his tears to see Major Minoru and the other soldiers standing at the entrance of the Outram Road jail. They were bowing to him.

They buried Edward that evening, in the small prison cemetery.

3

HANS

1
ALONE IN THE CROWD

January 15th 1944, morning
Seng Poh Road, Singapore

What little food he had in his satchel was now gone. Hans had eaten the rice in the cover of darkness, away from the eyes of other people. Sometime that morning, he knew he would have to forage for food again, or face hunger, and eventual starvation. Food—it was an ongoing factor in his struggle for survival. A factor which would continue to plague him, as well as the rest of the people in Singapore, for almost two more years.

But every time he thought of Papa, the tears flooded his eyes. He wanted to sob, to wail, to cry out loud, but he knew that he could not. People of the Tiong Bahru neighborhood were beginning to recognize him. The last thing he needed was to appear weak and become an easy pick to the other boys on the street. So far, the gangs had left him alone and he wanted it to stay that way.

Gangs did not make much sense to him. For sure, they owned strength in numbers, but whatever small scraps of food that they found had to be shared among all of them. Obviously, the gang leader or the bigger boys received most, if not all, of the food. That left the smaller members, who were usually the ones who could find food in the first place because of public sympathy, with nothing for themselves.

Nevertheless, Hans respected the street gangs although he would never join them. He could see that they espoused a sense of brotherhood, which seemed to be very important for some people.

Hans knew he had to be strong. Perhaps it was because of his promise to Papa, or maybe his inborn survival instinct was kicking in, but whatever it was, he knew he would not give in, or give up. He would spend his energy adapting to his surroundings.

Language had been an initial barrier, but one that he quickly overcame. Hans seemed to be able to grasp without much difficulty the finer nuances of Hokkien and Cantonese, where a slight shift in tone could change the meaning of a word altogether. In his experience, perhaps the most important street language in Singapore was Malay. While it was considerably easier to learn than the Chinese dialects, he also found it to be useful in communicating with people who were not Malay. Although Hans was able to pick up a few words in Tamil and Punjabi, which were the more common Indian languages in Singapore, what he knew was not enough to hold a decent conversation. That was where Malay came in handy—most of the Indian people in Singapore spoke it as well.

He also learned another way to better his chances of survival. Perhaps he had seen his father do it, or perhaps it was just in his nature. Without having ever heard the saying that one catches more flies with honey than with vinegar, Hans instinctively found that the best way to get something is by endearing himself to those who had what he needed.

This was the opposite of what many of the Chinese boys on the street were doing, where they sought what they wanted through coercion or even theft. While this worked to a certain degree, it usually was not successful more than once. All an old aunty had to do was summon the *Kempeitai* or any soldier on patrol and tell them that so-and-so tried to rob her, and the next thing, that so-and-so's head was rolling on the floor.

Later that morning, Hans noticed two Japanese officers were riding on horseback along the main road. While everyone usually made themselves scarce when any soldiers came by, Hans did not fear them. After all, the Major at Outram Jail had given him food before. Maybe these officers would be kind as well. Hoping for a handout, he followed the officers from a distance. He had bowed to them when they first noticed him, but after that point, they ignored him. The officers rode their horses to the front of a tea house, where they then dismounted.

Singapore, even then, was a place with automobiles in mind. Nobody rode horses on the streets—the only places for horses were the racecourse or the polo club. As such, there really was nowhere for the officers to secure their horses.

Seeing an opportunity, Hans stepped up to the officers. Standing stiffly at attention, he raised his right hand in what he hoped was a proper salute.

"Good morning, sirs! Would you like me to hold on to your horses while you go in?" he said.

The officers looked at each other and smiled. "Good idea, boy. Make sure nobody touches them," one of them replied. They handed him the reins and went inside the tea house.

Hans did not know how long they were inside, but it felt like a long time to him. He was getting tired of waiting, but he could do nothing about it. After some time, the officers came out. One of them handed Hans a sweetened rice cake.

"Well done!" the officer said.

Hans bowed. "Thank you, sir!" he said, handing him the reins.

The cake tasted heavenly. Sweeteners of any sort had been in short supply in Singapore since the start of the war. With Japan on the losing side, in 1944, such luxuries were even harder to come by. It was the first time in years, literally, that Hans had tasted honey. He tried very hard not to swallow the whole cake at once, wanting to savor it slowly instead.

Hans had discovered an advantage dealing with the Japanese. For one thing, they seemed to be kinder toward children than they were toward adults in general. They also seemed to appreciate good manners. Not the insincere, sucking up sort of manners, but genuine politeness. It appeared to be in their culture.

But the extra edge Hans possessed with the Japanese was that he did not appear to be Chinese. From what he could tell, the soldiers seemed to despise all Chinese, and found any excuse to mistreat them. Yet, at the same time, he was obviously not European either. In that way it was ironic, yet to his good fortune that with his Asian dark hair and sun-tanned skin, mixed in with certain Caucasian features, he looked as if he could be almost anything but Chinese or European, the very two races that he actually was. Most of the Japanese soldiers thought he was perhaps of Arab descent, maybe north Indian or even some sort of Malay.

Earlier on, Hans had made another observation about the soldiers: Not every one of them was ethnically Japanese. While it appeared that all of the officers and some of the enlisted men were actually Japanese, many of the privates were Korean or Manchurian conscripts. He also learned that some of these men were convicts who had enlisted for combat, in lieu of jail time.

The Japanese are a very structured people, with the concept of hierarchy well established in their lives. Their military system then had an especially strict hierarchy, where it became common—almost expected—for the senior ones to physically abuse the junior man on the totem pole. The Koreans and Manchurians were, unfortunately for them, at the bottom of that pole. In turn, they viewed the Chinese—all civilians really, but especially the Chinese—as below them, and therefore deserving of rough treatment. Essentially, they were taking the abuse from their superiors and, in turn, passing it on to any civilian whom they felt deserved it.

Hans observed that the worst abuses came from these men. He quickly learned to differentiate them from the regular Japanese soldiers, and to stay away from them. Being street-smart was one of the most important aspects of survival.

That evening, he went back to the familiar landing under the staircase at the Seng Poh Road apartment building. Nobody was there, so he sat down—staking his claim, as it was. It did not always turn out that way. If an adult or a bigger boy was there, he would have to find someplace else. Now, if it was a smaller boy, he had the option of going away, or telling the kid to go. However, if he let the smaller boy stay, it could be taken that he was weak or soft—a pushover. Usually, the smaller kid would leave, without a word. That was just the way of the street.

By that point, he was as filthy as any other street person. Sometimes when it rained, he went out and cleaned himself in the torrential downpour. Unlike temperate or colder climate zones, in the tropics it is not dangerous to get drenched in the rain. Actually, it can be quite refreshing. What was unwise was the act of going to sleep wet. Hans found that if he let himself get wet early enough in the day, he would be comfortably dry by nightfall.

He learned many things on the streets by asking questions here and there, but mostly by observation. It was just as he had done when he was younger, following Papa around, and learning by watching him.

Except that Papa was now gone.

Thinking about Papa was still very painful for Hans. But he never wanted to simply forget about the great man. In time, he knew he would be able to recall him to mind—all the things he said and did—without tears streaming down his face. Nobody would notice if he only became a little misty-eyed then.

Survival belongs to the fittest, as the saying goes. Not necessarily the strongest, or the smartest, for these virtues by themselves are insufficient in the art of survival. Fitness of mind, of being able to think on one's feet, was what saved this six year-old boy during those war years.

2
THE COWBOY AND THE INDIAN

Before the war came to Singapore, one of the things that Hans had enjoyed most was watching Hollywood westerns on the big screen. He really loved those movies. As a boy, he had fun playing Cowboys and Indians, carrying his toy carbine with him everywhere. Who didn't want to be John Wayne?

Watching the big screen heroes, Hans never imagined then that he would one day become a cowboy. Well, maybe not the John Wayne sort, but he became a cowboy in the true sense of the word.

March 3rd 1944, sunrise
Lower Delta Road, Singapore

In his daily quest for food and shelter, Hans had explored extensively the area between Tiong Bahru and the Outram Road jail to the east, covering more distance each day. In no time, he knew the ins and outs of the area, including all the small side streets.

Hans routinely watched the soldiers going about their duties, approaching them and offering to run errands in return for food. Sometimes, there was no pay-off for running these errands. In all fairness, it was not that the soldiers were trying to be mean. At that point in the war especially, they too were living on very meager portions.

That morning, he decided to try a different tack—maybe there would be better pickings in the opposite direction. Heading west of Tiong Bahru, he walked past houses and through open fields before reaching a road that appeared to run north and south. Since it made no difference to him—he was still exploring, after all—Hans turned south.

After some distance, he came across a small house built from wood, with corrugated metal pieces and *attap* for the roof. Behind the house was a shed—more like a small barn, perhaps—constructed of similar materials.

As Hans approached the dwelling, he could hear a woman's voice coming from the shed. The voice was speaking in Tamil-accented English, with an irritated tone. "*Aiyo-yo*, you bladdy animal! Why you always give me such a hard time, I don't know. Stop moving, you!"

Hans peered into the shed. An older, very dark-skinned woman inside was attempting to milk a clearly agitated and emaciated cow. She looked up at him.

"What do you want, boy? Can't you see I'm busy?" she said, flapping her hand at him in a go-away motion.

"Would you like me to help you, Aunty?" Hans offered.

The woman looked as if she was about to retort something nasty, but before she could say anything, Hans had walked gently to the cow and begun stroking its face. The cow settled down after only a few strokes.

"I say, that's jolly good, you know! You seem to be very good at calming her down!" the woman said, surprise evident on her face. With the cow distracted, she was then able to milk it without any further problem. When she was done, she turned to Hans and smiled.

"Much better! You don't know how much trouble this one gives me, but she's all I've got. Huh, Geetha? You're all I have left," she said, turning back to the cow and stroking it, almost trance-like.

Suddenly, she turned back to look at Hans. "I say, boy. Thank you for your help! What's your name?" she asked.

"Hans," he replied.

"Hans? What sort of a name is that? What is your whole name?"

"Hans Joseph Felix Schirmer."—Joseph had been added on at his baptism.

The woman looked at him strangely. "Well, I shall call you Joseph, then. You can call me Aunty Mary. Mary and Joseph..." She laughed at her own wit.

Hans smiled politely.

"So, Joseph. What are you doing wandering about here? Where are your Mummy and Daddy?" Mary asked, resting her hands on her wide hips.

Hans swallowed back his emotions. "My father is ... gone. I don't know where my mother is," he replied.

Mary nodded her head and frowned. "That's how it is these days," she said. After a while, she continued, "You seem to be very useful. Why don't you do some work around here, and in return you can sleep in here with Geetha at night and I will also cook for you something to *makan*. How does that sound?"

It was the best prospect so far. Hans thanked her.

After a few days, he was not so sure if it was indeed the best deal around. For one thing, he was no longer sure if Aunty Mary was quite alright in the head. One moment, she could be sickeningly sweet—you're the child of my dreams and all that—and the next moment she would be raging at him about how lazy he was.

She did not feed him all that well, either. However, it was apparent that she did not really have very much to offer. Nobody in Singapore did. In fact, Mary appeared to eat just as little as Hans did. Despite that, she still had a round, apple shaped body. Hans wondered about that.

He considered moving on, but in the end he stayed. Part of him knew that out there, nothing was certain. Part of him also felt sorry for her. As he came to know her story, he began to understand her a little better.

From the start, Hans had wondered why this strange woman was living by herself in the rundown shack, with not much more than a skinny milk cow among her possessions. However, he hated asking personal questions. If someone wanted to tell you their life story, they would. If not, then it was rude to ask. Yet, his curiosity may have shown.

One day, she sat him down. "Joseph," she began. She had this sing-song way of saying it, which made him shudder inside. He never really much liked the name in the first place, but she was only making it worse. "Joseph, you must wonder why Aunty Mary lives here alone, don't you?"

Hans shrugged. She went on.

"Before the war, we had money. This was not our house. This was the gardener's place. Come, I want to show you something."

She stood up and led him outside. They walked through an overgrown field for some distance, before reaching the burnt foundations of what had been a large house with a wide circular driveway in the front.

"This ... this was our place. When I married Mr Silva, he was already a successful businessman. He was very kind, very gentle. He showered me with all sorts of pretty things, you know. Such a wonderful man..."

Hans watched her as she spoke. Mary's eyes appeared very glossy and distant.

"We had one child—a boy," she continued. "Such happy times! I taught him to ride his bicycle right here. I remember when Mr Silva bought a brand new motorcar in 1922, and our family drove up through Malaya. Sometimes, he even went as fast as forty miles an hour, you know! That crazy man, I tell you!"

She paused to smile.

"Our son grew up, and so we sent him to England to study the Law. Then the war started over there and so he came back here. But then our war started here.

"At first, we thought the British would have no problems. You see, the Japanese only bombed downtown one time before Christmas, and then they did not come back. We thought it was because they were afraid to come back! But we were wrong. We did not know that the British were losing in Malaya, and that the Japanese would begin bombing Singapore again.

"One evening, around New Year's time, my son and I went out to do some shopping. My husband stayed at home. He said he had some business matters to attend to. While we were downtown, the sirens started going off. We had to wait until it was all over, before they would let us leave the shelter. When we came home, this was all that was left.

"My son went berserk! The bomb was a stray one, but it was a direct hit. There was nothing left of his Daddy. He joined the soldiers the next morning, even though I begged him not to do it. I never saw him again. After the Japanese took over, I found out that they had killed him near Pasir Panjang."

Hans listened silently, looking down at the driveway. He imagined a young Indian boy wobbling on his bicycle, trying his hardest not to hit his Daddy's parked car—the one that could go forty miles an hour.

"Well, that's my story. Our gardener and his wife ran away and left their cow behind. This is all I have left. Except for you."

Hans did not know what to say.

After a moment Mary said, "You know, life has brought us together somehow. You are all I have, and I am all you have. Would you like to call me your Mummy?"

Again, Hans did not know how to reply. *You are NOT my mother*, he wanted to say. That was when he realized that he was not even close to his own mother. Had never been, really.

Ever since the day he had to go on his own, he had not really thought about her. His Papa had been at the front of his mind all that time. Papa had been his everything.

Mary sensed his hesitation and frowned. "Well, it would mean something to me. But never mind—don't worry about it," she said, more than a little sullenly.

Hans felt bad for his hostess. Ever since he was little, he always tried to please others. He did not want to hurt Mary's feelings.

"Mother," he said.

Mary frowned. Then she laughed. "My goodness, don't call me that! So formal ... Mother!" she said. "My son called me Mummy, even when he was a big man."

Hans nodded. "What was your son's name ... Mummy?" he asked.

"His name was Joseph."

So began his stint as the cowboy. It was a strange period of his life. Hans tried his hardest to please Mary, but it was very difficult for him to address her as "Mummy."

He realized that he was being a little mean, but in his mind he began to think of her as "Blackie Mummy." Undoubtedly, he knew that she was a little crazy—who could blame her after all that she had been through—but nevertheless, he did not want to be her son. Why couldn't she treat him like some hired hand, just like in thc movics?

Hans did not like being stifled. He needed to roam, to see things. Every now and then, he would get distracted and wander. When he returned, Blackie Mummy would be beside herself and beat him severely. Then she would weep and hold him.

"Don't ever leave me, Joseph. Don't ever leave me," her voice echoed in his head.

He was too young to understand anxiety and mental imbalance. Although he did not like the way things had become, he also hated seeing her in that manner. Each time it happened, he resolved not to cause her any more anguish.

Until the next time something distracted him.

Like beautiful silver airplanes high in the sky.

3
SUPERFORTRESS

November 5th 1944, 0640 hours

Hans woke up to the sound of air raid sirens blaring in the distance. It surprised him. He had not heard that sound in a while.

The last time he remembered hearing the sirens was when the Japanese were coming, raining their bombs from high. But the Japanese had won the war then—they were the ones ruling here now. So who was it coming to bomb Singapore this time? Was it the British, coming back to fight the Japanese for what had been theirs?

At that time, Hans was sleeping in the house with Mary, no longer in the barn. He carefully crept past her room and went outside to take a look.

At first, he could barely make out anything. The sky was still mostly dark, with magenta streaks coming from the east. Then—in the direction of northwest—he saw the morning sun glinting off what appeared to be around fifty silver aircraft. They were of a design that he had never seen before.

He was excited, for he had always had an eye for machines. These were especially interesting to him because of their sleek, modern design. They were long and skinny in the fuselage, with equally long and skinny wings. At first glance, they did not seem that big to him. Altitude distorted the size perspective. But as he watched Japanese fighters climbing to intercept—mere dots in the sky—that was when he noticed how tiny they were in comparison to the bombers.

Before the fighters were able to reach combat altitude, another group of strange looking aircraft approached from the direction opposite of the bombers, swooping down to meet the Japanese. It was the most incredible sight he had ever seen.

The second group of aircraft—apparently these were fighters of some sort—were also shining silver. They appeared to have two engines, unlike the Japanese fighters, and moved with amazing speed. Hans had never seen anything quite like it. Who were they?

When the war began, the Japanese were the fastest guns in the sky. Now, they looked no better than the antiquated Buffalo fighters did at the time, going up against a superior enemy.

As of August 1944, the US Army Air Force (USAAF) 67th Fighter Squadron began operations out of the newly acquired Middlesburg airfield in Dutch New Guinea. Flying from there, the twin engine Lockheed P-38 Lightning long-range fighters could rendezvous with the B-29 bombers anywhere over Singapore, Malaya or the East Indies. They were the latest versions of the P-38 Lightning—the "J" and the "L" variants—with much improved range and performance over the "F" versions of 1942.

The bombers were completely brand new. Boeing's B-29 Superfortress was the first operational bomber with pressurized cabins. Unlike the crews of earlier bomber designs like the B-17 and B-24, the crew of the B-29 did not have to wear heavy insulated jackets and oxygen masks at operating altitudes. Electronic gun turrets and aiming systems were other innovations, along with increased range and payload.

USAAF XX Bomber Command squadrons began flying B-29s out of Kharagpur, India to targets in Sumatra, Singapore and Malaya in November 1944. This was their first raid on Singapore.

Hans watched the strange fighters—he did not know at the time what they were or who they belonged to—dive in and shoot down their adversaries with seemingly little effort. The Japanese did not even stand a chance.

While fighters tangled, the bombers flew on in formation, undisturbed. Beyond the hills, far to the north of where Hans was standing, came the rumble of distant explosions, followed by the sight of flaming balls that rose upwards and turned into rolling thick black smoke. It was an oily smoke. The black greasy fallout would be on everything around the Sembawang naval base area.

Filled with excitement, Hans ran back inside the house, where he found Mary in the kitchen, calmly putting breakfast together. She appeared altogether indifferent to the ongoing raid. Hans quietly sat down. Since she was not saying anything, neither would he.

After some time, she spoke softly, "Come, Joseph. Better eat some *chapati* before you get to work." Not a word about the bombs.

Hans came around to the dinner table to eat the flat bread, served with a little ghee—a fermented clarified cow butter. The piece of bread was small, but it was all he got because it was all she had. By that point, he was becoming a caricature of himself—a skinny kid with a big head. But all the children he came across were no better off, and in fact, some were in worse shape.

He thought it strange how Mary was behaving as if it was just another day, as if nothing important was happening, but it would not be the first strange thing she had said or done. He too acted as if nothing was happening, but resolved to find out what he could about the new aircraft, as soon as his chores were done.

Hans thirsted for information, but accurate news reports were hard to come by in occupied Singapore. The Japanese had outlawed the possession of private radio sets, under penalty of death. They had also prohibited the discussion of any pro-Allied news, but with people being people, the gossip just went on anyway. By then, just about everyone knew that Japan was losing the war, although it was obviously something that nobody dared to talk about in the open.

Even so, Hans knew of a place where he still might learn something—the marketplace.

Perhaps the younger generations will never have the opportunity to witness this phenomenon, for such places have become gradually fewer. But historically speaking, everyone knows that old men gathering in marketplaces are the best sources of gossip.

Hans innocuously moved among the groups of people at the Tiong Bahru marketplace, listening in on their conversations. Mostly, it was about benign and uninteresting topics. These groups tended to talk loudly and openly. He was looking for groups who were more subdued. Chances were, these groups had something more interesting to discuss.

Something forbidden.

He thought he heard one group quietly discussing something about aircraft, so he stopped to listen. Indeed, they were talking about the bombing raid of that morning. They also kept repeating a word that he was not familiar with—*bee kok*.

Although he had a million questions, he remained silent. After all, he knew that children should be seen and not heard. Hans waited patiently for the opportune moment. At one point, when there seemed to be a lull in the conversation, he spoke to one of the men—the one he thought looked the kindest.

"Uncle ... don't mind me, please ... but what is '*bee kok*'?" he asked.

The man turned to him in surprise, then smiled and said, "*Aiyah*, you don't know '*bee kok*' ah? American! John Wayne! BANG! BANG!"

Half-crouched, he mimed shooting a pistol in each hand—a gun slinging Chinaman.

His friends laughed at him. He grinned and "shot" at each one with his fingers. This made them laugh even harder, and some clutched their chests in response. One of his cronies must have had thespian aspirations. Not only did this one clutch his chest, but he also jumped up and staggered about in an exaggerated manner, shouting out, "*Aiyah*! *Aiyah*!" before collapsing on the ground, his arms splayed out. Hans and the old men laughed hysterically. Too many Saturday matinees for that one.

The old gunslinger turned to Hans, still grinning widely. "You saw the airplanes this morning? Those people are the Americans! They are the ones who are winning the war against Japan!"

Then he grew serious, looking about furtively. "Ah, boy! Better not repeat what you hear. Japanese soldier catch you talking about Americans, well..." He brought his hand down in a chopping motion.

Hans nodded his head. He had already seen for himself what the soldiers were capable of. Shortly after arriving in the neighborhood, he had come across a human head lying in a ditch. It was not the last beheading he would witness, either.

Americans! Those fascinating people with the fast horses and fast guns. The ones who could quickly draw and hit anything with their pistols. Now they were coming here with their fast planes, shooting down the Japanese. To a six year-old boy, they were just like the good guys in the Westerns!

What seemed even more amazing to him was that the mythical Americans always appeared to be able to shoot down the Japanese, yet without taking any losses to themselves. To his boyish eyes, they seemed invincible—very unlike the British who had taken such a shameful beating earlier in the war.

This was, of course, not entirely accurate. It was a war, and the USAAF naturally would lose one or two B-29s on some of those missions. Sometimes it was from flak damage, but mostly it was from accidents or fuel shortage. But since Hans never actually saw them take a hit, or go down before him, they seemed quite amazing in his eyes.

That said, actual USAAF losses were incredibly low during their operations over Southeast Asia in 1944 and 1945. The Japanese had considered Singapore to be a secured territory, so they shipped most of their pilots and equipment to the Philippines and Japan, where they knew the main showdown was going to take place. They just did not have much of anything left to throw at the Americans.

Lockheed P-38J Lightning

Boeing B-29 Superfortress

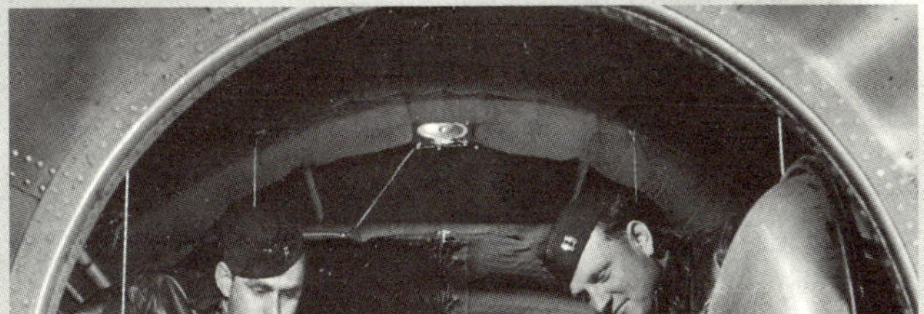

Inside the B-29's pressurized cabin.

4
THE AMERICANS

Throughout January to March of 1945, XX Bomber Command conducted daylight bombing raids over Singapore. The main targets were the naval base and the King George VI floating dock in the north end of the island, as well as the Empire Dock in the south. Other targets included the offshore oil refineries located on the smaller southern islands.

These air raids usually took place in the morning. Hans looked forward to the sight of aircraft even more than he did three years ago, when the Japanese came to bomb Singapore. The fact that he could have been hurt or killed by a stray bomb did not matter to him. It was simply the thrill of seeing the fascinating new aircraft in action again. He especially enjoyed watching the aerial battles between the fighters. Now that he was older, he fully understood that men were dying in the burning wrecks that fell to the ground. However, this time, the ones being shot down were the Japanese and he was fine with that.

Moral implications are usually considered after the fact. For a young boy, the different shades of morality can be a hard concept to grasp—it is even so for most adults. To Hans, since it was the Japanese who were responsible for his Papa's death, as well as the other atrocities he had personally witnessed, that made them the "bad guys" in this drama.

Yet at the same time, he knew that they could not all be bad people. After all, he had personally benefited from acts of kindness performed by certain Japanese individuals.

It was all very complicated.

But in the air, he had made a simple distinction. The Americans were the good guys; the Japanese were the bad guys. And the bad guys always lose in the end—that was a simple fact in any story. The evidence of this "fact" was confirmed in this child's eyes by the large number of plummeting, flaming Japanese fighters.

After those first few raids, the Japanese had no more serviceable aircraft to send up over Singapore. Even anti-aircraft fire was becoming thin—they were beginning to run low on ammunition. The Americans and their B-29s could come and go as they pleased. And that was when Hans began to see them coming in really low.

When the USAAF began their aerial campaign on Japan in June of 1944, they employed the same tactic that they had been using in Europe—daylight high altitude precision bombing. However, the air currents over Japan did not support that technique—accuracy was going out the window. Furthermore, conventional ordnance did not seem to be as effective on the mostly wooden Japanese structures as they had been on the mostly concrete European buildings. Mission success rates were unimpressive, to say the least. General Curtis LeMay studied the mission debriefs, as well as the geographical makeup of the target area, and came up with a solution—low level bombing using incendiary (napalm) ordnance.

Since late 1944, XX Bomber Command had been gradually deploying to the Marianas to join other groups for the all-out bombing of Japan. During that transition period, they began practicing their low level tactics on Singapore.

February 24th 1945, morning
A field around Redhill, near Lower Delta Road, Singapore

American bombers targeted the Empire Dock near Keppel Harbour that morning. As soon as the sirens began, Hans ran out to see what was happening. Within minutes, he could hear explosions in the distance, but did not see any aircraft flying above. The Americans were beginning to fly much lower than they had before.

Hans knew of an open field nearby that allowed a clearer view all around. He ran to it, before Mary could say anything. When he arrived, he saw that he was not the only one at the field looking for a show. Other boys and men were already standing there, looking south at the rising columns of smoke. These frequent raids, along with the absence of Japanese resistance, provided mounting evidence that the war was turning hard and fast against their oppressors.

The adults watched quietly, keeping their expressions to ambiguous headshakes. If they were cheering inside, they did not let it show. One never knows who is watching, after all. While the Japanese would probably not have done anything to a small child who oohed and aahed about the American aircraft, an adult seen cheering for the enemy would more than likely be found in a ditch later, minus a head.

As they continued to look south, everyone became aware of a roaring sound that seemed to be increasing in volume. Something was coming closer! For Hans, what happened next was a moment frozen in time. As he recalled it over the years, he could see it all in his mind's eye, playing back frame by frame.

Just as the roaring reached its zenith, a B-29 burst overhead, barely clearing the treetops. There was no containing the surprise for anyone. All present, adult and children, let out shouts of excitement.

It was the biggest thing Hans had ever seen. A hundred feet of shining aluminum and Plexiglas passed just over his head, propelled by four roaring engines that were mounted on wings spanning one hundred and forty feet. On each side of the B-29 fuselage was an observation porthole covered by a Plexiglas bubble, or blister. This design allowed a crewman to stick his head and upper body inside the bubble, and therefore be able to look outside in all directions.

As the aircraft passed over, Hans caught a glimpse of a young man—he had short blond hair and was wearing a khaki uniform of some sort—in one of the observation ports, looking at the people below him.

He looked a bit like Papa! For a moment, their eyes met. Hans waved. The American waved back. Then he was gone.

Small, shiny objects fell from the bomber as it roared away, the blast from the supercharged Wright Cyclone engines sending them in all directions. Everyone on the field ran toward the objects. Some were faster than the others. These ones pounced first on the tiny objects, screaming in ecstatic disbelief. Hershey's chocolate bars ... Packs of Lucky Strike cigarettes ... Wrigley's chewing gum...

Nobody had seen any of these things in years. On the black market, they could be as valuable as gold! A feeding frenzy ensued, with everyone grabbing what they could. Hans and the other young boys were even picking up the packs of cigarettes when they came across them, knowing that they could make a trade with the deprived soldiers later for something edible.

Low flying bombers appeared a couple times again on later days. Why were they buzzing the city? Hans had no idea then, or even later as an adult. It did not appear to have any tactical or strategic purpose, unless it was part of their training. Perhaps the pilots were testing the limits of the enemy's defense, or lack thereof.

Whatever the reason, the crew of these B-29s would drop some rations whenever they saw civilians gathering to watch. A small gesture of goodwill perhaps?

At first, the Japanese warned against picking up the goodies falling from the sky. However, they were as deprived as anyone else, so these warnings were half-hearted. In the end, one would often see Japanese soldiers running out among the civilians to partake in the falling bounty. Hans observed that the soldiers would give up just about anything for cigarettes. They readily traded their Hershey's chocolates along with a rice ball or two for just a few sticks.

It was his first taste of entrepreneurship.

March 30th 1945, approximately 0820 hours
Pulau Bukom, an island south of Singapore

In preparation for Japan, the B-29s came in low again that morning. Their first missions had been carried out from 20,000 feet. Now they were flying in around 3,000 feet, sometimes lower. The decreased altitude would also increase their chances of success—Pulau Bukom was a small target.

The crisp morning sun reflected off the aluminum and Plexiglas surfaces of the twenty-nine bombers flying on that mission. Although they did not expect to encounter any resistance, based on intelligence reports, the aircrew still kept an alert eye for enemy fighters or gunboats as a precaution.

Intel reports were correct—not a shot came their way. The B-29s flew over the island, dropping their load on the oil refinery plant and storage tank farm below. Ordnance away, the bombers climbed slowly back to 20,000 feet as they banked southeast, moving on to a new base in Dutch New Guinea. From there, they were to transition to the Mariana Islands, in range of the Japanese homeland. Behind them, secondary explosions continued while the oily black smoke rolled upward. Their time in Southeast Asia was over—that was XX Bomber Command's last mission to Singapore.

Thus began for Hans an infatuation with America, and all things American. From the time he first saw the USAAF aircraft, he knew that the Japanese Occupation could not last much longer. Every time he recalled the sight of the B-29 flying just over his head, he would describe it with one word, "Beautiful!"

After the war, as Hans learned more about the events that happened in the Pacific as well as in Europe, it confirmed for him that the Americans were the "good guys" in that war. As far as he was concerned, if it were not for the Americans, the British would have lost the war completely. In his eyes, he would continue to view the collective British as an overtly arrogant people who had made a mess of things in Singapore, and for that, he had little respect for them. Although he knew that his father had died at the hands of the Japanese, he still blamed the British for having let them in.

A little simplistic perhaps, but that was how he saw it.

Later on, in his early years as a police constable—during which British officers were still in charge of administration and training—he continued to witness their arrogance first-hand. The way he saw it, they were still behaving as if they had won the war single-handedly.

Obviously, Hans recognized that not all British people were that way. He spoke of one particular Superintendent who had always taken a personal interest in the men under him, and who had treated the locals with dignity. He remembered the old Colonel and a few others like him. But by and large, his observation was that many of the colonial British were still treating the locals poorly, up to the time they left Singapore at the end of the 1950s.

It was a different time.

5

BACK ON THE STREETS

Hans did not stay with Mary much longer after the bombings began. He could not. Maybe it was the bombings that had stirred something in her. Maybe it was Hans himself—eager to please, yet nobody's slave. For some reason or other, she was becoming increasingly unbearable to be around. Her erratic moods were now becoming noticeably more extreme. These days, even when he performed his normal chores as he always had, she would come after him and accuse him of not doing anything. From screaming rants and raves, she would then go into an almost catatonic state.

As bad as he had felt for her at one time, she was now beginning to scare him with her bizarre behavior. One night, he jumped awake from a bad dream—Papa was dying before him again. But the moment he opened his tear-filled eyes, he found himself staring into a big black face only two inches from his, the whites of Mary's eyes the only discernible feature. He screamed in terror.

"It's only me, Joseph," Mary said, no emotion in her voice.

Somehow, that did not comfort him. Quite the opposite, actually it terrified him. Why was she sitting up at night, staring at him only inches from his face?

Hans knew that he had to leave. He could no longer be party to the emotional blackmail that Mary was dealing. He was sad for her, and for what life had dealt her, but even at that young age, he knew that it was not something he had to fix. Or that he should even be trying to fix. He had his own survival to contend with.

So one evening in early 1945, he made up his mind not to return to Mary's house, after a day out in the fields. It was something that he had been contemplating for a while. He did not want her to come looking for him, or to prevent his leaving, so he made no mention of it beforehand.

Although he had lived with her for almost a year, during that entire time she never really asked him about his life, where he came from, or what he was doing before he showed up at her place. Because of that, he felt safe returning to Tiong Bahru, the place with which he was most familiar.

Being back on the streets once more posed the same old issues—he had to scrounge for food and shelter everyday again. On that first night back, he slept in the open, as all the usual places were taken. All night long, he shivered from the cold, all the way until the sun was well up in the sky the next morning.

The lack of nutrition, coupled with exposure to the elements, was taking its toll on his young body. He would later describe himself then as "a skinny kid with an old man's face" along with a bulging abdomen, distended from malnutrition. While the quantity of food in Singapore was abysmal to begin with, the nutritive quality of what one could find became the main issue. Hans ate what he could find—usually tapioca—in order to ward of the hunger pains, but otherwise, he starved.

When he was able to do so, he would drink some milk directly from a cow or goat udder. Or when he was fortunate enough, some kind soul would present him with an egg or two. However, this did not happen often enough to provide sufficient nutrition for a growing boy. He was only seven at that time and the effects of malnutrition would affect him for a long time after the war.

But the important thing was that he was free to come and go. Later on in his life, that need for freedom—for adventure—would become an integral part of his personality. Learning to survive on the street and the ability to adapt became factors that molded him in a positive way, however unfortunate those circumstances may have been. As an adult, he recognized that his never-give-up mentality had developed from the experiences foisted on him at that early age.

There were other life-lessons that Hans learned during this time. Because he was able to observe people under extreme circumstances, he learned more about human nature than a child his age typically would. Lessons from his parents about morals, kindness, reasoning, cause and effect—these did not seem to apply in this upside-down world. In their quest for survival, many people sold others out. Sometimes it was over a paltry amount of food, too.

However, not everyone behaved in that manner. Every now and then, Hans benefited from acts of kindness that would renew his faith in mankind. During the Japanese occupation, all civilians had as little as the next person. Yet, as rare as they were, there were still some who were willing to share what they had with others.

The Japanese also had as little to eat as the civilians. However, the one thing that remained very different for them was that they possessed unchecked power over the civilians. This predictably led to many abuses. Hans witnessed, on various occasions, the soldiers killing civilians for no particular reason other than random choice.

When he closed his eyes, he pictured one particular scene in his head, as bad as any nightmare repeating itself...

A squad of Japanese soldiers walking down the street, on a routine patrol. The more observant civilians, having seen the soldiers coming from a distance, discreetly disappear. Others, the ones milling around, quickly come to attention as soon as they see the soldiers, followed by a deep bow from the waist down.

Keep staring at the floor. Better not look up!

The soldiers stop to look at the bowing peasants. This becomes a sort of game for them. What would the stupid Chinks do if we just stand and stare at them?

After minutes of silent bowing—most people know that the only thing to do is to remain in that position until the soldiers leave—an inexperienced civilian, a young man, lifts his head carefully to see what the soldiers want.

One of the soldiers stamps forward, grabs the young man by the neck, pushes him to the ground. He screams at the man on the floor, while kicking at him viciously.

The young man covers his face and curls into a ball.

After the soldier is satisfied, or simply tired out—for one tires easily in the hot tropics—he stops kicking the man, unslings his rifle chambers, turns it around and shoots the man through the head.

The other people remain with their heads down. Hans can hear someone weeping quietly, keeping it controlled.

The soldiers leave, laughing and clapping each other on the back as if they had just been to a sporting match. Jolly good show!

Only after they leave do the people rush forward to tend to the fallen man. A woman screams and wails, her hands covered with her own son's blood and brains.

Hans could understand the basic premise that if someone actually did something wrong, then that person was liable to receive some form of punishment. Simple cause and effect.

However, when a soldier randomly kills just because he did not like that person's face, or simply to assert his authority, then that made no sense to him at all. Unfortunately, Hans saw that sort of senseless killing happening one too many times. It became obvious to Hans that there must have been no reprisal for these actions, otherwise the soldiers would not have continued doing so.

Hence, the lesson this young boy gained from his observation was that certain individuals, when unrestrained, were capable of actions that were beyond reason and belief. It was clearly not due to circumstance, for Hans had also observed soldiers who were equally low in rank behaving in a decent way. Hans was amazed with the complexities of human nature. Because such acts of kindness existed alongside the cruel brutality, he learned that you cannot hate a whole people. You just hate the actions of the individual.

It was the same in Europe. One could not say that all Germans were evil, only the ones who perpetrated, or even perpetuated, the horrors. It is too simplistic, as well as wrong, to label an entire race or group for the acts of some.

That said, the Japanese soldiers occupying Singapore were, generally speaking, a harsh lot. The Japanese military culture did not tolerate surrender. Death before dishonor was their code. In their eyes, to surrender was dishonorable, and they held their opponents to that same standard. Thus, they considered anyone in Singapore, military or civilian, as a dishonored person. As warriors, they may have honestly admired the battle prowess of their enemy, especially if that enemy displayed great valor in the fight. However, once the enemy surrendered or allowed himself to be captured, then as far as the Japanese were concerned, that one had also given up his honor. For that one, his own death was the only way to redemption.

One day in July 1945, Hans was to witness that rather extreme facet of the *Bushido* code of the warrior in action.

6
OPERATION RIMAU

A year after the success of Operation Jaywick in 1943, Ivan Lyon, who had by then been promoted to the rank of Lieutenant-Colonel, felt that another similar commando raid on the ships in Singapore Harbour was still a viable option. He returned with his men in October 1944. The code name this time was Operation Rimau—from *harimau*, the Malay word for tiger.

The basic premise of Rimau was the same as the previous operation—insertion to Dutch East Indies waters via submarine, then transfer to a captured fishing junk in order to get closer to Singapore waters. This time, they were equipped with newly designed electric powered submersible canoes for the final leg of the raid, and more mines. The plan was to repeat the previous mission, but with more firepower. Unfortunately, the success they had during the former raid was not about to repeat this time.

On October 10th, a Japanese boat patrol spotted their fishing junk. They closed in and hailed the Operation Rimau team for identification. There was still no real cause for alarm at that point, for the crew was in disguise and some of them spoke Malay. It had worked before.

Unfortunately, someone on Lyon's team panicked and fired the first shots. The surprised Japanese patrol shot back, at which point Lyon's entire crew joined in laying down a suppressive fire. Lyon and his men succeeded in destroying the patrol boat but their cover was blown. After scuttling the junk along with most of the submersibles and mines, Lyon ordered the majority of his men to evade detection until their submarine arrived to pick them up. Meanwhile, he and a few others would attempt an alternative smaller scale raid.

The small raiding party succeeded in sinking three Japanese ships moored in Singapore Harbour. They then escaped, hopeful that they could regroup with the others while waiting for the pre-arranged submarine rescue. It did not turn out that way. The Japanese, aided by Malay villagers, chased Lyon and his men from island to island. The commandos fought their pursuers when they had to, but otherwise retreated and remained hidden as much as they could. In the end, thirteen of the original twenty-three died either in battle or from mistreatment in captivity. The number of dead included their leader. On the 16th, Colonel Lyon was holding off a large number of Japanese troops, while covering the retreat of some of his men. He and another commando were shooting at the enemy from the cover of a tree when a Japanese grenade killed them both.

The remaining men evaded capture for a few months longer, but eventually the Japanese managed to round them all up, a few at a time. The men were then brought to Singapore, to the dreaded Outram jail. After interrogating the ten survivors, the *Kempeitai* conducted a mock trial on July 3rd 1945. Predictably, they found the commandos guilty of espionage.

Even though Japan was not an adherent to the Geneva Convention in the first place, the *Kempeitai* justified the execution of these men by stating that they had not been wearing conventional military uniforms, and were therefore not protected by the Convention.

It was very strange how the Japanese took such great pains to hide behind tenets of the convention when they chose to, and ignore it altogether at other times. For example, it never seemed to stop them from bayoneting uniformed prisoners, or shooting at downed Allied pilots floating helplessly in their parachute.

July 7th 1945, morning
Tiong Bahru district, Singapore

There seemed to be much excitement at the marketplace that morning. As Hans wandered around, he overheard some scuttlebutt about a Japanese parade for certain *angmoh* soldiers, but he did not know what that was all about. Curious, he decided to follow the crowd to see what was going on.

When he arrived at the junction of Tiong Bahru Road and Outram, what he saw was the tail end of a procession heading west. He followed along. It certainly appeared to be some sort of parade—Japanese soldiers with full uniform and arms surrounding a contingent of about ten European men wearing dark green coveralls.

The Europeans marched alongside the Japanese, towering over them. They did not look anything like the prisoners-of-war labor gangs that Hans had seen from time to time. For one thing, these men were not wearing the familiar khaki short uniforms. For another, they did not appear to be emaciated like the others he had seen from Changi camp.

The men must have been beaten at some point—some bruises were apparent—but otherwise they appeared mostly fit. They held their heads high, returning salutes from the Japanese officers as they went by. Hans had the impression that it was indeed some sort of hero's parade.

The procession continued west for a distance, the number of curious onlookers grew as it progressed. They marched past Tiong Bahru and Redhill, moving on to what would later be known as Commonwealth Avenue and Clementi Road. They came to a stop at a field near Dover Road. This was a long way from Outram—over eight kilometers, or five miles—and by then, a fairly large audience had gathered along the way. At the field, the Japanese offered drinks and cigarettes to the ten men, who in turn accepted these gifts. They knew why they were there; might as well have one last smoke.

That was when the pleasantries ended.

The soldiers tied the prisoners' hands behind their backs. They then forced one of the ten to kneel down with his head forward. In their interpretation of *Bushidō*, the Japanese warrior code of conduct, the Japanese were about to dispatch the prisoners in the honorable manner of warriors—beheading.

Unlike what one sees in samurai movies, this particular beheading was neither swift nor merciful. In the hands of an expert martial artist, the Japanese *katana*, or samurai sword, was capable of beheading even a large animal with one stroke. The executioners at this event were apparently not that skilled.

Hans watched as the Japanese soldier held a sword high over his head. With a shout, the soldier brought it down on to the neck of the first victim. His aim was bad—the blade slammed into the commando's shoulder. The victim fell over, screaming in agony.

The soldier grimaced—he had lost face. He began hacking at the fallen man's neck, hitting all over and using many strokes before the head finally came off.

The commando screamed for a long time.

The nine other men awaiting their own executions were forced to watch, as their friend died in that horrible manner. Some of them closed their eyes and muttered prayers, while others fell to their knees weeping.

The gruesome executions continued, one man at a time. For the crowd of onlookers, each one seemed to take forever. Many had to close their ears and turn away. One can only imagine what it must have been like for the condemned men.

At that time, Hans did not know who those men were, or what the circumstance was behind their capture and hideous execution. He could only surmise from their accents that they were either British or Australians. Whoever they were, he noted that they had carried themselves with pride, even up to death. It would be much later, as an adult, before he could learn about the men whose deaths he had personally witnessed.

What he learned later was that those men were part of a Special Operations force called "Z" Special Unit, which comprised of British, Australian and New Zealand commandos from the different branches of service. While most people will always remember the sacrifices of the US Marines throughout the Pacific, these men, who quietly operated behind the scenes, have been largely forgotten.

After slaughtering the ten commandos that day, the Japanese dumped their bodies into an unmarked grave. No more ceremony or honors. After the war, the Japanese attempted to cover up the incident but there had been too many witnesses.

The recovered bodies of the commandos from the field—along with those of Ivan Lyon and a few other Rimau members—later received full honorable burials at the Kranji War Memorial Cemetery, in Singapore. Today, there is also a small Memorial with the names of the ten men at the site of their execution, just off the junction of Clementi and Dover Road. Many Singaporeans living in the area walk by the memorial, but few pay attention to its significance—as a forlorn reminder of a brave but somewhat futile sacrifice.

It seemed particularly tragic that those men should have to die on that day in July 1945. Although there was no way of knowing it then, in another month, the war would be over.

But not before the world was to witness a new horror—the Atomic Age.

7
U-235 AND PU-239

When war began, the United States was well behind Germany in the field of nuclear technology and research. It was Albert Einstein who, in 1939, urged the American government to invest in that field before the Nazis could break through with viable atomic weapons. Even though he was a pacifist, he realized it was still better for the Americans to have the technology rather than the Nazis.

He knew what Hitler was capable of.

President Roosevelt listened and so the race for the atomic bomb began. By the time Germany surrendered in May 1945, the American team responsible for developing the bomb—the Manhattan Project—had not yielded viable nuclear weapons yet, but they were close. Very close.

There were two types of atomic bombs on the drawing board, one of which utilized Uranium-235, while the other used a transuranic (or heavier than uranium) element, Plutonium-239.

In naturally mined uranium, the most abundant isotope is U-238. That is to say, in any sample of uranium, ninety-nine percent of it is made up of that particular isotope. The remaining one percent is made up of uranium atoms with different neutron numbers, or isotopes.

In order to obtain the weapons grade U-235 (which has a 0.75 percent abundance in nature), one has to extract it from the uranium ore, a process which was especially time consuming then, as the men of the Manhattan Project were working with a brand new form of technology, much of which was still theoretical.

Plutonium, on the other hand, is not a naturally occurring element. It has to be manufactured by "bombing" uranium with neutrons. Again, the processing methods in the 1940s were especially time consuming. Hence, the long wait for America to obtain a working bomb.

However, the scientists had postulated that a relatively small amount of Pu-239 would yield a larger explosion than a comparable amount of U-235. The US Army was very interested in the development and experimentation of both types of bombs. By the middle of 1945, the two bombs were ready. No longer were they merely on the drawing boards; they had become a reality.

On July 16th 1945, a plutonium-fueled bomb—codenamed Trinity—was detonated in a desert in New Mexico. It was the first successful nuclear weapon. The Atomic Age was born.

The B Reactor at Hanford, Washington was primarily responsible for the production of Pu-239 that had fueled the Trinity bomb. From that production facility, more plutonium was available at the same time for another bomb. That other bomb was codenamed Fat Man.

After Germany surrendered in May 1945, the Allies turned their full focus on Japan. On July 26th— after the successful test of the first atomic bomb in the New Mexico desert—President Roosevelt issued the Potsdam Declaration, calling for the unconditional surrender of Japan, the alternative being "prompt and utter destruction."

Prior to the actual use of these weapons, the Americans were essentially warning the Japanese about the new atomic bombs, about the untold death they would bring. For their part, the Japanese neither accepted or rejected, or even contested the declaration. They simply ignored it as if it was of no consequence. This was the act of *mokusatsu*—killing it with silence.

The Allies could not be expected to sit around and do nothing in the face of such a diplomatic rebuff. The Japanese, in their proud way, had sealed their own fate. On the morning of August 6th 1945, the B-29 named Enola Gay dropped a single uranium bomb—codenamed Little Boy—on Hiroshima, Japan. It was the first nuclear weapon to be used in war. The first one used on humans.

Three days later, another B-29 named Bock's Car dropped the Fat Man bomb on Nagasaki. The second and last nuclear weapon used in war. Hopefully, the last one ever.

But the bombs had done their job. The next day, on August 10th 1945, Emperor Hirohito met with his cabinet to discuss surrender. Prior to the bombs, the Japanese were prepared to fight to the end, to die for their Emperor. Now, he urged his people to accept the unconditional surrender terms dictated in the Potsdam Declaration.

For some in his cabinet, this was simply unthinkable. They believed that the Declaration would mean the end of their Emperor and the Japanese right to self-rule. However, this was not true. The Declaration was quite clear in its wording that any Allied occupation forces were temporary and for peacekeeping purposes only. Furthermore, it stipulated that any removal of persons from office would be limited to those who had actively promoted the war. This did not include the Emperor.

In any event, the Emperor firmly made his wishes known that he did not want the fighting to continue, or for any further deaths of his people. After much discussion, the cabinet agreed to reply to the Allies. Japan would accept the declaration, with one caveat—the Emperor's sovereignty was not to be compromised in any way.

Despite the agreement, there were still a few who remained opposed to dealing with the enemy, even though the Allies were being much more generous than the Japanese had been at Singapore or the Philippines in 1942. It was much too humiliating for them. Rather than surrender, a group of die-hards in the army attempted a coup to seize control of the government. This inside struggle lasted a few days. The rebels did not prevail.

On August 15th the Japanese people heard, for the first time ever, the voice of their Emperor. His surrender speech had been recorded the day before and was now being broadcast over the radio. Hirohito spoke in the Imperial Language. It was not easily understood by the average Japanese person, but the message remained clear—Japan had lost the war.

There was no way that Japan could have hoped to defeat the United States itself, let alone the entire combined Allied forces. The Soviets, freed from fighting the Nazis in Europe, joined in the fray by deploying one million men to Manchuria. They invaded on the same day as the American bombing of Nagasaki—August 9th 1945.

Between America's technology and this mass of manpower, for Hirohito to continue the fight would have only resulted in the annihilation of his people, and he knew it.

In 1941, Japan had hoped for a quick knockout blow on the Allies, one which would persuade them to back off on the trade embargoes, and thereby allow Japan to be the superpower in Asia.

For a time, it seemed to be going that way, with the fall of Hong Kong, Malaya, Singapore, Dutch East Indies, the Philippines, Wake Island, and so on.

Three and a half years later, the tide had turned completely. Japan's navy, with all its capital ships, was at the bottom of the different seas. The air forces were reduced to a few aircraft, used in those last days primarily as suicide bombers—the *Kamikaze*.

In comparison, America's industrial and technological prowess had only grown exponentially since the days of Pearl Harbor. From the pitiful F2A Buffalo fighters at Wake Island—every one of them shot down in flames—to the F4U Corsair, capable of flying one hundred miles an hour faster than the Zeroes. From the bolt action M1903 Springfield rifle to the self-loading M1A Garand.

From conventional bombs to nuclear devices.

The "Enola Gay" coming back from Hiroshima.

The atomic bomb on Nagasaki –August 9th 1945.

8
COMING DOWN FROM NIITAKA

All throughout the first week of December 1941, Tokyo's diplomats were working hard with their American counterparts, in order to gain concessions for Japan without their nation having to go to war for it. At the same time, fully armed Japanese warships were already deploying for destinations in the Pacific and Southeast Asia.

In the event that negotiations were not favorable, Japanese commanders would receive a radio code—"Climb Mount Niitaka"—ordering them to commence hostilities.

The diplomats failed. The climb began. Then, in 1945, the Japanese had to come back down.

August 15th 1945
Tiong Bahru district, Singapore

The past week had been a strange one, with everyone behaving oddly. Hans compared it to stepping on an ant-nest. Something big had happened in Japan and the soldiers were unsure of what to do.

Rumors claiming that the war had already ended were circulating all around. Some people were saying that the Americans had won while others were claiming that it was the Japanese who had won. Whichever was true, Hans noticed that the soldiers seemed even more anxious than before. He steered clear of them.

There was one particular rumor that seemed to be too fantastic to be true. According to some, the amazing Americans had learned to control the elements, and had unleashed fiery destruction on Japan. One version of this rumor had it that Japan no longer existed. Was that even possible?

That afternoon, many of these wild rumors were laid to rest. His Imperial Majesty, Emperor Hirohito, announced on the radio that the Japanese government was ready to accept surrender terms, as dictated by the Allies. Furthermore, he confirmed that the Americans had "begun to employ a new and most cruel bomb, the power of which to do damage is, indeed, incalculable, taking the toll of many innocent lives."

It was very serious—not only the content of the speech, but the fact that the Emperor himself was announcing their defeat. From what Hans could gather, the Emperor never did anything like that. People did not look at him, and very few had actually heard him speak.

He was a god.

Now, the god had come down from his lofty place and spoken on the radio. Nobody knew what to do with that. After the initial shock had subsided, different reactions began taking place on the part of the Japanese in Singapore. On one end of the spectrum, there were many who were tired of the war, tired of having been away from home for so many years. Those individuals silently heaved sighs of relief. The important thing was to stay alive and go home. Make friends with the locals. No hard feelings, eh?

For some of the soldiers—especially the ones who had not abused their power—it was easy enough to let their guard down, and to become friendly with the locals. Not too friendly, however. Some of the Chinese were out for revenge, and they did not care if this or that soldier had been one of the good ones during the Occupation. They were ready to kill anyone in the imperial Japanese uniform.

As for the ones who had been notorious for their abuses—and people did not forget their faces—life would not be so easy. These ones tried to stay indoors or keep strength in numbers. Even so, they were not always safe.

On the other end of the spectrum, there were those who were taking the surrender as a loss of their honor. If they could not gloriously fight down to the last man, then they would end life at their own hands, rather than laying arms before the enemy's feet. Near the school hall building of the Saint Patrick's School in Siglap was an underground bunker, which was also used as an air raid shelter. A large group of Japanese officers congregated there on the evening of their Emperor's speech. After shouting their ceremonial *banzais* and having one last drink, they pulled the pins on their grenades.

Hans had not personally witnessed this incident, as Siglap was quite a long way from Tiong Bahru. He had only heard the report of it, as well as reports of similar mass suicides around the island. It seemed like madness! Why would anyone want to do such things?

He also began hearing alarming reports of a different nature: Acts of retribution by Japanese soldiers with nothing to lose, yet wanting to take out their frustrations on innocent people. This became a very dangerous time for anyone, adult or child.

It was not only the civilian population that needed to be cautious around the soldiers. During this time of madness, the already weak and emaciated prisoners-of-war in Changi were also hiding out in their barracks from the guards—drunk on homemade *sake* or beer—who were seeking to regain honor. But how does one restore his honor by kicking an already half-dead, unarmed man to death?

Similar actions were going on throughout Japanese occupied territories in the Asia-Pacific Theater, not just in Singapore. Acts of retribution against prisoners-of-war were not new. They had simply become more frequent and intense.

As early as 1943, when the tide of war began turning against Japan, some felt that the only way to save face was by punishing the enemy prisoners-of-war in their charge, as strange as that may sound. Although they were kicking men who were already down, this action somehow seemed to redeem their honor, from their strange point of view. Fighter pilot Major Gregory Boyington, of the United States Marine Corp's famous VMF-214 Black Sheep Squadron, witnessed this bizarre phenomenon during his time in captivity. In January 1944, Boyington was shot down during a combat mission, and subsequently captured by the Japanese. In his postwar memoir *Baa, Baa, Black Sheep*, he wrote that whenever there had been an American battle victory, certain camp guards would go through the barracks kicking and beating the prisoners. His experience was not unique. In December 1944, with US forces closing in, Japanese camp guards at Palawan Island in the Philippines herded a group of American prisoners into a small wooden air raid shelter. Once the shelter was full, they poured gasoline in through the vents and set the building on fire, to the pleas and screams of the men trapped inside. Seeing this horrible death before them, other prisoners tried to make a break for it, but camp guards gunned most of them down. Only a few managed to make it out to tell of this atrocity.

The mentality of such individuals, the ones who perpetrated these cruel acts, was beyond reason and completely illogical to begin. Once the surrender became official, such men grew even more unreasonable. As senseless as their own suicides were, it was unconscionable that they first had to take out their frustrations on helpless ones.

For young Hans, the idea of coming so far only to be killed by a stray bullet or at the hands of a grief-filled soldier going berserk seemed to be a very sad waste. As he observed the breakdown of order increasing over the weeks since the surrender, it only made more sense to keep a low profile. On some days, he did not dare leave the cover of his hiding place beneath the cement stairs. This obviously meant not eating or drinking during the entire time. Hans found that he no longer needed to go to the bathroom either—there was nothing for his body to eliminate.

His health and his strength were rapidly declining, but out of instinct, he knew that taking cover was still the better thing to do. He reasoned that since the Japanese had lost the war, then the British or maybe even the Americans had to be on their way. If he could stay alive until they showed up, he knew everything would be alright then.

Then one day, the shooting stopped. He could hear different voices—happier sounding voices. But he was not sure anymore. He had grown too weak to venture out, to see what was happening. As he lay in his hiding place, resting, he listened for signs of help.

9
THE RELIEF

September 5th 1945
Singapore

The first full contingent of Allied troops to return to Singapore was the British 15th Indian Corps. These men had just come from fighting the Japanese in Burma, and were all too familiar with the scenes of devastation—the walking skeletons, with their hollow faces and blank eyes, the crying children, with their bellies bloated from Kwashiorkor, brought on by a diet lacking in protein.

These were the sights that greeted the Allied soldiers.

The fact that the men of the 15th were familiar with these sights did not mean that they had become used to it. As they walked through the streets of Singapore, a few men tried very hard to hide the tears streaming down their faces. Others managed to mask their feelings, but for many of these men, they would go home after the war to wives who would hear them weep in their sleep for years.

Some men wept in their sleep for the rest of their lives.

As other personnel involved in the reoccupation—ones responsible for civil maintenance and other relief efforts—arrived on the scene, the soldiers' first military priority became the liberation of prisoners-of-war from Changi Prison, Selarang Barracks and other camps.

What they saw at these places made their blood boil.

Probably the hardest thing for the officers to do was to keep their men under control, to keep them from shooting the Japanese prison guards, when they wanted to do the very same themselves. But orders were orders. The enemy had surrendered. There were to be absolutely no acts of retribution against the Japanese.

Still, as the British soldiers watched the ghoulish sight of Allied prisoners staggering out of the barracks, with skin stretched drum tight against their bones—no fat and barely any muscle left—it became too much for even the most hardened ones.

Of the Indian men, there were those who wanted independence from Britain, and there were those who were still proud to be part of the Crown. But this atrocity transcended politics. Seeing what the Japanese had done to the English, Indian and Australian prisoners-of-war angered everyone. It was simply inhumane.

The first thing anyone wants to do, upon seeing a starving person, is to offer all the food they can. The first thing a starving person wants, upon seeing a rescuer, is to ask for food. However, the rescuing party had already received their instructions. If not properly administered, food will kill the body that has—out of survival—shut itself down and become accustomed to smaller quantities.

As difficult as it was to refrain from slipping an inmate something to eat, they knew that they would only be killing them in an act of kindness. Nevertheless, it became increasingly difficult for the soldiers to have to look at these feeble men and hear them say, "You bastard! Why won't you give me something to eat?"

At this, the soldiers would reply, "Hang in there, mate. The doctor's got to look at you first."

This reply would usually do nothing for the hungry man, and he would continue to look dolefully at the soldier, as if he had caused his suffering.

The same challenge faced anyone who was trying to bring relief to the civilian population. How much food can a malnourished body take at a time? When is it too late to help?

September 6th 1945, afternoon
Seng Poh Road, Singapore

Pieter Maartensen, a young Pharmacist Mate from a Dutch Merchant Navy ship, was one of the many Allied volunteers helping to locate and assist survivors. As he walked down Tiong Bahru Road with his group, made up of doctors and other pharmacist mates like himself, he began to feel more and more overwhelmed by the sea of grinning faces and outstretched hands. With the intense tropical heat searing all around, his head was starting to spin as well.

Seeing an opportunity, he ducked down a side street to escape the chaos. He had only meant to take a quick break, before diving back into the relief work, but instead he found himself walking down the street and looking at the dingy buildings.

Piet, as he called himself, sat down in front of a walk-up apartment to rest from the oppressive heat. Truth be told, his heart was not quite in it. Volunteering for the relief seemed to be the right thing to do, but he was finding it increasingly difficult to remain focused. There were just so many in need of help, and it had become very overwhelming. Piet knew that he was behaving like a spoiled crybaby. Unlike many, he had evaded much of the hardships of war.

Having observed Hitler's phenomenal rise to power in the 1930s, Piet's father saw the writing on the wall for Europe. Because of their Jewish ancestry, he knew they could not stay much longer. With that decision made, Piet's family very narrowly escaped Nazi occupation of the Netherlands when they moved to America at the end of 1939, shortly after the invasion of Poland. Feeling as if he was shirking his responsibilities, Piet later joined the exiled Dutch Merchant Navy and trained as a ship's Pharmacist Mate, which brought him to Singapore.

And now he had a job to do. *Come on now, time to go...*

He was about to get up when he thought he heard a sound behind him, something like a cough. He turned to look at the staircase behind him, but there was nobody. Not that he expected to see anyone there—the people were gathering along the main road, where the relief station had been set up. Piet stood up slowly.

Then he saw it—a small hand. Someone was hiding under the stairs! Piet got down on his hands and knees. He carefully picked up the small boy from under the stairs, cradling him like an infant. *Oh dear God! The poor thing is so thin!*

The boy looked to be about five or six, but it was hard to tell. His body was shriveled, yet the abdomen remained distended. The face seemed to be that of someone much older. *Not Chinese or Malay. Eurasian perhaps. I wonder if he speaks English?*

"Hello, little one. My name is Piet. Do you speak English?"

The boy nodded, his eyes half shut.

"What is your name, then?"

"Hans..."

"Hans? Are you Dutch?"

The boy weakly shook his head and coughed. "Papa ... was German," he said, in between coughs.

Piet pulled out a canteen from his web belt, unscrewed the cap with one hand, and carefully put it to the boy's lips. After only a few sips, the boy closed his eyes.

Oh God! Don't die in my arms!

Piet set the boy down on the sidewalk. He knew that he should go and find the doctor first, but something compelled him to take action on his own instead. Fishing around in his first-aid satchel, he found some vitamin lozenges. He placed a couple in the boy's mouth.

"Hans, wake up. You need to take these. You can suck on them or chew them." Piet said.

Hans opened his eyes slowly. He sucked on the lozenges at first, and then he slowly began chewing the orange-flavored vitamins. They tasted like candy. He closed his eyes and smiled.

Piet smiled as well. *He seemed to like them. Maybe I should let him have more. After all, they are just vitamins. What harm can they be?*

Piet placed two more lozenges in the boy's mouth. Hans chewed on them with weakened teeth. Piet picked him up and cradled the thin body as he began walking back to the main road. It was time for them to find the doctor. He had taken no more than a few steps when Hans began coughing again. Then the boy scrunched up his face in pain and clutched the obscene belly. Piet picked up the pace and ran, carrying Hans to the main road. When they reached the relief center, Piet looked among the sea of faces for his ship's doctor—not an easy thing to do in the large crowd. Having located the doctor, who was with a group of people under some trees, he waded through the crowd to reach him.

"Doctor van Dijk! This boy needs help!" Piet yelled as he pushed through the throng of people.

The doctor barely glanced up from his work. He muttered something that sounded like, "So does everyone in this bloody place."

Piet stood in front of the doctor, cradling the groaning boy. Doctor van Dijk, while still tending to an elderly Chinese man with a head wound, sighed and looked up. He glanced at the tiny boy in the Pharmacist Mate's arms.

"What's wrong with him? Don't tell me ... did you feed him something?" he said.

"A few vitamins, Doctor."

"What! You know you should have brought him here first. You're not a physician, Piet!" Doctor van Dijk scolded. Then more gently, he said, "Piet, you may have done more harm than good. The boy is starving. The ascorbic acid must feel like hell in his empty stomach. You have to feed him like an infant. See if he will take some milk, then. Now, go!"

Piet felt chagrined. "Is there nothing else you can do for him, Doctor?" he asked.

"Damn it all! I've got my hands full, as you very well can see!" the doctor snapped, but immediately regretted his words. He looked upward and sighed again. Speaking in Dutch so as not to be understood by the locals, he gently said, "Look, we can't save everyone. You know that, Piet. We just have to do the best we can. Go get a baby bottle and some powdered milk, and do what you can for the boy. Remember—feed him very slowly."

Piet nodded and walked to the supply tent, carrying Hans with him, to find the milk and infant supplies. Having found what he needed, he sat down to nurse the boy with milk from a bottle.

He grew worried after some time. The boy had only taken in a small amount of milk, a bit at a time, but then he seemed to fall into a deep sleep. Although Piet could feel a steady pulse and hear his shallow breathing—which was somewhat reassuring—he remained frustrated that there was nothing else he could do.

For some reason, he could not put the boy down. He was feeling a serious responsibility for him, a bonding of sorts. At the same time, he knew that he was not pulling his weight with the first-aid dressings and other tasks that he had volunteered for.

Piet then had an idea to fashion a sort of sling from utility belts, which would allow him to carry the sleeping boy in front of his torso, while he performed his duties. Every now and again, he checked the boy's pulse and other signs. *So far, so good...*

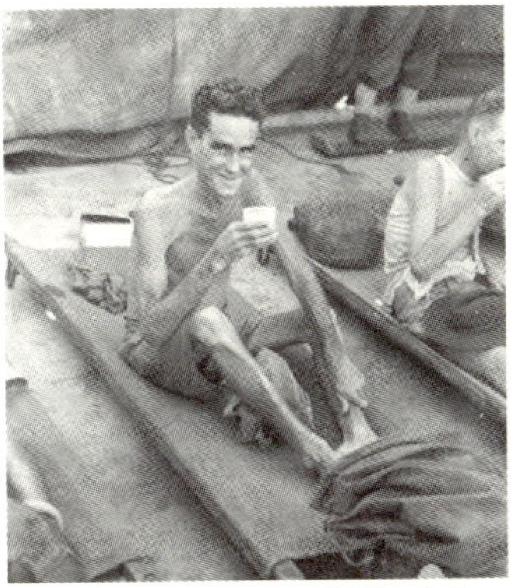

Liberated Australian Prisoners of War (*above and below*).

10
THE ROAD TO RECOVERY

This went on over the next few days in that same manner—Piet carrying out his tasks with Hans strapped to his chest. Anyone who saw them smiled at the sight.

As often as he could, Piet checked on the boy's vital signs for changes, or to see if he needed more milk. Just like a sleeping infant, Hans sucked on the bottle at certain times but not always. The important thing remained that the boy was slowly receiving some nutrition.

The milk was also settling in the boy's stomach more than it had at first, which was certainly a very good thing. Piet thought back to his first evening with Hans. More than likely, it was the combination of the vitamins and the milk, but whatever it was, the result was not good. Hans had diarrhea shortly after his first feeding, and it ran down his legs and on to Piet's boots.

Oh, bloody hell! What do I do now? I've never cleaned up a child in my entire life!

Piet had grown up rather spoiled as an only child. His family was not close to their relatives, so he had never had any experience with children younger than himself. He was at a loss as to what to do. They did not teach anything about diapers in medical training!

However, the human nurturing instinct kicks in when needed. Piet cleaned the boy up, starting with the mess at first, and ending up with giving him a whole body sponge bath. He then made a diaper of sorts from an arm sling, before taking Hans to the relief station to obtain some clean clothes.

Having observed him the past few days, Doctor van Dijk was worried about Piet. He could see that the Pharmacist Mate was becoming much too attached to the boy. That was never good—the doctor had seen this sort of thing happening before. The next time he saw him, he would pull Piet aside to have a few words, try to reason with him.

During a break, he saw Piet come into the meal tent, carrying the boy. He waved the young Pharmacist Mate over. "Piet, you know you should leave the boy at the relief station. Let one of the nurses watch him. You've done all you can," the doctor said softly in Dutch.

"Doctor ... I feel personally responsible. I'm the one who found him. Then I made a mistake, one which may have made him very sick. So no, doctor. I will take care of him myself."

Doctor Van Dijk raged at Piet. He was tired, and on top of that, he was a Dutchman with the proverbial temper. "Damn it, you bloody fool! He's not a puppy you found so that you can take him home, you know. You're getting too attached to the boy! That's always a mistake. Have you thought about that? For one thing, what if he dies? Yes, that's what I said—dies! What are you going to do then? Think you'll be the same again?"

He paused to let that sink in, before going on. "Now, if the boy lives, he will have to go back to his family. If he has no family, then it is the Englishmen's problem. Either way, you have to leave him. You can't take him home with you! What, you think a half-breed like that will be welcome in your father's house?"

Piet had trouble controlling his equally fiery Dutch temper. But the doctor was right. He was also the boss. Piet took a deep breath before speaking again. "Sir, you are correct in all that you say. However, I respectfully insist on watching the child myself. He is not hampering my work in any way. Most of the time, I am just running supplies for you or someone else, and he weighs nothing. If he dies, then I know I did all I could, as you've said before. But if he lives, then I will turn him over to the authorities here, when the time comes."

"Just like that, eh?"

"Sir, I will do just as I have said."

The doctor could see a certain cold resolution in Piet's eyes, and he knew that the young man had meant every word.

"All right then, you foolish boy. Don't say I didn't try to warn you," he said, stern but with a smile.

After carrying Hans around for five days, there was a moment when Piet thought he had lost the boy. Usually, as he carried him strapped to his body, the boy lay against his chest, like a sleeping infant. Remaining restful but not lifeless. Also, he was used to hearing the boy making sounds in his sleep.

Initially, Piet did not notice the moment when Hans had first become limp. The loose neck with the flopping head was what had caught his attention. When Piet could not feel a pulse, he began to panic, but then he caught himself. This was what he was here for.

Training, training... have to remember training! Dropping to one knee, he laid the boy down on the ground—chest down with face to one side—and applied pressure to the back, inducing artificial respiration. Piet focused his thoughts away from the image of the boy's face.

Done this before ... count ... just like training...

After some time, Hans coughed and opened his eyes. He stared blankly for a while, before turning to look at Piet. Slow recognition formed in his eyes, followed by a small smile.

"Do you have any food, please?" the boy asked.

Piet, still kneeling, leaned back and sat down, exhausted. He smiled back with his eyes closed, unable to stop the tears. "Hans, do you like peanut butter?" he suggested.

"I don't remember, sir."

"Well, I think you will like it."

The road to recovery began slowly for Hans. Having been afflicted with malnutrition during a crucial formative period, some of the effects of that ordeal would continue to be with him for a long time. His dental health, for instance, remained poor for the rest of his life.

As soon as the administrative staff was able to ascertain his full name, the names of his parents and when he had last seen them, they began a search for his mother immediately. Just to be sure, they also included an investigation into the records at the Outram Road jail, though they did not mention this to Hans. Since the boy already believed his father to be dead, there was no point in giving him any false hope otherwise.

In the meantime, Hans followed Piet around, who in turn continued to carry out his first-aid responsibilities while keeping an eye on the boy. His appetite remained larger than his actual ability to digest food, so his consumption needed to be carefully monitored.

September 12th 1945
The Padang, Singapore

There was definitely a different atmosphere in Singapore in those days. More Allied personnel had since landed to restore order, and the Japanese were preparing for the official surrender. Although it was going to be a long road to recovery—for both the people as well as the nation—everyone could finally feel the oppressive hand of the Japanese occupation lifting.

On the first Monday after the Allies had returned to Singapore, thousands of people gathered in the area surrounding the parade field in front of Municipal Building to witness a moment in history. Three years and seven months earlier, triumphant Japanese troops had marched there, signifying the British capitulation. After that parade, the people of Singapore watched as contingents of British and Australian POWs—armed with brooms—were put to work sweeping the public streets, further signifying their humiliating defeat. This time, the tide had turned and it was the Japanese who were there to surrender.

The British military in 1945 looked very different than it had in 1942. The khaki shorts were gone, replaced by a full-length dark green battle dress uniform. The Royal Marines lined the streets, armed with a new sort of weapon—the Sten submachine gun, with its unique side-loading magazine. The men were also very fit, well fed. They looked like real soldiers.

In comparison, the Japanese contingent bore a worn down appearance. Their dress may have been meticulous, but their countenance was that of a defeated group. Hunger from reduced rations over the course of the Occupation had affected not just the civilians and prisoners-of-war but the Japanese soldiers as well. They were ready for it all to be over.

The Japanese, led by General Seishiro Itagaki, did not turn to look at the jeering crowd or the guards of honor on the parade ground—men from British, Australian, Indian and Gurkha regiments. Instead, they marched face forward, single-file, into Municipal Building, to meet with Lord Louis Mountbatten—Supreme Commander of Allied Forces (Southeast Asia)—who would accept their surrender.

Present that morning were also many who had endured the privation of prison life under the Japanese. Witnessing their former enemy surrender would not erase the pain that they had been through, but it would help to close one chapter of their lives.

General Percival, who had surrendered Singapore in 1942, was not one of them. He was still in Japan, where he had been able to witness the main surrender of the former enemy, aboard the battleship USS Missouri in Tokyo Bay on September 2nd.

The surrender ceremony that day represented the Japanese forces in Southeast Asia. It was one of many taking place throughout the different occupied territories, over the period of August to October 1945—from Burma to Manchuria, from the Indian Ocean to the South Pacific.

The Japanese surrender of forces in Southeast Asia, at Singapore's Municipal Building—September 12th 1945.

11
REUNITED

September 13th 1945, afternoon
YWCA Building, Singapore

Florence did not appreciate the term "Displaced Individuals." Unlike the hundreds of truly homeless women around her, she knew that she had a place to go back to. After all, the house on Ubin was still there. Unfortunately, it was not as simple as that. For a multitude of reasons—none of which made any sense to her—the returning British administration officials did not allow her to take possession of the house on Ubin. Something about the "rightful occupant having been deceased" or some such nonsense. Words like "will and testament not found" and "probate." It was all very confusing.

Basically the fact remained that, despite being the surviving spouse of that "rightful occupant," it did not necessarily grant her ownership of the place. She was, for all intents and purposes, homeless.

So there she was, stuck at the YWCA until somebody could work something out. While it was obviously better than the *Kempeitai* prison at the YMCA, she still felt like she was in a cage of sorts. Again, another obstacle in life. She was getting quite sick of it. Why is any moment of reprieve always followed by misery?

On that day, a Tuesday, a young fair-haired *angmoh* soldier came in after lunch looking for Florence. After asking around, staff members directed him to where she was sitting.

"You are Florence Schirmer, madam?" the English soldier inquired, removing his beret.

She nodded, apprehension on her face.

"Mrs Schirmer, I regret to inform you..." he began. "Oh, dash it all—this is so hard! Your husband died while in enemy captivity. I am truly sorry, madam."

Florence nodded. "I had expected as much," she said.

"Oh," the soldier said. What else was there to say? Clearing his throat, he continued, "But there is some good news, however. We seem to have located your son. He is alright, you know."

"Hans?"

"Yes, madam."

"Where is he?"

"At a refugee center not far from here. A Dutch medical team is looking after him. He was terribly starved, but he is eating now, and the doctor believes he should make full recovery, madam."

"Thank God! What happens now?"

"As I understand it, you are about to be moved to a more appropriate dwelling. One that can accommodate you and your son. In the meantime, perhaps we could arrange for you to meet him, say tomorrow."

"Where is this place? How do I get there from here?"

"Don't worry, I will send someone to pick you up first thing tomorrow morning. How does that sound?"

September 14th 1945, morning
Tiong Bahru market, Singapore

Piet knew this day was coming. He had to remind himself that he was a medical professional, and that he had done his job. Why then, did he dread what he was about to say to the boy?

Because you allowed yourself to do the very thing Doctor van Dijk warned you about. He was right, of course, the old goat. I am much too fond of the boy.

Hans followed a few steps behind, watching everything quietly. Although he seemed much stronger, and was now able to walk to places on his own, he remained rail thin, with his abdomen protruding awkwardly.

Piet sighed. He had to do this.

"Hans, come here please."

Piet sat down on the edge of a curb. Hans sat next to him.

"How is your stomach this morning? Better?"

The boy nodded.

"Good. You need to eat. Get strong again. Take the medicine that the doctor gives you."

All right Piet, get to the point with him.

"Hans, it is time for us to say goodbye."

"Goodbye? But why, Piet?"

Piet forced himself to smile, to look happy for the boy.

"Good news—they have found your mother! She will be coming for you later today. Isn't that wonderful?"

For some reason, Hans did not seem at all elated. The only thing he said was, "Oh."

"Oh?" Is that all you can say? Why aren't you excited?

"Aren't you happy at all, Hans? Your mother is coming to see you today!"

"I can't remember what she looks like, Piet."

It was now Piet's turn to say, "Oh."

How long has the poor boy been out here on his own? Nobody should have to live through such things!

After a moment of silence, Piet spoke. "It will be alright, Hans. You are going home. You will be fine."

They seemed such empty words.

Hans shrugged. "I wanted very badly to go back to our home, the one on the island. But now I don't. Papa won't be there anymore."

Piet did not know what to say. He swallowed the lump in his throat and blinked rapidly.

Why doesn't the boy cry? I'm sure he wants to, but his eyes are so cold. Did he forget how to cry? The poor child!

"Piet, are you going away, too?"

"I will be going back to my ship soon. After that, I don't know. Eventually Holland, I suppose."

"Can I go with you?"

"No!"

Hans looked down quietly. Piet mentally kicked himself for not having handled the situation well.

"Hans, your place is here. With your mother and your family, right here in Singapore. You can't come with me, little one. Hans, the war is over; everything will be alright. Your Mama will come and get you. You will go to school and have friends. Everything will be alright. You just wait and see!"

Will it really? The boy lost his father. He lost his childhood. My God, the things he had seen!

While Piet was speaking, Hans also thought about what Papa had said the last time he saw him. He remembered his promise to his father—to go on living, to never give up.

He silently mouthed, "Alright, Papa."

To Piet he said, "Should I stay here with you, or should I wait for her in the tent?"

"I think it will be better if you wait for her there."

The Jeep—American lend-lease equipment to Britain—pulled to the side of the road, across from a large white tent on Tiong Bahru Road. The driver, an army private, engaged the parking brake.

"That is the administration center, madam. You should start there first," he directed, pointing to the tent.

Florence thanked him, climbed out of the jeep, and began walking slowly to the tent. What would she find there? What did her son look like now?

There were so many faces milling around the tent. Hopeful Chinese boys looked at her. Each one was thinking the same thing: Is she my mother?

When they realized that she was not, they turned their faces away—some sad, some angry.

So many faces! It overwhelmed Florence. She stopped a nurse.

"My son is Hans Schirmer. Do you know him? Where can I find him?" she asked.

Fortunately, everyone there knew him. His name was not a common one and most of the staff had come to think of him as Maartensen's pet. The nurse replied, "Oh, I just saw him a minute ago. Let me see ... Ah, there he is!"

Florence looked in the direction that the nurse was pointing. She saw a familiar face. But it was so much thinner than the last time she had seen it. So much older, too.

Just then, the boy stood up. Florence could see the stick-like appendages and the bloated belly—obscene reminders of the abuse he had been through. Alone. All by himself.

She shrieked, "*Aiyah*, Hansel! Look at you, *lah*. You poor thing!"

Hans looked up suddenly at the sound of the familiar voice, the thoughts in his head clearing up like clouds in a strong breeze. He turned to see a young Chinese woman at the entrance of the tent.

That had to be his mother, he realized.

Hans had not heard anyone call him by that name in a long time, it seemed. A very long time.

Papa used to call me that!

Memories came flooding back to him. Of how things used to be...

Papa carrying him on his shoulders. The salty odor of the sea, mixed with the pungent smell of petrol and exhaust smoke. The sound of the Seagull engine. Nasi Lemak on a banana leaf. Are you still hungry, Son? Be good now. Don't scare the chickens, Hansel.

POM! A wild boar tumbling to the ground dead. Wah! Good shot! Good shot!

Birthday at Robinson's. Would you like a catapult?

Mickey Mouse doing his magic. Broomsticks dancing in a line. See how I fix the engine, Son. There used to be tigers around here, did you know? Hansel! Oh, no Papa! They beat you up. I will always be with you, Hansel. Remember that, my Son.

I love you, Papa...

Hans looked up from his reverie to see his mother standing in front of him.

"Oh dear, Hansel!" she said, shaking her head.

Somehow it made him angry, hearing that name again.

"Please don't call me that. I am not a little boy anymore," Hans said, and looked away.

Florence stared at her son, not knowing what to do. He was, as he had asserted, not a little boy indeed. She was looking at a stranger.

12
AFTERMATH

Things would not—could not—ever be the same for anyone who had been at all involved in that epic moment in history, known thereafter as World War II.

The Schirmers were just one of many families in Singapore who had been torn apart by the decisions and actions that were made ultimately by men far removed from the battlefield. Actions that would affect countless other families and individuals alike, in varying degrees.

The war would devastate some completely, while others would arise from the ashes and make names for themselves. To his credit, young Hans Schirmer became one of the latter, growing up to be a good man the way his dying father had hoped.

Sadly, Hans and Florence never became close, as a mother and son should be. Candidly, he later reflected that he always had too much of an independent streak, and that he could be very willful as a child. Perhaps that was an inborn trait, but more than likely, it was something inculcated by the will to survive that he had honed during the war. In any event, there was not much closeness even before then.

For her part, she was frustrated with the same hand that life kept dealing her, time after time. At an early age, she had lost wealth and security because of her selfish and abusive father. Then when she thought she had escaped that, she found herself trapped as a young, unprepared mother. The war was the final straw that ripped everything she had from her.

In the end, she was not granted occupancy of the Ubin house, despite being the widow of the owner, and Hans never found out what became of the place. They never returned to it. For a period, they lived in a resettlement village, made up of temporary dwelling huts that lacked indoor plumbing. He distinctly remembered the outdoor communal pits with coconut trunks straddled across, used as toilets. For Florence, the prospect of starting over with nothing—and in her mind, shackled to a dependent child as well—was completely unbearable.

She often gave in to fits of rage, severely beating her own child with anything close at hand. But each time this happened, Hans stubbornly held out, refusing to give her the satisfaction of seeing him cry, which only infuriated her more. There were many times when she beat his back with a stick until the stick broke, while he instinctively curled up in a ball to defend his face and hands. Exhausted and left without an operable device of punishment, she would then storm off.

Hans recalled this one time when Florence's kindly but simple old mother came to his aid, as he lay on the ground with the skin on his back torn to shreds. Unfortunately, what she did then was of no help but quite the opposite. Trying to be of comfort, she applied Tiger Balm to his injured back. An excellent product for sore muscles but never to be used on broken skin, the stinging ointment caused him to jump and scream. Years later, he could tell the story with a laugh, saying that the Tiger Balm ironically had caused more pain than the actual beating!

Whenever she witnessed these violent acts, the old granny shook her head and softly chided her daughter to not be so mean, but it remained ineffective. She appeared to also be in fear of the angry, frustrated Florence.

There were times, usually after a beating, that Hans would run away and camp in the jungle for days on end. Whenever he returned, he typically received another beating, which would prompt him to go back to the jungle again. It was no way for a young boy to live, but he refused to submit to his mother's fits of rage.

As soon as he was able to emancipate himself, after high school, he left home to join the Singapore Police Force in 1957. The pay was lousy, but they offered free room and board, which was all he needed. Finally on his own, he had his whole life ahead of him.

Florence remarried after the war, this time to a Chinese businessman named Lim, and they had a son born to them in 1947. Mr Lim was an amicable, easy-going sort. Perhaps this easy-going nature was also his downfall, for he was apparently not very diligent in maintaining his finances. For a short time, they were fairly wealthy and comfortable, but he lost everything soon thereafter. Florence could not believe that it was happening to her again, and raged at her husband, Hans, or anyone who came in her way. They divorced in the early 1950s.

She went on to find happiness with an older Chinese man, an attorney, or barrister, as the English term applied then. He was a steady, quiet, kindly man who was also sensible with his finances. They too had a son—Aaron—who was born to them in 1960. The old man was a very kind gentleman. He regarded Florence's other sons almost as his own, and treated them well.

By this time, Hans had his own lodgings, but he made a point of coming by to visit regularly. Ultimately, it was out of a sense of duty to his mother, although he grew to have immense respect and fondness for the old gentleman. Unfortunately, the old gentleman died of cancer in 1978. Of all the men she knew, Florence said that he was really the only one she truly loved.

As she grew old, all her sons continued to take care of her in one way or another. Hans provided financial support, but it remained difficult for him to be close in any other way, after the years of abuse. He was keeping his promise to his father, to look after her as the oldest son.

Florence admitted that her favorite had always been the youngest son, Aaron, and she went on to live out her final years with him. In February 2010 she died of natural causes, with Aaron holding her in his arms. She was eighty-nine years old.

Tan Teck Imm's family continued to raise Carl Johann and Franz Eugene, even after the end of the war. For some reason, Florence no longer felt an attachment to the boys and did not even want to think of them as her own sons.

The boys grew up separately, cared for by two of Tan's daughters and their families. At the age of eighteen, Carl joined the fledgling Singapore army and for a time, led a somewhat rough life.

Later in life, the two brothers found solace in religion and became zealous ministers for the Calvary Charismatic Church. They married well, had children and lived peacefully, despite some sadness at their own mother's rejection of them. Carl had a daughter, Charmaine. Eugene had two sons, Fritz and Roy. Eugene succumbed to cancer in 2008. Carl has been battling ill health for the past few years. He underwent bypass surgery in 2010 and his health remains compromised.

Hans, Carl and Eugene would see each other once in a while, perhaps at Christmas or at Chinese New Year, but they were never close as a family. The Schirmer brothers of Singapore had to forge their own paths in life separately. More casualties of war.

Their father's remains were exhumed from the Outram road prison after the British return, and laid to rest at the Bidadari Cemetery. Over the years, Hans visited the grave often, to clean up around the marker, and then stand in front of it in silent reflection. He always regretted that Edward had never gotten the chance to meet his grandchildren.

Today, there is no more Bidadari Cemetery. Land scarce Singapore needed to make room for the living, so in 2008 the government paid for the exhumation and cremation of those buried there.

Edward Henry Schirmer's remains are now interred at the Choa Chu Kang Columbarium

But what became of the others in this epic? Of course, their story bears telling as well. After Singapore, General Yamashita spent two years in Manchuria. Then in October 1944, Tokyo sent him to the Philippines with a promotion. In the meantime, his nemesis Tojo had resigned as a result of Japan's failing in the war and was no longer able to keep Yamashita in obscurity.

As a full general, Yamashita faced the invading forces of US General Douglas MacArthur. The showdown became a mirror image of the Malayan campaign, and this time, Yamashita was the one with more men but a weakened air force and navy. It became a campaign of attrition on the part of the Japanese. Yamashita endured heavy losses, but he would not surrender until after Emperor Hirohito's famous broadcast of August 15th 1945. On September 2nd, Yamashita surrendered his forces to the Allies.

He then faced the American Military Tribunal for war crimes. Yamashita was cleared of personal culpability in the atrocities committed during his commands in Malaya and the Philippines, as it was established that he did not authorize such acts. Nonetheless, the Tribunal still found him guilty of war crimes and sentenced him to death. The precedent made during the trial was that he remained ultimately responsible for the actions, be it directly or indirectly, of his men.

Tomoyuki Yamashita died on February 23rd 1946, the hangman's noose around his neck. When asked for any last words, he gave a short speech, whereby he acknowledged his responsibility as commander over his men and therefore willingly accepted his death without shame. He ended by thanking the Americans profusely, especially his defense council, for their kindness toward him. It was an honorable gesture, one that his samurai ancestors might have approved.

On a side note, the whereabouts of Edward Schirmer's custom Drilling gun remains a subject of conjecture. Perhaps an American serviceman found it and took it home as a souvenir. Or maybe it remains stashed with the fabled "Yamashita's Gold"—the alleged cache of treasures that many believe is still buried somewhere in the Philippines. Who knows?

With the fall of Singapore on February 15th 1942, all remaining Allied servicemen as well as Colonial government officers faced imprisonment for the duration of the war. Unfortunately, most of them did not make it out. Generals Percival and Heath, as well as Governor Thomas, were some of the survivors. They were detained in Changi immediately after the surrender for a six-month period. Then in August of 1942, the Japanese transferred all senior officers to Formosa (present day Taiwan), where they would stay for two years. They ended the war in cold Manchuria, a long way from tropical Singapore.

General Percival was present at Yamashita's surrender, a great turn of events. There is an account of that meeting which states that Yamashita had reached out to shake Percival's hand, as a vanquished foe. However, Percival snubbed him, refusing the hand. According to that same account, Yamashita wept from the shame.

Percival retired from military service in 1946. Although he had won the respect of many fellow prisoners-of-war, the public as a whole would unfortunately only remember the mousy man blinking nervously before the Tiger of Malaya. Unlike many of his peers, he never received the knighthood.

Arthur Percival died on January 31st 1966 in Westminster, England. He was seventy-eight.

Great Britain would never fully recover the majestic glory of the past. The British Empire had already been in financial dire straits from the cost of World War I, as well as the burgeoning costs of maintaining colonies worldwide. The drain of World War II only served to pull the nation further into debt, a legacy that continues to plague the once great empire. Even before the war, there had been stirrings in the colonies to break away, to gain independence. India was the jewel that they could not afford to lose, but that one already seemed inevitable.

Then the Japanese came along and dealt the British an unrecoverable blow. Of all things, an Asian race had shattered the prestige, the appearance of indomitability and superiority of Europeans. An Asian race that was once caricatured in Western newspapers as bowlegged, bucktoothed, shortsighted "yellow monkeys."

Perhaps of even more humiliation for the British was the fact that the Japanese had defeated them in Malaya and Singapore with an invading force that was half their number.

The image of British invincibility immediately shattered in the eyes of Asians. No longer in awe of their colonial masters, they began to seek independence for their own nations in the years following 1945. In places where seeds of nationalism had already sprouted before the war, such as in India, the effects of World War II only served to foment that desire.

The same sort of thing happened in Africa and other parts of the globe, affecting other European colonists as well. Some nations had to gain their independence by way of armed struggle—French Indochina, Dutch East Indies, Portuguese Angola ... the list goes on.

Others were to gain their independence by way of peaceful charter. The British colonies of Malaya and Singapore are an example of this. It did not mean that their road to independence was without bumps. Undoubtedly, there were interspersed periods of civil unrest during the years after 1945, but these were mainly caused by internal struggles among local groups. As far as the British were concerned, they relinquished control without a fight, and provided the much-needed assistance during the interim period.

By 1955, Malaya and Singapore were partially self-governed. After a brief and uneasy period of merger with the newly formed Federated Malaysia, Singapore broke away to become a sovereign state in 1965. Today, Singapore is among the most technologically advanced nations in the world. Citizens, as well as visitors, enjoy a high standard of living in a very clean and modern city, with a relatively low crime rate. Despite the nation's small size and limited manpower, their military is one of the best armed in the region. This is to ensure that Singaporeans alone, not foreigners, would be the ones responsible for their own defense. Never again would they allow themselves to be so shamefully invaded, conquered and occupied, as in the days of 1942.

EPILOGUE

My father, Hans Schirmer, the inspiration of this epic tale, was always the consummate adventurer and story-teller. True to form, he went on to have many more experiences during his years in the Singapore Police Force and beyond. While it would no doubt take another book to chronicle everything, I hope this epilogue sufficiently brings out the highlights of the rest of Dad's story.

When he left home to become a police officer, there was no way that he could foretell the life of adventure ahead of him. However, the birth of a nation is oftentimes marked with tumultuous moments. Singapore had its share of such moments—the Communist insurgency, the racial riots, and the 1962 to 1966 confrontation with Indonesia, otherwise known as the *Konfrontasi*. Dad saw action in all these events, starting as a beat-walking constable in 1957, then later on as a detective. He also saw stints in the Riot Squad and the Special Branch during his police career.

In the late 1960s, there were still moments of unrest in Singapore. The Communist threat was not yet over. During this period, the US was seeking friendly nations in Southeast Asia and other parts of the world, in their war against Communism. Singapore was one such nation.

Around that time, Dad was an undercover surveillance officer in the Criminal Investigation Department (CID), tasked with monitoring known Communist agitators. Because of that, he and a few other officers were chosen to learn techniques of discreet monitoring and photography from the American CIA. Naturally, he enjoyed that training, and felt privileged to work with the Americans.

Dad also shared with me some harrowing tales about the gun battles that took place during his service. In the early days, Singapore police officers were armed with the ineffectual British army .38 Webley & Scott revolver. This equipment almost cost him his life on more than one occasion, due to the weapon's lack of stopping power. Later on, the department switched to the more effective American police .38 Special Smith & Wesson revolvers. Ironically, he never had to use his weapon in combat after the switch.

Hans Schirmer's name may never have been in the headlines, and for as many people who have known him in his life, there are multitudes more who do not. However, his contribution toward the forming of a fledgling nation cannot, and should not, be ignored.

He was a true Son of Singapore.

On a side note, his small place in history was not relegated only to action-packed adventures or violent moments. In February 1965, during his Riot Squad days, he was on duty the night The Rolling Stones played at the Singapore Badminton Hall. It was the last performance of their Australasian tour.

I enviously thought of that assignment as an unbelievable opportunity, but he hated it! He could not stand the music, and he could not believe the teenage fans either. Crazy girls screaming for a bunch of long haired, skinny drug addicts was how he saw it. Unbelievable!

Sometime while he was in the Police Force, Dad learned to dive and he became a professional diver on the side. During the 1960s, he had the opportunity to dive down to the sunken HMS Prince of Wales. He described it as a beautiful but sad wreck sitting on the murky sea bed.

Despite the protected designation as a War Grave, he could see that treasure hunters had already been there and removed many small souvenirs, such as the bells and Aldis lamps. He found that to be an appalling disrespect.

While doing commercial salvage work, Dad was always filled with immense awe for the beauty that is underwater. However, he also knew of the dangers. On one of his jobs, he survived a shark attack by holding his air tank out in front of him. When the shark bit the metal tank, it became discouraged and left him alone. Once again, he had cheated death. I realize that these anecdotes do sort of make my father out to be like some Forrest Gump character—the guy who was there at every historical moment.

But these things did happen and my mother was there with him in those days.

In 1960, a mutual friend introduced Dad to a beautiful, determined young Chinese nurse. Marlene came from a small, predominantly Fuzhou Chinese village in Perak, Malaya, the youngest of five siblings. She had moved to Singapore in 1957 to attend the nursing college, and upon graduation, elected to further her career there.

They married in 1966. My sister Patricia was born in 1967 and I came along in 1970. Forty-four years later, my mother Marlene continued to be his loving source of companionship and strength.

For being someone who had experienced so much tragedy—losing his own father at such a tender age, growing up hungry amidst the scenes of war and *Kempeitai's* atrocities, abused by his own mother—my father could easily have become a very disturbed soul. On the contrary, he was the most loving, caring, protective and yet extremely fun husband, father and friend that I ever knew.

There was the one thing that I did not understand, until I was much older and able to put some pieces together. When we were little, I remember Dad taking my sister and me to the movies to watch a *Looney Tunes* feature film. He always enjoyed watching those cartoons, laughing along with us at all the funny bits. He also seemed to enjoy the old *Tom and Jerry* cartoons. But for some reason, he did not seem to be as enthused about the Disney animated films.

I believe it might have had something to do with the way he associated them with his father—a bittersweet feeling. When shows like *Dumbo* came on the TV, he would go and find something else to do. Each time, he smiled and said he wasn't really in the mood for "kid's stuff." I never asked him about it. For as close as we were in many ways, and for how much we talked about his growing up days, I think it was still difficult for him to reconcile certain things.

In any event, I have always felt it was amazing how well-balanced Dad was, despite his circumstances while growing up. While we were never really close to our extended family—the cousins, uncles and aunts—we were very tight as an immediate family. Dad was very devoted to us, and we were his "little tribe."

Just like his father, Dad loved the sea, and he loved hunting. Due to the many restrictions, it was not always easy to go hunting in Malaysia, and completely out of the question in Singapore. However, boating was always accessible, and it became our regular form of recreation when I was growing up. Our family spent many weekends together on the boat, and I have the fondest memories of that time in my life. At other times, we indulged in Singapore's favorite pastime—eating. People eat to live, but Singaporeans live to eat. Dad always liked that saying and was a firm believer in its wisdom.

In 1972, he left the Police Force and entered a career in sales. Initially, he worked for a furnishing and interior decoration firm. Later on, he ventured into the field of industrial chemicals and oilfield supply, working for a Japanese petrochemical company. Despite his experience during the war, he never held a grudge against the Japanese people in general. Always a quick learner, Dad started his own oilfield supply and service company in 1976. It was a good time to be in that line of work, and he made lots of money during the oil exploration boom of Southeast Asia in the 1970s.

In 1979, he tried something different when he opened a Country Western Bar and Restaurant, an unusual find in Singapore. However, he knew his clientele—the American oil riggers—and what they wanted. The Ginivy Country Western Bar served the best Tex-Mex cuisine and featured the best local country western cover bands in town. My parents worked back to back over the years, making friends with customers from different parts of the world and giving them a feeling of comfort, hospitality and above all, a home away from home in the middle of Singapore.

They finally sold the business in 2002, having made their fortune. It had been a satisfying life. Over the years, they had watched their two children grow up and five grandchildren being born. It was time to kick back.

When they were still working, they had purchased two condominiums in Malaysia. One was on Tioman Island, a fabulous diving spot and interestingly enough, located about seventy-five kilometers south of the HMS Prince of Wales wreck. The other was at a place called Sebana Cove, a resort with a marina and golf course located up a quiet river in Johor. They usually went there on weekends to escape the bustle of Singapore. That was around 1995. When they retired in 2002, they began spending more time in Sebana. This allowed them to play on the river anytime with their boat and jet ski, take leisurely strolls, or drive to the nearby village Sungei Rengit for food. To basically enjoy each other's company, for the rest of their lives.

Dad's adventures continued. He liked exploring the mangrove tributaries of the river on his jet ski, and he did this on a daily basis when they first went to Sebana. On one of his jaunts, he came upon a herd of wild elephants bathing in the river. He then had to beat a hasty retreat when they charged at him! To this day, his friends laugh about that one.

For Dad, another benefit of owning property in Malaysia was having the accessibility to hunting. His best friend and hunting partner was Nathan Isaac. They had known each other from their days in the police force, after which Nathan had gone on to become a successful attorney. Over the years, they roamed the jungles and plantations around Johor together in an army surplus Land Rover, hunting wild boar. Sadly, Nathan died of a heart attack secondary to renal failure in 2009. Dad never hunted again.

Hans and Marlene's little paradise came to an end tragically on Saturday, June 19th 2010. That day started out as a perfect one for them. After their customary morning walk, they headed to the village for breakfast, followed by a feast of his favorite fruit—the pungent durian.

Dad had even won a modest cash prize that morning in the lottery. Mom sometimes bought tickets for it but never won anything. He typically never bought lottery tickets, but did so this time on a whim and had won! It was uncanny how perfect that day had started out.

They kissed goodbye and parted company later that morning. She went back to the condominium, while he went on to have a fun day at sea with a friend on his beloved jet ski. The narrative of what happened thereafter depends on who tells it. In summary, at some point his friend had lost control of his boat, which then ran over Dad while he was in the water at a speed of about forty knots.

Apparently, he was still conscious when a boater in a passing motor yacht pulled both him and his friend out of the water. Unfortunately, in the panic that ensued, there was no attempt at first-aid measures that might have otherwise saved his life. It was a ridiculous end for a man who had survived so much. He bled to death approximately twenty minutes after the accident, just as they reached the marina. Mom was waiting there at the jetty with her first aid kit. Somebody had called her but had given no details except to say that "someone was cut."

I can only imagine the shock and horror she felt, at seeing her own husband's body being lowered onto the jetty before her. However, she refused to give in to hysteria at that moment; her practical training as a nurse took over. She closed his eyes and straightened his limbs before rigor mortis could set in. Then she said goodbye to her best friend.

At the funeral a week later, a Chinese man in his seventies wept openly for he had known Dad from back in the 1950s, when they were still young detectives in the Police Force. Friends and family flocked to say goodbye to Dad and to offer their support for Mom. Even shop owners from Sungei Rengit and the outlying areas showed up. In the previous ten years or so, my parents had become very much part of the community around Sebana, and everyone felt the loss deeply.

Such was the profound impact that Hans Schirmer had on people—a man who inspired and moved anyone having the privilege to know him.

Dad always felt that he had been blessed in life. Every time something looked bad, it ended up all right for him. He believed that his Papa had kept his word and was watching out for him somehow. He once told me that if he had to go, he would prefer it was at sea, doing what he loved. I guess he went the way he wanted.

Nevertheless, nobody was quite ready for it. For an old guy, he was extremely active and enjoyed his life immensely. He was seventy-two but with a young heart and body, with so much more life to live, so many more adventures to experience, so much wisdom to impart.

For all that you have taught me and done for me, I thank you Dad. Thanks also for all the wonderful stories. Sorry I took so long to write them down for you.

I will love you always.

In memory of Hans Schirmer (1938–2010).

Edward Henry Schirmer, from the photograph taken with General Yamashita in 1942. Unfortunately, the actual photograph was destroyed after the war. Florence was worried about being accused of collaboration with the Japanese.

Hans Schirmer, age nine, and his mother Florence (1947).

Hans Schirmer in his high school days, age 16 (1954).

Hans Schirmer, age 19, looking serious just after high school (1957).

Trainee Hans Schirmer, at the Police Training School, age 19 (1957).

Hans Schirmer looking dashing on a Suzuki Police Interceptor, age 27 (1965).

Constable Schirmer, age 20 (1958).

Hans Schirmer working as a photographer for the Criminal Investigations Department (around 1967).

Hans and Marlene at a dance not long after they met in 1960.

Just before Hans and Marlene's marriage in 1966.

The author, Edmund Schirmer, and his father, Hans Schirmer, at Changi beach (around 1972).

Hans SchirmerHunting wild boar in Johor (around 1998)

Hans, age 71, and Marlene, happily retired in Sebana (around 2009).

A very active 72-year-old Hans and his favorite toy—a water scooter (2010).

ABOUT THE AUTHOR

Edmund M. Schirmer is an upcoming writer. Born in Singapore in 1970, he attended the prestigious Saint Joseph's Institution there before moving to the United States at the age of 21. Today, he resides in the Tri-Cities area of southeastern Washington.

Always an avid writer, his main interest lies in World War II history and the effects of that epoch on individuals and societies.

The passing of his father cemented in him a desire to chronicle the momentous events of World War II as seen through his father's eyes, to document the experiences of a passing generation, before they are lost and forgotten.

Extensively researched to corroborate his father's account, *When There Were Tigers In Singapore* is Schirmer's first novel.